WHAT IS AUTHORIAL PHILOLOGY?

What is Authorial Philology?

Paola Italia, Giulia Raboni, et al.

https://www.openbookpublishers.com

© 2021 Paola Italia and Giulia Raboni. Copyright of individual chapters is maintained by the chapters' authors.

This work is licensed under a Creative Commons Attribution 4.0 International license (CC BY 4.0). This license allows you to share, copy, distribute and transmit the text; to adapt the text and to make commercial use of the text providing attribution is made to the authors (but not in any way that suggests that they endorse you or your use of the work). Attribution should include the following information:

Paola Italia, Giulia Raboni, *et al. What is Authorial Philology?* Cambridge, UK: Open Book Publishers, 2021, https://doi.org/10.11647/OBP.0224

Copyright and permissions for the reuse of many of the images included in this publication differ from the above. Copyright and permissions information for images is provided separately in the List of Illustrations.

Every effort has been made to identify and contact copyright holders and any omission or error will be corrected if notification is made to the publisher.

In order to access detailed and updated information on the license, please visit, https://doi.org/10.11647/OBP.0224#copyright

Further details about CC BY licenses are available at, https://creativecommons.org/licenses/by/4.0/

All external links were active at the time of publication unless otherwise stated and have been archived via the Internet Archive Wayback Machine at https://archive.org/web

Updated digital material and resources associated with this volume are available at https://doi.org/10.11647/OBP.0224#resources

ISBN Paperback: 9781800640238
ISBN Hardback: 9781800640245
ISBN Digital (PDF): 9781800640252
ISBN Digital ebook (epub): 9781800640269
ISBN Digital ebook (mobi): 9781800640276
ISBN XML: 9781800640283
DOI: 10.11647/OBP.0224

Cover Image: Ludovico Ariosto, Frammenti autografi dell'*Orlando furioso*, Biblioteca Comunale Ariostea, Ferrara c. 26r, Classe I A. Courtesy Biblioteca Comunale Ariostea, all rights reserved. Cover Design by Anna Gatti.

Contents

Preface	vii
Introduction to the English Translation	ix
Acknowledgments	xi
Introduction	xiii
Paola Italia and Giulia Raboni	
A definition of authorial philology	xiii
The critical edition in authorial philology	xiii
(Authorial) philology and critics (of variants)	xiv
From Petrarch's *Canzoniere* to modern texts	xvi
History, methods, examples	xvii
One discipline, different skills	xviii
Digital editions and common representations	xx
1. History	1
Paola Italia and Giulia Raboni	
1.1 Author's variants from a historical Perspective	1
1.2 Methods throughout history: from Ubaldini to Moroncini	3
1.3 Authorial philology and criticism of variants	6
1.4 Authorial philology and *critique génétique*	11
1.5 Dante Isella's authorial philology	13
1.6 Authorial philology in the digital era	18
1.7 Authorial philology in the latest decade	22
2. Methods	29
Paola Italia	
2.1 The text	29
2.2 The apparatus	37
2.3 Variants	47
2.4 Marginalia and alternative variants	57

| | 2.5 | Diacritic signs and abbreviations | 59 |
| | 2.6 | How to prepare a critical edition | 62 |

3. Italian Examples 71
Paola Italia and Giulia Raboni
    3.1 Petrarch: The *Codice degli abbozzi* 71
    3.2 Pietro Bembo: The *Prose della volgar lingua* 76
    3.3 Tasso: The *Rime d'amore* 83
    3.4 Alessandro Manzoni: *Fermo e Lucia* and the *seconda minuta* 89
    3.5 Giacomo Leopardi's *Canti* 98
    3.6. Carlo Emilio Gadda's work 107

4. European Examples 113
    4.1 Lope de Vega's *La Dama Boba* 113
    Marco Presotto and Sònia Boadas

    4.2 Percy Bysshe Shelley's *Poems* 122
    Margherita Centenari

    4.3 Jane Austen's *The Watsons* 133
    Francesco Feriozzi

    4.4 Marcel Proust's *À la recherche du temps perdu* 139
    Carmela Marranchino

    4.5 Samuel Beckett's *En attendant Godot / Waiting for Godot* 149
    Olga Beloborodova, Dirk Van Hulle and Pim Verhulst

References 161
Glossary 181
List of Illustrations 187

Preface

Almost a century after its birth, and after the publication of many editions across the whole gamut of Italian literature, authorial philology has only recently been recognized as an autonomous discipline — as one separate from traditional philology (philology of the copy, which specifically studies variants introduced through transmission); as having its own history and its own methodologies; and as able to provide increasingly refined research tools that can deepen our knowledge of texts through the analysis of their internal history. In this way, authorial philology has led to critical achievements of major note.

This renewed interest is due, on one hand, to the high degree of theoretical evolution achieved by the discipline in the context of Italian literature, in which pioneering critical editions have been produced and have established themselves as effective reference models even with regard to the European scene. This interest is also due, on the other hand, to the ever-growing technical developments in the methodologies by which variants are represented and in the tools for reproducing manuscripts. In recent years, such tools and methodologies, with the introduction of the digitalization of images, have revolutionized the work of philologists, offering far superior fidelity compared to the physical reproductions of the past, and giving the possibility to work interactively on the image, not only by enlarging single papers or details, but also through the synoptic vision of witnesses housed in archives and libraries that are often very far apart. Also notable here are innovations in applying graphic contrast filters that allow the researcher to achieve visual results that are far superior even to those provided by the direct consultation of the manuscript.

This book aims to provide the first synthetic overview of this discipline, charted through its *history* (see Chapter 1), which has not yet been systematically investigated so far, through the *methods* (see

Chapter 2) used in daily philological work, and above all through concrete *examples* set out in chronological order (see Chapter 3). We will examine the problem of authorial variants in critical editions of some of the most important works of Italian literature, from the fourteenth to the twentieth century, from Petrarch's *Codice degli abbozzi* to the *Rime d'amore* by Torquato Tasso, from Giacomo Leopardi's *Canti* to Alessandro Manzoni's *Fermo e Lucia*, and onto Carlo Emilio Gadda's novels and short stories. In an Italian context, these authors' names are intricately bound up with the work of the philologists Gianfranco Contini and Dante Isella, who promoted a fruitful interaction between criticism of variants and authorial philology, with Isella developing this interaction into a full-fledged philological discipline with its own system of representation in his philological work and teaching. The development of this discipline is also indebted to the major achievements of the philological school of Pavia. We, the authors of this book, carried out our training in Pavia, where we found a stimulating environment enlivened by the contributions of major scholars such as Cesare Bozzetti, Franco Gavazzeni, Luigi Poma and Cesare Segre. There, with many of our fellow students we gathered the fruits of that active decade between the end of the sixties and early eighties, a period recalled by Isella himself in a lecture held in Pavia in 1999.

On that occasion, Isella expressed the hope that someone 'would take the initiative to historicize the overall picture and carefully retrace the times and the facts, identifying the directions in which we have been going so far and recognizing the specific character of the Italian school in relation to the theoretical positions and editorial initiatives of other countries such as Germany, France and Spain' (Isella 2009a: 241). He also recalled how most editions of '*in fieri* texts' were constituted 'by works undertaken in the Pavia area', works that had allowed the development of 'ecdotic models and criteria that can be perfectly used without us having to invent each time different, untested solutions' (ibid.: 244). This book aims to offer a first contribution to this yet unwritten history, and to also act as a token of gratitude for such a great teacher.

Milan, 2010
Paola Italia and Giulia Raboni

Introduction to the English Translation

At a time when written creativity no longer manifests itself through pen, but rather through keyboard, the growing interest inspired by authorial variants has led us to promote the English translation of the manual which, in 2010, first presented the history, methods and most significant cases of authorial philology, the branch of philology that deals with variants due to the author's intentional desire to change the text, rather than with its transmission.

Before authorial philology was 'officially' founded by Dante Isella, and even before Gianfranco Contini theorized and practiced his 'criticism of variants' in the 1930s by working on autographs by Italian authors such as Petrarch, Ludovico Ariosto and Giacomo Leopardi, but also on Marcel Proust and Stéphane Mallarmé, the existence of authorial variants had already been recognized in classical texts by Giorgio Pasquali.

The peculiarity of the 'Italian case' has two main bases. The first is the existence of a large number of autographs bearing authorial variants, starting from the 'Codice degli abbozzi' (the twenty pages that testify to the first version of Petrarch's *Canzoniere*, containing corrections to 57 of the 365 poetic texts of the collection, which Petrarch decided to keep 'non illorum dignitati, sed meo labori consulens' ('not for their merit but for my effort'; *Rerum Familiarum Libri*, I, 1: 10). The second and more substantive is the fact that, since the seventeenth century, these materials have been preserved and considered objects of worship, as can be seen in Federico Ubaldini's 1642 edition of the *Canzoniere*, which contained not only the final version of the text, but also its drafts found on the 'Codice degli abbozzi', rich with corrections and variants, which were later contemptuously defined by Benedetto Croce 'scartafacci' ('a scratchpad', implying the lack of any literary interest). One could therefore say that genetic criticism was born in Italy in 1642 and developed, from the very beginning, a very sophisticated technique of representing authorial variants, which later found an effective system of formalization in the method elaborated by Dante Isella.

This pioneering book offers a history of authorial philology, as well as a methodical set of instructions on how to read critical editions, and a wide range of practical examples. The volume expands upon the conceptual and methodological basis laid out in the first two chapters, and applies the 'authorial philology method' of representing variants not only to the most important Italian authors — from Petrarch to Carlo Emilio Gadda — but also to some significant examples taken from European Literature: from Lope de Vega to Percy B. Shelley, from Jane Austen to Marcel Proust to Samuel Beckett.

In introducing to an international audience the method of editing authorial variants, we thought it would be useful to broaden the view to European examples (Chapter 4), and to propose cases of authorial philology taken from the most significant poets, novelists and playwriters of modernity, whose chapters have been written expressly for this edition — and we are particularly grateful to them — by their specialists: Marco Presotto and Sònia Boadas (Lope de Vega), Margherita Centenari (Shelley), Francesco Feriozzi (Austen), Carmela Marranchino (Proust), Olga Beloborodova, Dirk Van Hulle and Pim Verhulst (Beckett).

For this new edition, we have also updated the chapter devoted to the innovations represented by the digital environment (Chapter 1.6: 'Authorial philology in the digital era') and written a new chapter on the developments of the discipline in the last ten years and its future prospects (Chapter 1.7: 'Authorial philology in the latest decade').

By presenting a thorough account of the historical and theoretical framework through which authorial philology developed, this book reconceptualizes the authorial text as an ever-changing organism, subject to alteration and modification. At the same time the account allows us to extend to other literatures (and to other disciplines which deal with autographs bearing authorial variants) a philological and critical method that has developed in Italy and which prompts us to consider important questions concerning a text's dynamism, the extent to which an author is 'agentive' in his/her gesture on the white page, and, most crucially, concerning the very nature of what we read.

November 2020
Paola Italia and Giulia Raboni

Acknowledgments

We would like to thank some friends with whom we have shared a passion for philology, who discussed with us the topics covered in this book over many years and who helped us with suggestions: Simone Albonico, Paolo Bongrani, Stefano Carrai, Ferruccio Cecco, Andrea Comboni, Roberto Leporatti, Maria Maddalena Lombardi, Massimo Malinverni, Donatella Martinelli, Luca Milite, Giorgio Panizza, Giorgio Pinotti, Rossano Pestarino, Claudio Vela and our students of the Italian Philology courses in Parma and Siena, who were its first, attentive readers.

We are grateful to Carolina Rossi (Preface, Introduction, Chapter 1), Luca Mazzocchi (Chapter 2), Francesco Feriozzi (Chapter 3) and Katherine Kirby (Chapters 4.1, 4.2, 4.4) for having produced the English translations for these respective sections of the book, and we would particularly like to thank Simon Gilson for having further revised it.

We dedicate this volume to the memory of Franco Gavazzeni (1935–2008) and Dante Isella (1922–2007).

November 2020
Paola Italia and Giulia Raboni

Introduction

Paola Italia and Giulia Raboni

A definition of authorial philology

Authorial philology — a felicitous term coined by Dante Isella (Isella 1987) — differs from philology of the copy (which studies variants introduced through transmission) because it examines the variants introduced by the author himself/herself on the manuscript or on a print. These are variants that bear witness to a change in the author's will, to a more or less significant change of perspective regarding a specific text. Hence, the object of study of authorial philology, on the one hand, consists in the study of how a text is elaborated, a text whose autograph has come down to us and which bears traces of authorial corrections and revisions (and is therefore an *in fieri opus*) and, on the other hand, the object of study involves the examination of the various editions themselves, be they handwritten or printed, of a work. Of course, from a material point of view, very different situations can arise. The most emblematic case of authorial variants is an unpublished manuscript, but there can also be authorial variants on printed copies or on apograph copies (made, for example, by a copyist), or we might find that the traces of the reworking process may not be directly testified by the autograph interventions but 'recorded' by the non-authorial manuscript tradition or by the prints.

The critical edition in authorial philology

In philology of the copy, setting up a critical edition means creating a text that comes as convincingly close as possible to the lost original.

In authorial philology, instead, it means deciding which text to pick as copy-text and reconstructing, through appropriate systems of representation, the corrections made during the gestation or revision of the work. When confronted with a text, therefore, the philologist's work has two aims:

- *establishing the critical text*, that is, to decide which reading to pick as copy-text;
- *reconstructing and representing* in the clearest and most rational way the process of correction of the text itself.

Authorial philology therefore takes us directly into the writer's workshop, leading us to know their secrets, their 'recipes', and allowing us to penetrate the inner workings of their texts. It is similar to the evidential process, in which we have objective data offered by our witnesses that must be connected and understood in the most rational and logical way possible, using all the elements we have at our disposal: letters, notes, other texts, knowledge about the literary environment, about the author's linguistic skills, style, etc. This is a sort of *ex-post* reconstruction of what happened in the author's mind to bring the work to fruition.

What is the purpose of this reconstruction? Given that we already have the text and could base our study on this alone, what other information can allow us to know about the factors that preceded or accompanied the text during its history? This is the key question which leads us to consider the critical implications of this branch of philology, the so-called *criticism of variants*.

(Authorial) philology and critics (of variants)

If, then, authorial philology investigates the process of how a text is elaborated, criticism of variants represents the critical application of the results of such philological study. Both disciplines focus their attention on the creative moment concerning the genesis of the text or its evolution, and both make assumptions, on the basis of the extant materials, about the relationship between the author and the text. The study of this relationship does not only concern the time of the creation of the work, but also what follows its printing, including the more or less numerous and complex revisions which affect the printed text.

Philology is concerned with the representation of a text along with its corrections and variants; criticism deals with the interpretation of this collective information. Both modes of enquiry, description and interpretation, are closely intertwined, not least because the descriptive process is neither neutral nor limited to the literary aspect of the text, but requires one to take into account many different factors — historical, cultural and linguistic — that contribute to how we interpret and connect up the data in a reconstruction which is, in itself, an act of critical interpretation. We will see how the very evolution of the discipline leads to an increasingly interpretative philology, moving from the preference for synchronic and photographical apparatuses (i.e., methods for the representation of corrections) towards a diachronic and 'systemic' apparatus.

As we can see, then, we are dealing with a new way of looking at the texts, a new kind of approach which has only recently become an autonomous discipline. What distinguishes authorial philology and its critical application from other methods of literary criticism? The answer is, above all, the consideration of the text as a living organism that can evolve. In the past, the text was considered as a fixed, unmoving object, the result of a moment of creative genius that cannot be explained rationally and has to be evaluated largely as an artistic product according to different aesthetic canons. In authorial philology and criticism of variants, the text is instead considered as an expression of a process of research, whose final product is simply the result of subsequent 'approximations to a value' (according to a well-known phrase by Contini) — a value which is not absolute but relative, dependent on the relationship with the preceding texts.

This new approach modifies the aesthetic evaluation of a text as well. The text is not sharply judged according to the simple alternative 'poetry'/ 'non-poetry' as proposed by the idealist philosopher Benedetto Croce at the beginning of the twentieth century. Rather, the text is constantly related to its internal history, which is embedded in its existence as a final product. It might be useful to start with a definition given by the founder of criticism of variants, Gianfranco Contini (in 1947; see now Contini 1982: 233–34):

What significance do the authors' corrected manuscripts have for the critic? There are essentially two ways of considering a work of poetry. One is a static perspective, so to speak, that thinks of the work as an object or result, giving a characterizing description of it. The other is a dynamic one, which regards it as a human product or a work in progress and dramatically represents its dialectic life. The first approach evaluates the poetic work in terms of a 'value'; the second perspective evaluates it in terms of a never-ending 'approximation to a value'. This second approach, compared to that first, 'absolute' one, might be defined as 'pedagogical', in the most elevated meaning of the word. The interest in later versions and authorial variants (as with the *pentimenti* and repaintings of a painter) fits into this pedagogical vision of art, since it replaces the myth of the dialectic representation with more literal and documentarily-founded historical elements.

As we can see, this is not solely a philological problem, but also a philosophical one, even though it is striking that the critical, ideological and philosophical implications only began to be discussed after some tangible attempts had been made to prepare editions based on authorial philology.

From Petrarch's *Canzoniere* to modern texts

The study of the elaboration of a text — from the first idea and the drafting of early preliminary sketches to the construction and refining that accompanies its genesis and subsequent evolution — is the critical approach that brings us closest to the author's choices, eventually allowing us to evaluate more deeply his/her poetics. This is difficult to do for ancient and medieval texts, where the 'vertical' transmission — i.e., based on copies made from the original manuscript, which is lost — has cancelled and blurred the possible traces of any different authorial will. On the contrary, the reconstruction of the development of the variants — i.e., the adjustments and corrections made to the text while it was first being written, or later in time — is possible when the autograph documents have been preserved. In Italian literature, this means from the time of Petrarch's *Canzoniere* (*Rerum vulgarium fragmenta*), of which we possess not only the idiograph of the final version, but also the so-called *Codice degli abbozzi*, which is a composite autograph manuscript preserving both initial and intermediate redactions of various poems in different stages of their elaboration. The *Codice degli abbozzi* is a fundamental testimony, not only because of the importance of the documentation it preserves and of the canonical value of Petrarch's *Canzoniere* for the whole development of Italian literature, but also because the *Codice* shows an awareness of the act of writing literature that differs from that seen in previous medieval literature (including Dante, for whom no autograph is preserved). Such awareness implies on the author's part a special care for the preservation of his/her own papers and for their dissemination.

The presence of autographs — accompanied or replaced after the invention of printing in the 1450s by printed editions that the author may or may not have edited — is increasingly attested from this period onwards, and reaches its peak in the modern age, becoming the norm in twentieth century, when specific conservation centres have been established for autograph manuscripts, developing proper storage spaces and consultation policies and criteria for such purposes.

History, methods, examples

This work aims to follow the developments of the discipline of authorial philology, developments which have been fully clarified only recently, after almost a century of its history, thanks to a theoretical effort that has resulted in a substantial bibliography over the last few years. The main purpose of this book, in accordance with its introductory and didactic character, is however to provide a clear account of the methods of this discipline in its practical application by listing the fundamental elements of the critical edition and analysing some relevant cases.

The choice of the editions that we will analyze in their chronological order is based on the principle of presenting a case history of circumstances and critical methodologies that is as broad as possible, in order to offer innovative proposals regarding at least one of the following problems that the editor faces in dealing with a text:

- *Defining a base-text* (what redaction should be privileged? Should we take the one corresponding to the first authorial intention or to their final intention?): there are many different proposed solutions, as we can see by comparing the two cases

of Pietro Bembo's *Prose della volgar lingua* (see section 3.2 below) and Giacomo Leopardi's *Canti* (see section 3.5);
- Distinguishing *writing stages* (to be represented in the apparatus) and *intermediate versions* (which have to be published in full): this is the problem raised by the so-called *Seconda minuta* of *I promessi sposi* (see section 3.4);
- Dealing with the problem of the *'untouchability' of the text* and of finding criteria for *representing the variants* (as can be seen again in the critical edition of Bembo's *Prose della volgar lingua*);
- Explaining the relationship that a single text can have with a greater textual 'whole' as in the case of organized collections of poems, such as Petrarch's *Canzoniere* and Tasso's *Rime d'amore* (for which see section 3.3).

In each of these examples we have tried to highlight the advantages and possible side effects of the editorial choices undertaken, so as to encourage a reflective approach and offer further points for consideration. In this context, it is important to remember that the perfect critical edition does not exist, but within certain established criteria (coherence between text and apparatus; the need to avoid contamination between different chronological writing stages; the rationale for every editorial intervention on the text, etc.) each edition raises specific issues that can be resolved through individual philological solutions.

One discipline, different skills

We have already said that, as with philology of the copy, the practice of authorial philology requires different skills related to the author and his/her time. Useful information for interpreting and therefore properly 'restoring' a text includes both data that is historical, documentary and biographical (dating of the versions and their chronological sequence as they can be assessed through external elements) and a close knowledge of the *genre* (metrics, stylistics, etc.). Palaeographic expertise (the ability to assess the authorship of the autograph and knowledge of the author's graphical habits, etc.), archival expertise (an understanding of whether, for instance, the order of the papers is original or has been modified) and knowledge of the history of the language (the *usus scribendi* and the evolution of the author's linguistic habits) are fundamental as well.

In this regard, the philologist also has to be a literary historian, a scholar of metrics and stylistics, a palaeographer and codicologist, an historian of language, one able to combine a very careful and detailed analysis of the object of study with an understanding of the general historical context, including the history of culture, of literary production and also publishing production, of the printing practice of the time, etc. In many specific textual cases (e.g., as with part of the witnesses of Petrarch's *Canzoniere*), the interweaving of both a given author's own innovative re-working and of textual tradition often makes it necessary to use both the methods of authorial philology and of philology of the copy. Likewise, for texts dating from after the introduction of printing, a particularly important contribution has been made by Textual Bibliography, a discipline with origins in Anglo-Saxon scholarship that was later introduced and developed in Italian Studies.

The study of how printed editions were prepared, and above all the acknowledgement of the existence of *different* exemplars of the same edition, testified to by so-called *stop-press corrections*, allow the editor to establish the author's degree of involvement in the printing process. As a consequence, it is possible to evaluate how reliable an edition is both in its overall structuring of the text and in its single readings (editor's interventions and possible censorship or alterations must be carefully taken into consideration), as well as with regard to the linguistic aspects of the text, which are often affected by a process of normalization which is not always due to the author.

Obviously, the more complex the textual circumstances are, the more difficult it will be to include in a single visual representation the whole set of information. For instance, when we are dealing with macroorganisms such as collection of poems or short stories, or epistolaries, there may be, just like in philology of the copy, *organic witnesses* (i.e., manuscripts or print copies that contain the entire collection of texts) and *disorganic witnesses* (i.e., copies with single texts in earlier versions that are sometimes autonomous from the overall project of the collection). There are also particular interventions connected to wider projects of revision which require us to evaluate the relationship between the individual correction and the wider writing phase. In this case, too, two different perspectives have to be combined: one 'from afar', which allows us to embed the single text in an organic whole, and the other 'from close up', which analyzes the single text as an autonomous organism. The case-study of Petrarch's *Canzoniere* and its different forms over time is the most conspicuous example in this sense. It is no accident that, even though various studies in the last decades have been devoted to its structure, no critical edition has been produced so far that is able to embrace the entire process of its elaboration. Similar problems arise in many other traditions, and, in several instances, modern editors have introduced unacceptable contaminations between global structure and single adopted readings of the poems, or have largely deliberately ignored the author's ordering.

Digital editions and common representations

One possible solution to these problems might come from digital editions, which allow us to represent the textual tradition in ways that enable a focus on specific elements as well as the textual whole, for a more direct and, at the same time, more synoptic representation of the textual tradition. Digital editions are able to visually render the passage from one 'system' to another, by means of virtual technologies that simulate the gradual increments made to a text.

The above-mentioned idea of a text in progress suits very well a representation *in fieri* as offered by hyper-textual editions. In this way, the various 'movements' of the text can be visually represented through specific uses of space and colours.

Nevertheless, even though the value of studying the Italian *scartafacci* is well established nowadays (see Chapter 2 for the debate about this at the beginning of the twentieth century), the study of variants is in fact deeply conditioned by the lack of shared editorial criteria, both within Italy and outside. This makes it difficult to use editions, since with each edition, one has to deal with a new system of diacritical marks and symbols, without being able to rely on any form of standardization.

One consequence here is that, whereas the Italian philological school is undoubtedly very active in preparing critical authorial editions, the use of variants as a way of making incisive comment on texts is still lacking, although it has become more and more popular in the last few years. At the same time, far less use is made in Italy compared to France of various kinds of apparatus in order to characterize the author's *modus operandi* and the creative and elaborative mechanisms underlying the text (for the *critique génétique*, see Chapter 3).

A judicious balance between a practical approach and a more general critical concern is the best way to create more accessible and readable editions, above all with the aim of clearly offering the largest amount of available data, by having recourse as far as is possible to common systems of textual representation, while at the same time respecting the fact that every text is singular and unique. According to Isella (2009a: 245):

> the critical edition of an *in fieri* text is different from time to time: it depends on the different materials on which we work (loose papers, notebooks of any kind, autographs, idiographs, copies made by others — for instance, some lines and redactions by Montale are only known through photocopies, and so on). Because the phenomenology of the text that has multiple redactions or is *in fieri* extremely varied and articulated, it is necessary to establish common rules, as with classical philology.

1. History

Paola Italia and Giulia Raboni[1]

1.1 Author's variants from a historical perspective

In his seminal book *Storia della tradizione e critica del testo* (1934), Giorgio Pasquali laid the foundations for revising Karl Lachmann's philology. In this book, Pasquali replaced the dream of a very 'accurate and mechanical' philology as proposed by Lachmann with a more historical and documental approach to the transmission of texts. Pasquali also notably pointed out the possible occurrence of authorial variants in classical texts as one of the areas where textual criticism needed to be corrected and expanded. Pasquali adumbrated the possibility that some variants that were believed to be due to transmission might actually be ascribed to later redactions by the author, whose original manuscript was obviously lost. Pasquali made this consideration by analogy with the state of Italian literature, which Michele Barbi had remarkably emphasized in those same years with his studies on the tradition of vernacular texts, studies that were later collected in his volume *La nuova filologia e l'edizione dei nostri scrittori da Dante a Manzoni* (1938).

Pasquali downplayed somewhat the significance of this situation in the next edition of his book (1952) because of the way other philologists, after the 1934 edition, had begun to propose excessively simplistic attributions of intentional authorial variants. All the same, the same scenario occurs at the origins of Italian literature given that the manuscript tradition of texts often contains variants that give grounds for us to suspect the author's intervention. For example, the poems of

---

1 Paola Italia wrote sections 1.3, 1.4, 1.6, 1.7 of the text; Giulia Raboni wrote sections 1.1, 1.2, 1.5.

Dante's *Vita Nuova* seem to have undergone a redrafting designed to produce a consistent organism at the moment of their inclusion in the book (which is formally prosimetric — that is, a mixed text containing poems framed by prose narrative). In paragraph xxxiv, Dante himself refers to the existence of a double beginning of the sonetto 'Era venuta nella mente mia', but depends on conventions, giving the first and highly influential authorial testimony of his own subsequent re-elaboration of this composition. While in this case, as with variants in many other texts, we can often only speculate, the situation is different when we face the autograph of a text, as we find for Petrarch's *Canzoniere* (see section 3.1) or Boccaccio's *Decameron*. For Boccaccio, we have not only the autograph of the final version, the MS Hamilton 90 codex kept at the Berlin State Library, but also the previous version transmitted by the Parisian BnF MS Italien 482, housed at the National Library of France.

The status of authorial variants changes with the invention of the printing press, as the phenomenon becomes notably more common and can be distinguished with variants that arise from tradition. During the Renaissance there are some famous cases of authorial variants: Ludovico Ariosto (for his chivalric epic, the *Orlando furioso*, we have not only the three printed editions supervised by the author himself but also autograph fragments), Niccolò Machiavelli, Baldassarre Castiglione, Giovanni Della Casa, Pietro Bembo, and finally Torquato Tasso, whose *Rime d'amore* represents even today one of the most interesting philological problems (see, once again, section 3.3). What is more, some of the outstanding literary texts of the eighteenth century — the works of Giuseppe Parini, Vittorio Alfieri, Vincenzo Monti — exist in authorial manuscripts, which allow us to reconstruct the stages in their development and the processes of textual correction.

However, manuscript witnesses increase and abound from the nineteenth century onwards, also thanks to a greater availability of paper which in the preceding centuries was a rare and precious commodity. Works by Ugo Foscolo, Giacomo Leopardi, Alessandro Manzoni, Ippolito Nievo, Giovanni Verga, Giosuè Carducci, all survive as a rich set of handwritten documents, taking us from the first germ of the text to the final copy before printing. In the same way, it is possible to retrace the internal history of the works of Giovanni Pascoli and Gabriele D'Annunzio and the great Italian poets and prose writers of the twentieth century, such as Eugenio Montale, Giuseppe Ungaretti, Umberto Saba, Vittorio Sereni and Carlo Emilio Gadda.

Beginning in the second half of the twentieth century, we can add to handwritten documents those that are typed first with mechanical typewriters, and then with electric typewriters. Photocopies take the place of copies made by copyists and, for the first time, mechanical means become part of the process of textual production. Such technologies involve different phenomenologies of transmission and correction of the text, which end up influencing the authors' process of working as well. These examples offer only a foreshadowing of the great revolution of the finale decade of the last century, dominated by a change in the production of literary texts, with the progressive (though not definitive) abandonment of handwriting and its replacement by computerized word-processing, that is, a way of writing that is completely different, both in how the text is conceived and how it is revised.

1.2 Methods throughout history: from Ubaldini to Moroncini

Authorial philology and its application in the form of criticism of variants has only come into existence with a coherent set of analytical tools, both methodological and critical, from the beginning of the twentieth century. This was the result of a theoretical and philosophical reflection that has brought with it an innovative way of considering how the literary work is made. At the same time, it is true that the focus on authorial variants has not come about suddenly, but has had a long genesis ranging across the history of literary criticism and beginning at least with Bembo's work as editor of Petrarch and a theorist of the language, and to some extent as a figure indebted to an earlier tradition. As demonstrated by Gino Belloni (1992), the way Bembo compared variants in his comments on Petrarch's poetry in the *Prose della volgar lingua* was a practice already used by Giovanni Pontano in his *Actius* (1495–1496), where the character of Azio-Sannazaro quotes some lines from the *Urania* (by Pontano) in a double version, to demonstrate how to amend the text in order to obtain the desired result of 'hastening' the poetic lines.

This is an important passage. It is unlike other parts of Pontano's treatise, where the concrete example of how to compose poetry is made through the manipulation of Virgil's lines where we are given the actual line, yet its elements are manipulated in order to prove how the author's use of *dispositio* is the most suited to achieved the desired stylistic effect, according to a method already used by Cicero and Dionysius of Halicarnassus. Instead, in this passage, Pontano's variants come directly from the author's workshop and are actually proven by handwritten versions of *Urania* that survive in the autograph manuscript Vaticano Latino 2837.

Given the fact that we know that there is an availability of other elaborations of the text by the author, a shift from fictional to real data takes place here, thereby paving the way towards a criticism of variants based on the information offered by the tradition. It is within this trajectory that we should place Bembo's analysis of Petrarch's variants. Such an analysis does not involve a theoretical change compared to Pontano's time, but is simply due to a different availability and access to materials. Bembo's example is important both because it soon draws its own disciples and because it opens the way to a greater attention to variants connected to different redactions and to the opportunity of a more accurate reading of the texts. It is evidently a turning point which cannot be disconnected from the more general cultural change and the different kinds of texts printed in those years.

It is no coincidence that, while studies of this kind on Petrarch continued, this sort of approach to an *in fieri* text would have been developed from the three editions of Ariosto's *Orlando furioso* (1516, 1521 and 1532). Works on Ariosto's variants by Simon Fòrnari (1549), Giovan Battista Pigna (1544) and Ludovico Dolce (1564) focus the discussion, with some difference among them, on didactic terms, postulating an 'implicit improvement' of the text, as Bembo's comments on Petrarch had done. In other words, in altering the text, the author shows his/her ability to refine it. Such a perspective, however, still lacks the ability to connect the various tesserae in the system of corrections to one another in order to provide a more comprehensive definition of 'poetics' (as pointed out by Segre 2008: 133–64).

A different and more advanced solution, and substantially not imitated until the twentieth century, is the one represented by Federico

Ubaldini's edition of *Rime di M. Francesco Petrarca come estratte da un suo originale*. In this edition, dated 1652, the philologist undertakes a graphical representation of Petrarch's corrections. Compared to the previous 'criticism of variants', this edition presents a striking degree of accuracy and innovation in reproducing in its entirety the readings in the *Codice degli abbozzi* with fitting typographical solutions in order to highlight deletions and drafting revisions. This is no longer a selection of *loci critici* as the aforementioned cases were, but a tool providing a complete vision of the correcting process, consisting in a 'documentation' offered without the filter of a preliminary critical judgment.

Ubaldini's edition, later employed by Ludovico Antonio Muratori in his Petrarchan commentary, would be reprinted in 1750, and then used until the 1891 diplomatic edition by Karl Appel, setting a trend for one of the earliest pioneering and seminal editions of authorial philology, namely that produced by Santorre Debenedetti in his *Frammenti autografi dell'Orlando furioso*. Debenedetti's work had the merit of taking up again in Italy the cause of representing autograph texts, bringing about — as we will see — Gianfranco Contini's reflection on Ariosto's working method and the debate on the 'critics of *scartafacci*' (that is, a form of criticism based on rough drafts).

As we are now seeing, criticism of variants and authorial philology have their origins in a series of reflections and considerations on topics of perennial discussion. This is itself a strong sign of the persistence of a tradition, although a 'subterranean' one for a long time, and of the relevance of this kind of study. Another major contributing factor, from the end of nineteenth century, that should be noted here is the Italian Unification and the consequent discussion on the national literary heritage, especially concerning works deemed to be politically and linguistically 'usable'.

The main object of nineteenth-century studies is Manzoni's great historical novel, *I promessi sposi*. A great number of scholars devoted their attention to Manzoni's novel, investigating in particular the linguistic differences between the so-called '*Ventisettana*' and '*Quarantana*' editions (see section 3.4): see Luigi Morandi (1873 and 1874), Riccardo Fogli (1877 and 1879) and Policarpo Petrocchi (1893 and 1902). The research was also extended to the first redaction with Giovanni Sforza (1898 and 1905) and Giuseppe Lesca (1916), up to Michele Barbi, who conceived a general plan (Barbi 1939) for the publishing of Manzoni's works which came to fruition in the 'Classici Mondadori' edition by Alberto Chiari and Fausto Ghisalberti (1954).

However, it was a *dilettante*, a passionate enthusiast for his object of research, Francesco Moroncini from Recanati, who made the most decisive effort to represent fully authorial variants and to provide an exhaustive apparatus. Having produced first an annotated edition of Leopardi's *Canti*, Moroncini published a critical edition of the same collection in 1927, creating a typographic system suitable not only for the representation of text variants of manuscripts and prints (up to the definitive Starita edition in 1835, which he used as the base-text), but also for the complex series of notes that surround Leopardi's autographs. These notes are known as the *varia lectio*, and include genetic versions, variants, notes that 'certify' the language employed by identifying examples from the Italian literary tradition, and literary sources. Taken together, the notes are an essential complement in understanding the genesis and development of the *Canti*.

Moroncini's work is the real starting point both for the rich reflection on Leopardi's autographs that has developed from Contini and Giuseppe De Robertis onwards, and for an increasingly refined elaboration of the authorial philology apparatus that is so well exemplified in this edition of *Canti* (see section 3.5). Moroncini's edition in effect proposed something — in the words of Gianfranco Folena — 'far beyond the editor's intentions, a new idea of the poetic text and a new complex and problematic criticism of the relationship between synchronicity and diachronicity, system and evolution, *parole* and *langue* in poetry' (Leopardi 1978: xi).

1.3 Authorial philology and criticism of variants

After a decade in which Moroncini's admirable work was more often praised and cited than seriously studied, in 1937, Santorre Debenedetti published his critical edition of some autograph fragments from *Orlando furioso*. The fragments consist of four major scenes added to the text of 1521 (the first edition, which was not very different, was printed in 1516): Olimpia's story; the 'Rocca di Tristano' episode with Merlino's prophetic frescoes; the Marganorre's narrative; and the story of Ruggiero and Leone — which brings the total number of Cantos from 40 to 46. These fragments — except the last one that has reached us in an apograph copy — survive in 'many notebooks and remnants of notebooks, handwritten by the poet [...] with different degrees of elaboration' (Ariosto 1937: viii), kept (with the exception of some papers) at the Municipal Library of Ferrara.

Debenedetti's edition tacitly follows some of Moroncini's own criteria. Despite not offering a systematic solution, Debenedetti tries to answer the main problems of authorial philology. One of these is how to deal with incomplete texts and with a manuscript documentation that is autograph but might not be fully reliable. For example, Debenedetti amends spelling errors but leaves unchanged 'the wrong readings that Messer Ludovico undoubtedly thought about in that way' (ibid.: xxxix). Another problem is how to distinguish between authorial variants that are made in the first act of composition and those that come later: with regard to these variants, Debenedetti argued that 'since it may be a change made during the writing of the line, or when the line was completed, it would be good to distinguish between the two' (ibid.: xxxviii).

In the same year, Contini wrote a review essay on Debenedetti's edition for the journal *Il Meridiano di Roma* ('Come lavorava l'Ariosto', later collected in Contini 1939). This essay is universally considered to be the founding act of criticism of variants. The authorial variants of the *Orlando furioso* offer the philologist some constant, recurring elements that may allow one to describe Ariosto's poetics in a way which does not clash with the Benedetto Croce's celebrated characterization in his *Ariosto* (1918 then collected in Croce 1920), where harmony is identified as its founding principle. In his review essay, Contini also tackles the more general problem of what it means to study text corrections and their aesthetic and philosophical implications. He does this through the above-mentioned definition of the 'dynamic way' in which the art work may be seen, as a 'never-ending approximation to a value' (Contini 1982: 233).

Due to the major influence exerted by Croce's thought and aesthetic on Italian culture, not even a renowned scholar such as Contini could operate on strictly literary and philological platforms, so that the new 'criticism of corrections' (the technical term he used before replacing it with the more well-known 'criticism of variants') was introduced as a 'pedagogical version' of Croce's criticism. Criticism of variants is therefore not in opposition to Croce's method and it could reach the same conclusions, though starting from a different approach which considered the text in a dynamic rather than static way.

Assuming that the task of criticism was to identify the 'poetics' of the text, and that, according to Croce, 'poetry' meant 'lyrical insight' (rather than the external superstructures which stained its purity), this exercise could only be carried out on the final text as delivered to the printer by the author in its final version. Every reflection around the previous writing stages was a merely linguistic or documentary exercise, useless for the 'critic': 'the work of art has a completely ideal origin, which comes from its presence itself' (Croce 1947: 93–94).

It is interesting to note that the subsequent dispute with Croce will not refer back to this essay by Contini or to Debenedetti's edition (and for which Contini's review essay was, in some way, a 'justification'), but to another text, which was, in its own way, in favour of a dynamic view of the work of art. The text concerned is the paper published by Giuseppe De Robertis in 1946 in defense of the first version (now known as *Fermo e Lucia*) of *I promessi sposi* edited by Giuseppe Lesca under the title *Gli sposi promessi* (Manzoni 1916). After its publication, Lesca's edition had been strongly criticized by the celebrated philologist Ernesto Giacomo Parodi (1916: 9). Quoting Contini's words in an article intended to defend Lesca, De Robertis implicitly acknowledged Lesca's role in creating the so-called criticism of corrections, supporting his philological effort (see section 3.5) and, more generally, his way of studying how literary works were made.

The debate inflamed the literary journals of the time, in the framework of the intellectual fervour of the post-war years. In 1947, Croce launched a major attack upon the fledgling disciple of criticism of variants with an article entitled 'Illusione sulla genesi delle opere d'arte, documentabile dagli scartafacci degli scrittori' (Croce 1947). The article was published in *Quaderni della Critica*, the recognized journal for supporters of Crocean critical orthodoxy. In this paper, Croce argued that it was completely useless to investigate authors' manuscripts if one wished to evaluate the text's true 'poetry'. Contini's reply was almost immediate, but it was, so to speak, like 'shooting the messenger' so as to reach the person who sent the message. In fact, one year after Croce's article, Nullo Minissi had come to its defence with the essay 'Le correzioni e la critica', published in the journal *Belfagor*. In this work, Minissi — without having read the original paper by Contini on Ariosto and only knowing De Robertis' paper — had branded the new critics and its leader as useless and detrimental to Italian culture.

Contini's essay titled 'La critica degli scartafacci' (which appeared the same year in *Rassegna d'Italia*) reveals that the target was higher than Minissi, with whom the skirmish was purely literary. Here Contini strongly reaffirms that the new criticism was not founded in opposition to Crocean criticism, but as a 'pedagogical' version of it ('I was opposing "directions" to "fixed boundaries"'), one which starts from the same assumptions, as rightly pointed out by Isella (2009a: 5–6):

> If the 'poetry created' does not naturalistically identify 'with the letter of the text (or the brushstrokes on the canvas)', if indeed its 'value' is to be understood, in strict orthodoxy, 'as a transcendental and non-physical presence', it follows strictly speaking that 'it can be found fully realized in the text' as opus perfectum, 'as well as in the movement or approximation to the text', considered in its making.

Nevertheless, Contini's cultural background — which brought together Debenedetti's philology with de Saussure's structuralism and Spitzer's linguistics — led him naturally not to consider within authorial variants the poetical *quantum* added to the text. This was a 'didactical' attitude that was still found in Moroncini's stance, who declared critical editions to be helpful for teaching young people the directions in which the authors moved, as they transitioned from incorrect to correct modes of expression. On the contrary, Contini's propensity was to study the text as a system, where change to a single part effected change to the entire text, like a chessboard, where moving a piece (the single variant) alters the structure of the entire game (as Gadda had argued with an evocative image in *Meditazione Milanese* in 1928). For this reason, Contini argued that the analysis of authorial variants could not be carried out as individual samples but should rather be achieved by means of categories, by correctional systems, by directions, with the purpose of giving a dynamic characterization of the author's poetics.

Needless to say, such a dynamic vision of the work of art could not be confined to purely national borders. The earliest applications of this new method of text or textual analysis are indeed devoted both to Italian and French classics. Italian works include Contini's essays on Petrarch ('Saggio d'un commento alle correzioni del Petrarca volgare', 1941, printed in 1943, now in Contini 1970) and on Leopardi ('Implicazioni leopardiane', 1947, now in Contini 1970), where, starting from the analysis of the poem 'A Silvia', he showed the deep logic of textual corrections in Leopardi's text. As for his work on French literature, it is worth remembering the 'Introduzione alle *paperoles*' (i.e., paperworks) on the variants of Marcel Proust's *Recherche* in 1947, and the essay 'Jean Santeuil, ossia l'infanzia della *Recherche*' (now in Contini 1970). When Proust died in 1922, only the first four parts of the *Recherche* had in fact been published. The other parts — *La prisonnière* [1923], *La fugitive* [1925], *Le temps retrouvé* [1927] — had been published by Proust's heirs on the basis of his papers without any proper philological criteria, and this therefore presented a significant problem which would eventually be resolved in the new edition issued in 1987–1989 by Gallimard. What is more, the new dynamic understanding of texts elaborated by Contini has to be put in relation to a 'Mallarméan consciousness', which came to him from the very heart of modern poetry through European symbolism ('Saggio d'un commento alle correzioni del Petrarca volgare', in Contini 1970: 5):

> The poetic school founded by Mallarmé, which has in Valéry its theoretician, by the way it considers poetry in its making interprets it as a mobile and non finishable, never-ending work, of which the historically existing poem represents a possible section, whose primacy is not theoretically justified and which is not necessarily the last. This is from the point of view of the producer, not of the user.
>
> However, if the critic considers the work of art as an 'object', this represents a concrete object only within his critical interpretation, this 'objectification' providing a theoretical justification for the critic's attitude of self-denial vis à vis the work of art; considering the poetic act will lead him to dynamically relocate his formulae, to seek directions more than fixed boundaries for the poetic energy. A guideline, and not a border, enclose authorial corrections; only today the Mallarméan consciousness, together with the standardized reduction of personality imposed by the aesthetics of expression, allows a rigorous and poetically fruitful study of it.

1.4 Authorial philology and *critique génétique*

Authorial philology, then, develops a new way of conceiving texts as the result of a different approach to literature, even from a philosophical point of view. Authorial philology and criticism of variants indeed understand a text's poetics not as a 'fact', an established 'value', but as an 'approximation to a value', which includes and stems from all the texts that preceded it (the *avant-textes*).

The term 'avant-texte' has found some fortune in Italy, but it has often been used with different meanings. Introduced by Jean Bellemin-Noël (1972), this term is employed in France to signify 'the set of preparatory materials collected, decoded, classified: from simple list of words to notes, sketches, first minimum drafts, until and on to actual versions' (Stussi 1994: 198). At times, the term is extended to cover areas that are not strictly philological, such as the mental journey of the author, which is at times considered part of the avant-texte.

In Italian authorial philology, the term *avantesto* refers to the entire set of materials preceding the text. In this sense, it is possible to distinguish:

- materials that do not have a direct relationship with the text (such as lists of characters, literary projects, lists of words, etc.);
- materials which have a direct relationship with the text (such as early versions and later drafts that precede the actual text).

Two different kinds of critical edition derive from this distinction: the French one that is better known as *edition génétique* or genetic edition, and the German-Italian one that is generally defined as *edizione critica* or *critico-genetica*, that is, as a critical edition or a critical-genetic edition. The genetic French edition is distinctive in its editing all the avant-textes, from initial notes to late corrections on printed proofs. It makes no distinction between these two different types of avant-texte and it does not subordinate one type to the other. Examples here are the edition of Paul Valéry's *Cahiers*, published in twenty-nine volumes between 1957–1961, or the edition of *Un Coeur simple* from the *Corpus flaubertianum*, published by Giovanni Bonaccorso in 1983 for Le Belles Lettres in Paris. The *edition génétique* is a representation of the history of the text through single 'pictures': each one 'photographs' a provisional status of the text's history without any distinction between apparatus, preparatory materials and the text itself.

On the other hand, the German-Italian edition tends to give greater importance to the process of correction of the version selected as copy-text or base-text. For this reason, such editions consider only the part of the avant-texte which has a direct relationship with that 'product'. In other words, the *edizione critica* (or *critico-genetica*) focuses on the evolutionary itinerary of the text, that is, the variantistic process leading from the readings contained in the apparatus to the version selected as copy-text (or vice versa). That is the reason why the special character of an Italian critical edition produced by authorial philology the double textual system that it presents to the reader, one which occupies two different typographical areas: the *text* and the *apparatus*. The latter is always dependent on the former, even graphically, as the apparatus is found either in the footnotes of each page, at the end of the text, or in a separate volume. Materials that do not have a direct relationship with the text are not included in the edition but these are usually published in a subordinate position, either in an appendix or, in the case of particularly voluminous materials, in a separate volume.

When undertaking the edition of an *in fieri* text, the philologist should not so much 'record in slow-motion' the act of writing, which would smack of disingenuous presumption and might well be pointless, for actually not even the author knows all the steps that have happened in his or her mind, from the first idea of the text until its final version, because s/he cannot recall them in detail. What the philologist should rather do is to translate the obscurity of the manuscript into clear signs representing, whenever possible, the compositional history that s/he was able to reconstruct and — far more significantly — that constitutes his/her hypothesis of what happens 'before the text', all that which leads the text to what it is. In other words, through the analysis of manuscripts one should not attempt to divine the mental journeys of the author, but rather to develop 'standards of formalization of the apparatus and [...] systems able to best render the elaborative process of the writer (with all its internal stages, properly distinguished and correlated), both for manuscripts and prints' (Isella 2009a: 16). Consequently, if the philologist makes a hypothesis based on the study of variants, the apparatus is nothing but the concrete application of this or, we might say, the scientific law that describes in a rational and economic way the series of empirical phenomena observed. Like every scientific law, it is to be considered valid until some data emerge that it is unable to explain, and that therefore invalidates the apparatus or obliges the philologist to propose simple adjustments of it.

For this very reason, any attempt at formalization has an experimental character, and it is impossible to provide a single apparatus for what is a non-homogeneous series of phenomena. What is more, since each author has his/her personal set of habits in terms of corrections, style, poetics, compositional strategy, it will be necessary to develop on a case-by-case basis a method suitable for representing such habits.

As mentioned above, the ultimate apparatus (just like the ultimate critical edition) does not exist. What may be fine for one author, does not work for another. Verga does not correct like Gadda, whose correcting habits are paradoxically much more similar to the habits of Bembo, although Gadda and Bembo cannot be brought together from any other point of view. When we have more works of authorial philology and this discipline is more codified, perhaps it will be possible to write a history of Italian literature based on its authors' various systems of correcting themselves and their relationship with their own manuscripts. New and interesting results would come from this study since in comparing a writer and his/her text we can get useful information on his/her poetics and even on his/her ideas on the world.

1.5 Dante Isella's authorial philology

The publication of *Le carte mescolate. Esperienze di filologia d'autore* by Dante Isella in 1987 created a watershed in the field of critical editions of authorial texts both for *in fieri* works and for works attested to by multiple redactions (see sections 2.1.1 and 2.1.2). The successful term *filologia d'autore*, or authorial philology, which is now commonly used in Italian Studies, derives from the title of this volume in contrast to the previous denomination *fenomenologia dell'originale* (phenomenology of the original) used by D'Arco Silvio Avalle (1970).

Isella was a student of Contini at the University of Fribourg. From the 1950s, he worked in the field of textual editing and its presentation of authorial variants. In particular, he produced a series of editions for texts from the sixteenth century to contemporary times, which were increasingly refined in terms of how the critical apparatus was elaborated. Each edition he prepared was characterized by different issues, and this allowed him to develop editing tools in each case. The opening piece of the volume — 'Le varianti d'autore (critica e filologia)' — was Isella's inaugural lecture delivered when he took up the Chair of Italian Literature at the ETH at Zurich, and is a first attempt to provide a history of authorial philology. Isella retraced the theoretical birth of the discipline from the controversy between Benedetto Croce, Giuseppe De Robertis and Gianfranco Contini (see section 1.3), underlining Contini's fundamental role. Contini's position is compared, on the one hand, with the aesthetics of Croce. Isella notes here that Contini had already emphasized, in his essay on Ariosto, a sense of perfect complementarity with Croce's work, seeing the examination of the variants as having a sort of control function in relation to the 'characterizing' descriptions typical of Crocean criticism. And, on the other, he compares Contini's approach with Leo Spitzer's stylistic criticism, which is corrected and verified by comparing the author's individual language not so much with a theoretical linguistic norm, but with the author's subsequent linguistic and textual choices.

Contini supplemented and systematized this frame of analysis by drawing on the contributions made by structuralism and this allows him to overcome the 'atomistic' idea of single variants (typical of the contemporary critical position of Giuseppe De Robertis), in favour of a systemic conception of the correcting process, one which proves particularly fruitful in the analysis of Leopardi's poetry. This results in a series of philological endeavours that characterize Italian criticism of the 1940s. In the following chapters of the volume, Isella aims to exemplify these innovations, shifting the focus from theory to practice. This change of focus implicitly leads him to modify decisively the relation between philology and criticism to the advantage of the former. From that point on, philology is considered not only equal and complementary to criticism (and already this is a major advance when compared to the ancillary role Croce had given to philology), but is also viewed as being by itself capable of providing new critical perspectives, through its elaboration of its own methodology. In other words, compared to Contini, Isella is much more of an editor. For Contini in fact never directly worked on authorial editions, except for the *Opera in versi* by Montale, edited with Rosanna Bettarini, and the collaboration of Montale himself, and his critical work takes place retrospectively on the material offered by genetic editions, such as the edition of Ariosto's *Orlando furioso* by Debenedetti or Leopardi's *Canti* by Moroncini and then Peruzzi. The examples Isella gives deal with very complex cases, and the preparation of the apparatus is based on a reasoned chronological ordering of the papers and the interpretation of the ways an author's habits and modes of correcting develop. Ecdotics itself — the science that deals with the problems related to the editing of texts — is therefore an interpretative act, which demands a greater responsibility on the editor's part, as the editor must adapt the methodological aspect to his/her reconstructive hypothesis. It demands the shift to more analytical and more flexible tools for representing variants that can be adapted to different textual conditions.

Three other chapters of Isella's book are dedicated to explaining some notable cases, in order to provide a template or model for a 'hypothetical handbook' of authorial philology. The next chapter ('Le testimonianze autografe plurime'), the most succinct and methodological in the volume, describes three complicated cases of authorial philology: Tasso's *Rime d'amore*, Parini's scattered poems and Manzoni's first drafts of *I promessi sposi* (the aforementioned *Fermo e Lucia* and the so-called *Seconda minuta*). The following two chapters deal in a more comprehensive and analytical way with Tasso's rhymes and Parini's *Giorno*. Isella always focuses his attention on the peculiarity of the textual condition of the works he examines, and comes up with new proposals, strictly related to the interpretative framework.

In the cases of Tasso's collection of rhymes and of the different versions of Parini's poems, Isella insists on the necessity of distinguishing between different compositional phases that correspond to different authorial arrangements, and he creates apparatuses which are functional to representing the variantistic process. To this end, Isella introduces, in the case of Parini's *Giorno* (1969), the distinction between *genetic apparatus* and *evolutionary apparatus*. The former includes the genetic elaboration before the copy-text; the latter testifies to the variants that follow it without taking shape in a completed and coherent revision (thus giving evidence of a writing phase which is completely different from the one represented by the following drafting status). On the distinction between *genetic* and *evolutionary* apparatuses, see section 2.2.1.

The quest in the apparatuses for an adequate and effective way of formalizing the set of variants responds to an attitude inspired by a sense of adherence to the text; an attitude which, in Isella's words, resembles the way in which a seismograph is sensitive to the registration of the movements of the earth. Any formalization must be properly modelled on the author's particular correcting practice. Gadda's typical procedure is to increase the sentence *ex post* through insertions and writings on the side of the page, and is therefore representable in a rather photographical way, not idiomatic. Manzoni's working method is instead characterized by logical implications that are developed from a 'base' sentence. The syntactic organization of these implications in new segments entails the replacement of the first draft with a different wording and requires a more cohesive representation that allows the visualization and the comparison of the whole structure subject to variation, according to a hierarchy of compositional phases as comprehensive as possible. This is what has been done with the apparatuses for Gadda's texts on the one hand and of *Fermo e Lucia*'s critical edition on the other. The latter is significantly directed towards an interpretative representation that gives priority to the comparability between long passages of the text over a punctual and topographic indication.

Some years separate these two projects: they were directly carried out by Isella or by his school students, and they further refined the editorial criteria. From the edition of Gadda's *Racconto italiano di ignoto del Novecento* in 1983, Isella was able to clearly state the distinction of a triple textual filter: (1) apparatus, (2) marginalia, (3) alternative variants. This filter is used for the complete edition of Gadda's work published by Garzanti's series 'I libri della Spiga' since 1988. Though not all texts are provided with an apparatus, for all of them a Note provides exhaustive information on the drafting and editorial scenario. The edition of Verga's *Malavoglia* produced in 1995 by Isella's student Ferruccio Cecco (Verga 1995, 2014) introduces some fundamental techniques in the establishment of linear apparatus for prose texts. In Cecco's edition, a *diachronic apparatus* is experimented with for the first time. In this kind of apparatus, parts of the text are arranged in a chronological order, separated and hierarchized by a number until the last phase (the copy-text) with minor variants in parentheses. This is a concise and highly critical form of representation, since it is not always easy to decide, especially in the case of long prose sentences, which elements are introduced at the time of writing and which are added later. In order to establish their timeline, the philologist should take into account every graphic, topographic, linguistic and semantic indicator which is available. In this edition, Cecco deals with, and successfully solves, the problems raised by the representation of the avant-texte and the need to distinguish in those further variants of the print, as compared with the final manuscript, the interventions that can be attributed to the author (evidently testified by drafts now lost) from those that can be attributed to the typographer.

From then on, these solutions have been taken and improved by other editions connected to Isella, a great promoter of philological workshops especially since his teaching years in Pavia. We already mentioned, on the one hand, the workshop on Tasso's rhymes launched in Pavia by Lanfranco Caretti in collaboration with Luigi Poma, Cesare Bozzetti and Franco Gavazzeni and, on the other hand, the Gadda workshop, to which a workshop on Verga was later added on account of Carla Ricciardi's, as well as Cecco's, participation. Another workshop was that on Manzoni, producing editions, in Pavia again, of the treatise *Della lingua italiana* by Luigi Poma and Angelo Stella (1974), of the *Scritti linguistici e letterari* by Luca Danzi and Angelo Stella (1991), of the *Scritti letterari* by Carla Ricciardi and Biancamaria Travi (1991) and even of the *Inni sacri* by Franco Gavazzeni and Simone Albonico (Manzoni 1997). Thanks to Isella's initiative, many editorial series were created that proposed critical editions of texts existing in several authorial redactions. This is the case with the 'Classici Mondadori' (and then of the 'Meridiani'), 'Studi e strumenti di filologia italiana' by the Arnoldo and Alberto Mondadori Foundation, the National Edition of D'Annunzio's works, and then the 'Fondazione Pietro Bembo' series, which was created by Isella with Giorgio Manganelli and continues to be directed by Pier Vincenzo Mengaldo and Alfredo Stussi. These series contained significant studies and emerged from other centers of excellence close to Isella's interests, in particular from scholars associated with Domenico De Robertis.

In light of what we have seen, the overall picture is an extremely positive one for Italian philological studies, which is at the cutting edge in this particular field. And yet we should not ignore the fact that — as Isella himself lamented it in a speech held in 1999, now collected in the new edition of *Le carte mescolate* (Isella 2009a: 235–45) — these editions have frequently not produced a lively debate or increased the volume of related studies, as one would expect. One reason for this is in part due to the tight connection of ecdotics with criticism in editions that are highly interpretative in character, and this may perhaps have led to a feeling of momentary overload. However, another reason stems from the difficulty in consulting apparatuses which are often extremely complex. This is a problem that could at least partly be solved by adopting, as far as possible, shared rules (on the problematic nature of some apparatuses, see the examples given in Stussi 2006: 196–257).

1.6 Authorial philology in the digital era

Starting from the 1930s, with the introduction of typewriting, and then from the 1970s with the widespread use of photocopies, authorial philology has had to deal with the introduction of new writing materials and devices altering the processes of production, revision, editing and printing. Consequently, it has had to develop new standards for representing corrections. One only needs to consider, for example, phenomena such as the different series of corrections represented by handwritten variants on a typewritten document, the possibility of assessing the relation between witnesses on the basis of the typewriter used, the use of white concealer on typewritten documents, the many kinds of photocopies that are useful in the reconstruction of the sequential order of macro-texts, and so forth. All these problems are constitutive features of the philology related to twentieth-century texts, as can be seen in section 3.6, which is dedicated to Gadda.

Only since the 1980s and 1990s, with the introduction of word processing, did we begin to witness an epochal change in the forms of communication, generated by the processes of conceiving, writing and revising the digital text that are completely different from what happens with handwritten texts. This shift is analogous to the great change represented by the invention of printing. Nevertheless, at present, we are still not dealing with literary works that belong entirely to the new mode of production, that is, works that are conceived, designed, written and revised exclusively in digital form. Rather we are dealing with transitional products, works of literature of a generation straddling both handwritten and digital production. It is important not to confuse these two realities.

Adopting Peter Shillingsburg's judicious distinction (2006), we might say that it is one thing to embrace new technology in order to make critical editions of literary works belonging to the Gutenberg generation, and yet completely another to conceive of a new philology meant for literary works belonging to the Google generation. *From Gutenberg to Google* is indeed the title of Shillingsburg's acclaimed book in which he discusses the delicate transitional phase between these two historical moments, and reflects on the criteria that are suitable for providing a reliable critical edition of a text published on the world wide web (see Italia 2007a). The enormous body of texts available online makes the formulation of a standard protocol ever more urgent for literary works belonging to the Gutenberg era and edited in the Google era. Building such a set of protocols, will allow a common platform for both the critical editor and the reader whether a specialist or not. The editor will continue to assume responsibility for establishing which version is to be selected as copy-text (even if on the web), and its features, while the reader will select the information provided by the electronic infrastructure according to their interests and the queries made to the text.

From this point of view, it does not make sense to talk about the need for a 'new philology'. Even those who are learning to read today and who, in fifteen years, will probably find *Don Quixote* on the web, will still be able to count on Francisco Rico's edition, without the need to establish a new critical edition of the text for the web. If these same people are fascinated by the poetry of Petrarch's *Canzoniere*, they will be able to discover the amazing genesis of that text through Laura Paolino's edition of the *Codice degli abbozzi* (see section 3.1), perhaps with the support of a *Just in Time Markup — JITM* program. On the other hand, the so-called Google generation texts, i.e., those entirely conceived, designed, made and read (or listened to) on the web, raise other issues. These texts will no longer be made of paper, but of bytes and pixels. We should truly consider a new kind of philology in this case, and this will be a task that will fall to the next generations.

Let us examine at any rate how the introduction of digital technologies has led to certain innovations in the framework of the 'old' philology that have completely changed what it means to do philological work. The first major change is in the phase of collecting and studying the witnesses, and it concerns the digitalization of manuscript materials. Such materials can be studied both on the autograph and on a digital medium, thus overcoming the historical problem of witnesses often being stored in archives and libraries that were very far apart and that of the quality of their reproductions as well. A high-definition digital photo (which can be easily made, even with a digital camera) allows us to enlarge the image up to ten times its natural size, to rotate it, to modify the colour and the contrast or even to read under deletions what would normally unreadable to the naked eye (see the DVD of the latest critical edition edited by Gavazzeni [2009], as discussed in section 3.5). A great advantage of digital editions is also the possibility of archiving off-line and on-line any kind of manuscripts, typescripts and printed documents related to a text. Through such editions, the reader can trace the philologist's work much more easily than in the past and follow it directly on the documents, concretely testing the working hypothesis offered by the critical edition.

A second change in the work of the philologist dealing with authorial materials affects the establishment of the critical edition, and this concerns the possibility of using a digital rather than paper-based medium in representing the genesis and evolution of the text. Experiments of this kind carried out so far, now fairly numerous (see www.filologiadautore.it), show the rich opportunities given by hypertextual editions in representing the historical stages of a text and the dynamics underpinning the corrections. Unlike the paper-based edition, the online one allows us to use internal or external hyperlinks, as well as chromatic markers, in order to represent the text's multiple layers and various phases of composition. As we shall see, all such elements in the printed edition were rendered by typographical (monochrome) markers and by means of symbols and abbreviations. Here, too, the large amount of information that can be archived on the web overcomes the difficulties that come from using a paper-based medium, for which the philologist had to devise the apparatus in a way that took into account the cost of printing. This is not to say that new editions should be repetitious and overly abundant, but rather that they make the handling of multiple witnesses much easier, thanks to the great availability of storage space and the ease of making a digital synoptic comparison between multiple documents. In this way there is no longer any need to find a difficult balance between text and apparatus, as shown in the solution of the *Fermo e Lucia*'s philological issue (on this, see section 3.4).

Digital technology has also introduced great advantages in how we can use critical editions both for teaching purposes and for specialized study, due to the immediate availability of the online editions that can be viewed, studied or even downloaded on the computer if enabled. We should not forget that authorial philology has always been a prerogative of a scholarly and refined but also very expensive kind of publishing, one which employs extremely sophisticated typographical techniques. The increased use of digital tools is therefore a true democratic revolution. The availability and the user-friendliness of editions produced at an international level is another advantage. In this way, Italian authorial philology is able to measure itself against the use of imaging and study techniques for variants developed in other countries, and not only in Europe, setting in motion a virtuous circle of communication. This will allow the work produced in Italy to emerge from the isolation it has experienced so far and the international scientific community should be able to come up with increasingly shared protocols and techniques of representation as well, the true foundation of a scientific method.

The latest developments on the web, consisting in the use of work platforms and information exchange, have ultimately led to a real methodological innovation. The overcoming of geographical distances between scholars enabled them to engage directly with one another's work and to share the contents and the virtual spaces from various platforms in real-time, in a sort of constant seminar. This new way of working offers extraordinary potential on a global scale (see the experiment on Gadda recalled in section 3.6) that will bring even more changes to the philologist's work by bringing it from an individual (if not solipsistic) dimension to a scenario in which knowledge is shared and is available to the entire scientific community.

1.7 Authorial philology in the latest decade

In the last ten years, also thanks to the diffusion of the discipline in the Italian philology classes of Italian Bachelor's and Master's degrees, and to the impulse given by digital philology, authorial philology has undergone notable development. This development has produced new critical editions (such as the original unpublished version of *Eros and Priapo* by Carlo Emilo Gadda, Milan, Adelphi, 2016 and the critical editions of *Storie ferraresi* by Giorgio Bassani, such as *Una notte del '43*, Siciliano 2018b, 2019), new studies (Italia 2016, Caruso 2020) and the series of books *Filologia d'autore*, launched in 2017, which collects volumes dedicated to 'How ancient and modern authors worked', starting with *Come lavorava Manzoni* (Raboni 2017) and *Come lavorava Gadda* (Italia 2017a, soon to be translated into French), followed by similar works on Gabriele D'Annunzio (Montagnani and De Lorenzo 2018), Francesco Guicciardini (Moreno 2019), Giosuè Carducci (Caruso and Casari 2020), Giovanni Boccaccio (edited by Maurizio Fiorilla, forthcoming) and Niccolò Machiavelli (edited by Pasquale Stoppelli, forthcoming).

What is more, in 2010 the website www.filologiadautore.it was founded, and has now become a digital environment for information, updates and training in authorial philology, and a repository of Wiki editions (WikiLeopardi and WikiGadda, whose main pages have had more than 750,000 contacts). The website is consulted daily by all those looking for an introduction to the discipline. Also relevant to this development are studies of the history, methods, reviews of the critical reference texts, and the Catalogue of Digital Critical Editions produced by Greta Franzini (https://dig-ed-cat.acdh.oeaw.ac.at/).

The website contains, in the 'Authorial Philology Exercises' section, examples of editions of autographs with corrections by Gabriele D'Annunzio, Luigi Pirandello, Pier Paolo Pasolini, and Elsa Morante. The site presents both the 'French-style' genetic edition — a *diplomatic edition* which is the first step for a correct deciphering of the manuscript and for the synoptic vision of the original and its transcription — and a *critical edition* adhering to the method of authorial philology, with the diachronic reconstruction of the series of phases (1, 2, 3) and sub-phases (a, b, c) being given. In addition to these exercises, there is the 'How to Prepare a Critical Edition' section (section 2.6 in this book), which is carried out on Giacomo Leopardi's *Alla luna*, which is an apparently simple, but actually very complex case because, on the fair copy, Leopardi made, in three different years (1819, 1820, 1821), three different layers of corrections, with three different pens (which are distinguished in the critical apparatus using letters) and a final series of corrections, probably meant for the 1826 edition of his poems (intitled, *Versi*), in red pen (a layered representation of the corrections is given in the digital edition Ecdosys Leopardi, cf. Giuffrida et al. 2020).

The method of authorial philology provides the best possible interaction between philology and criticism, as it makes it possible to represent the correcting movement in diachronic form, by phases — divided, if necessary, into sub-phases and internal bifurcations — and to compare the variants not only, as has been done so far, from a lexical point of view, but also from a syntactic point of view, a procedure that is impossible with the synchronic and photographic representation offered by genetic criticism. An analytical study of the variants, carried out on syntactic categories, will make it possible to extend the criticism of variants, for the first time, to the study of the genesis of the syntax of the sentence, and to establish new categories, to be added to those identified by Gianfranco Contini in 1937 in his essay 'Come lavorava l'Ariosto' (later collected in Contini 1939), with which authorial variants (especially lexical variants) are normally studied: lowering or raising the style, increasing dialectality, introducing more dignified forms, introducing forms of direct speech, etc.

Thanks to the advantages of the digital medium, the relations between authorial philology and genetic criticism, which in the 1990s had been rather lukewarm, have been strengthened in a common effort to enhance philology in general, by promoting seminars, conferences and specific studies on the genesis of texts. One could say that the disappearance of manuscript variants, now that creativity is no longer developed on white paper but on computer screens, has aroused a new interest in authors' corrections, and has overcome the old methodological differences. The study of authors' variants has also taken on an interdisciplinary perspective, with various projects of stratigraphic analysis of manuscripts, and with digital philology projects (such as Philoeditor Manzoni, see Di Iorio et al. 2014), which have pushed authorial philology to dialogue and collaborate with other philologies, with a view to extending the study of authorial variants to all disciplines based on the evidence of the document: history, philosophy, science, physics.

Thanks to the collaboration with ITEM, directed by Paolo D'Iorio (founder and coordinator of one of the main digital archives of authorial papers, Nietzsche Source), it has been possible to collaborate with an international network of scholars to consolidate studies of authorial variants worldwide and to collaborate with the working group on eighteenth-century Italian manuscripts directed by Christian Del Vento, within the Équipe Écritures des Lumières directed by Nathalie Ferrand (Ferrand and Del Vento 2018, and Ferrand 2019). Genetic critics' interest in the 'Italian case' culminated in the monographic issue of *Genesis* (Del Vento and Musitelli 2019) dedicated to Italian manuscripts from Petrarch to Antonio Tabucchi. While, in the last ten years, on the French side, authorial philology has built relationships that have allowed a fruitful dialogue with genetic criticism, on the Spanish side the diffusion of the discipline has been even more significant, as shown by the Spanish translation of *What is Authorial Philology?* published in the journal *Creneida*. The challenge of the next few years is to extend this network of relationships to other branches of philology, i.e., to the study of authorial variants in Europe, a project launched by Dirk Van Hulle and Olga Beloborodova: *Towards a Comparative History of Literary Drafts in Europe* (forthcoming, 2021).

The establishment of a stable and lasting network of relationships will allow, despite the plurality of methodologies of representing corrections, a sharing of good practices in order to achieve, in a short time, a crucial objective that can only be realized in collaboration with other philologies. The first, already signalled by Dante Isella, but unfortunately not yet achieved, is to establish a common system of representation for similar textual phenomena: acronyms and abbreviations have indeed not yet reached a shared standard. A good example for this is deletion, which since classical philology has been represented with inverted angle brackets (>xxxxxx<), while some critical editions use a different mode of representation, with some of them even opting to use regular angle brackets (<xxxxxx>), which would normally represent the opposite of a deletion, that is a textual integration by the editor meant to resolve a mechanical or textual lacuna. This inevitably leads to misunderstandings and difficulties in deciphering the apparatuses, creating an easy target for anti-philological polemics.

This is all the more urgent not only to prevent the scholar, and the general reader, from having to learn a system of representative signs from scratch each time and to memorize it when reading the edition, but also because standardization has become necessary to allow the automatic querying of data through digital text analysis, and the extraction of data on the basis of shared parameters. It is obvious that, as the discipline stands today, when faced with editions that use widely different systems of signs, such standardization is still a long way off.

It could be argued that XML/TEI marking provides a set of parameters dedicated to the representation of corrections which can constitute a shared system. But if TEI marking is applied to different representations of the same phenomena, it will replicate, in the digital world, the original dissimilarity found in physical editions. Moreover, the TEI marking, when used for authorial variants, has the drawback of not allowing double marking, tag overlapping, and automatic collation systems can be used only partially and only on texts with a very low rate of variation, and above all for variants that do not imply transpositions, since the systems do not automatically recognize the positioning of the transposed text portions. Despite the desirable speed of automatic collation, it is necessary to intervene to manually correct the portions of text that the computer cannot recognise syntactically and semantically. This is further complicated by the impetus imposed by the digital medium, towards an increasingly 'Bedierian philology' (Raboni 2012) — in which the document prevails over the text — that has led to the diffusion, especially in the Anglo-Saxon sphere, of the so-called *documentary editions*, that in traditional philology terms are hyper-diplomatic transcriptions, despite being often presented as critical editions (see the critical view in Pierazzo 2014).

It is no coincidence, in fact, that for more complex manuscripts, such as those of the Charles Harpur Archive, edited by Paul Eggert, the 'graphs' method (Ecdosys), elaborated by Desmond Schmidt with Domenico Fiormonte (Fiormonte 2015), has been used instead (Schmidt 2015), because it makes it possible to identify the different correcting layers and represent them in progression, breaking the bi-univocal relationship between text and apparatus, and replacing the parcelling out of the witnesses, provided by the *apparatus*, with the ordering of the different correcting phases, which can be displayed synoptically in the digital edition. Choosing between TEI marking and the marking with the 'graphs method' corresponds to choosing between a photographic and synchronic representation versus a dynamic and diachronic one, and shows that digital philology shares the same problems as analogical philology. We note two in particular: 1) a single shared model that can be adopted on the Internet has not yet been identified, despite the numerous attempts to model and extend the infrastructure to the single editions; 2) there is not yet a procedure to provide digital editions with a sort of 'certification' that allows us to distinguish scholarly editions from non-scholarly texts.

Authorial philology has also undergone considerable development thanks to the use of digital technologies for manuscript analysis that improve the legibility of manuscripts using the most sophisticated techniques: analysis of stratigraphies of corrections, under-erasure readings, readings under cartouches that cannot be removed. Collaboration with optics and photonics has allowed us to benefit from the progress made in recent years in the field of imaging: stratigraphies represented through spectrometric analysis, the use of terahertz waves, and 3D representation of the third (or 'Z') dimension, time, which can give, for manuscripts of particular importance, a new procedure of reproduction and conservation (see the THESMA PROJECT, developed at the University of Rome 'Sapienza' in collaboration with the Department of Physics, as well as the YouTube channel devoted to authorial philology, and Leopardi 3D, which aims to reconstruct the stratigraphy of the manuscript, understood as a three-dimensional object, and to allow an analytical study, even by non-experts).

The sharing of methods of representation for correctional phenomena is a necessary condition to reflect on the compositional modalities that might be common to different authors, and on the existence of *common writing patterns*. In this regard, in Bologna, a working group called Manus-creative has been set up, bringing together researchers from different historical periods linked by the study of manuscripts with digital technologies: from ancient manuscripts, to medieval and humanistic manuscripts, to modern and contemporary manuscripts (up to typescripts with manuscript corrections, which are comparable to manuscripts), to investigate the possibility that there could be a 'grammar of correction'. It is a fact, however, that the definition of such *correction schemes* is possible only by being able to compare corrections that have been represented with diachronic-systemic apparatuses, not with synchronic-photographic apparatuses. The first studies carried out on modern authors, from Manzoni to Bassani, lead us to believe that there may be a connection between some aspects of the ideology and poetics of the authors and the formalization of their creative thought on the manuscript (Italia 2017b).

The extension of the method of authorial philology to writers of other literatures could enhance the value of investigating creative thinking through the study of variants, and make it possible to understand whether the methodology of correction depends on the language used or on the genre chosen or on the relationship between the author and his/her own writing. However, there is also another objective that can only be achieved through collaboration with other disciplines. While it is true that the changeover from writing on paper to digital writing might cause the 'extinction' of authorial philology, as the study of authors' corrections for the writing of the 2000s will concern exclusively digital variants, it is also true that a new boundless area of investigation is opening up to authorial philology. The study of authorial manuscripts can indeed be extended to non-literary disciplinary fields that are based on the evidence of manuscript documents which have not yet been investigated with a philological method, from history, to economics, to law, to philosophy. One thinks of the extraordinary results obtained, precisely thanks to the analysis of autographs, in the study of Nietzsche's thought (Nietzsche Source is a sure reference model for digital archives), or that of Gramsci (the ecdotic model established by Gianni Francioni for the *Quaderni dal carcere* and the authorship studies carried out by Maurizio Lana and Mirko Degli Esposti). Recently, the drafts of Benedetto Croce himself, a proud opposer of Contini's criticism of variants, have been analyzed for a sort of counterpoint, with interesting critical results (Tarantino 2005). But we are yet to see the diffusion of research practice on the authorial variants of texts related to the 'hard' sciences, such as physics, mathematics, natural sciences and, more generally, the history of science. Expanding the study of authors' corrections to a broader conception of authorship means entering more deeply into the paths of creation, and together with the methods we have now refined for understanding and representing variants, not only on paper but also in digital editions, it will allow us to investigate scientific creative thinking and relate it to the genetic dynamics of non-scientific texts, as well as to solve authorship problems involving scientific texts.

This opens up very ambitious challenges for authorial philology: 1) to extend the study of variants to the wider dimension of syntax; 2) to establish a set of common procedures in the representation of similar textual phenomena; 3) to work towards a European perspective to build relationships with similar disciplines; 4) to enhance the critical paper editions already produced and often lying unused in the stacks of libraries and give them a new digital life, sharing them in an international research dimension, and finally 5) to extend the philological method to disciplines where a genetic study of authorial texts can be extremely productive, not only to broaden knowledge about the creative thinking of authors, but also to spread a philological attitude, which is the best antidote to save new generations from a passive, unconscious and, therefore, irresponsible use of texts.

2. Methods
Paola Italia

2.1 The text

Authorial philology is concerned, as we have seen, with the edition of the original, that is, of the manuscript written directly by the author (an autograph) or written by someone else under the author's supervision (an idiograph), and of the prints edited by the author. There are many different cases, each of them carrying with it problems that are difficult to summarize in a general overview. To put it simply, the areas in which authorial philology proves most useful can be divided into two fundamental categories: the edition of *in fieri* texts, which comes under a category more precisely referred to by Cesare Segre as genetic criticism (see Gavazzeni and Martignoni 2009), and the edition of texts *in multiple versions*, which falls into the so-called criticism of variants.

2.1.1 Edition of *in fieri* texts

Let us start with the case of a text attested to by one manuscript, be it an autograph or an idiograph. The manuscript can be clean (as in the case of a fair copy), or it can bear traces of a reworking process. The edition of a *clean manuscript* is similar in many ways to the edition of a single-witness text in the field of traditional philology (which studies variants introduced through transmission). Of course, an autograph is to be treated differently than an idiograph. An autograph directly exemplifies the author's writing and phonetic habits. In an idiograph, in contrast, the copyist's mediation can introduce alterations and/or standardizations, resulting in forms which are alien to the author's habits. There is a particular problem with regard to errors, which can also be found in autographs. Errors especially occur when authors copy down their own work, that is, when a text is transcribed by an author from a previous document. There is a variety of positions on how errors should be dealt with, ranging from absolute compliance to the text of the autograph to the correction of everything that can be considered no more than a mistake. Whatever the decision, editors have to point out clearly their interventions.

When there are *variants* on the *single manuscript* preserving a text, the philologist will have to establish critically the text and decide which kind of apparatus will better represent the variants found on the manuscript. The question 'Which version should I choose as copy-text?' can be answered in two ways.

1. The philologist can decide to transcribe the *base-version*, that is, the very first version of the text in chronological order. Any further variants will be collected, from the first to the last, in the apparatus (which will be called *evolutionary*).

2. Alternatively, the philologist can take as a reference the *last version as it can be reconstructed from the manuscript*. The apparatus (which will be called *genetic*) will collect the corrections through which the author came to the final version of the text, from the last to the first. As we will see, it is also possible to represent the corrections in a progressive way, that is, from the first to the last, the last being the one chosen as copy-text.

In the case of *unfinished texts*, it is necessary to make very difficult choices, especially when the text has not come to a final revision.

2.1.2 Editions of texts in multiple versions

Of course, the situation is different when a work is preserved in more than one authorial version (manuscript and/or in print). In such a case, philologists must ask themselves whether or not the preserved versions are comparable. If they are, the whole elaboration process can be represented in the apparatus with respect to the writing phase which has been chosen as copy-text. If not, when the versions widely diverge (as in the case of Alessandro Manzoni's *Fermo e Lucia* — *Seconda minuta* — *Ventisettana*: see section 3.4), or when it is preferable to look at them separately for study purposes (as with Giacomo Leopardi's *Canti* in the Gavazzeni edition (Leopardi 2009a): see section 3.5), the philologist can edit each and every compositional phase, presenting the internal variants for each, and create a separate apparatus, establishing a connection between the last stage of each phase and the following stage.

All such situations can be more or less complex. Authors may have come back at different times on their manuscripts, reused parts of a previous version, or worked simultaneously on different versions (something like this can happen nowadays when an author works on photocopies or on the print-out of a file). What is more, the original manuscript may have been lost, but the version it contained may have been preserved in the 'indirect' tradition, that is, in non-authorial ways, or ones not directly depending on the author. In this last case, authorial philology and philology of the copy should work together in order to distinguish any error introduced in the transmission from the actual authorial variants. It is necessary to identify accurately the case under study and make well-motivated choices, taking into account not only the socio-cultural background, but also the appropriateness and effectiveness of the representation (e.g., how easily text and apparatus can be read). As we are starting to see, then, it can be difficult to know which text should be chosen as copy-text, and this choice will always have far-reaching implications, both on the ecdotic and the literary/cultural levels.

The author's last will?

Let us begin with a concrete example. Let us say that a text was republished by an author several times and in different formats. If a publisher appointed us to edit a modern edition of this text, which edition should we prefer? The first, the second, the third, or the last one? The choice is not easy to take. Until the last century, it was standard practice to publish the text which reflected the so-called 'author's last will'. This would mean, in our case, that we should opt for the last edition published by the author. However, objections to the concept of the 'author's last will' have been raised in recent years, gradually breaching the *communis opinio* which elevated this notion almost to the status of a dogma. In order to tackle the various aspects of this problem, it is necessary to distinguish two levels:

- first, we have to take into consideration any element in favour of or against the adoption of the 'author's last will' when establishing which is the reference-text;
- then, when the reference-text has been decided upon, we have to think about the criteria to follow to respect the 'author's last will' for each single reading.

Our belief is that the two phases regarding the 'author's last will' — that is, the overall textual setting of the text for the publication of the work and the editorial intervention in the case of each chosen reading — should be treated separately (on this, see Italia 2005). The first level concerns the idea of themselves and of their own work which authors may have expressed throughout their life by means of an editorial plan, be it carried out or only envisaged in their mind, as well as the form in which authors may have delivered that idea to readers. The textual choice is indeed a very hard one for the editor precisely because it has a bearing on the new image of an author and of their work which is necessarily established by a new edition. Bruno Bentivogli and Paola Vecchi Galli have commented on the role of the editor in twentieth-century editions: 'It falls on the philologist to determine the most appropriate editorial strategy for the text and to promote with the publication its most authoritative source: the source may not be identified with the definitive or last version of a book, but perhaps with the most "groundbreaking" and "innovative" one for readers' (Bentivogli and Vecchi Galli 2002: 163).

The second level concerns the editorial procedure that we need to apply to the individual readings, and involves linguistic, graphic, and typographic questions. Despite being related to the language and style of every individual author, these matters can be addressed, at least to some extent, in a general way. Twentieth-century critical editions feature a wide range of interventions. Although there are significant differences between one edition and the other, it is possible to identify a few constants, which one day will hopefully lead to the adoption of a universal and standard set of regulation within the academic community. We will now present the problem as it is posed in Stussi (2006), who was the first to examine the elements in favour of and against both choices. The elements in favour of the 'author's last will' (i.e., republishing the last version of the text published when the author was alive) can be traced back to three main motivations:

- the *authorial motivation* calls for the respect for the personal choices made by the author, a 'feeling so commonly widespread that it has easily come to dominate the publishing field too' (Stussi 2006: 191): from this viewpoint, the 'last will' seems to provide the readers with a work perceived as 'more authentic';
- the *historical motivation* maintains that the diachronic perspective given by the adoption of the last version of a work allows us to better understand the history of the text and consider it as a historical process: from this viewpoint, the 'last will' seems to provide the readers with a 'more useful' work in terms of interpreting authors and their work;
- on the grounds that the passage from the first to the last version can be seen as a process through which the work moves towards a more evolved stage, the *critical-evolutionary motivation* implicitly looks at the last edition more favourably than it does previous ones: from this viewpoint, the 'last will' seems to provide the readers with a 'better' work.

However, all the motivations in favour of the 'author's last will' can be overturned:

- *authorial motivation*: the last will does not always reflect the true intention of the author. Stussi has noted, for instance, that there might be 'restrictions to the expression of that will in connection with the hereditary succession', or 'evident mental disturbances, constraints etc.' (2006: 191). The textual 'primacy' of the first edition exclusively lies in the value attached to it by the author, who links to that edition their own idea of themselves and of their own work;
- *historical motivation*: the historical perspective can be better appreciated if we consider the process in a diachronic way from the first to the last edition. Only the comparison between

the editions can offer historically verifiable information on the language and style of the work, which are otherwise flattened out and oversimplified by a final synchronic image. The first edition also allows us to appreciate the 'critical reception' of the work and to acknowledge its 'tradition', that is, how the work has had an impact on the literary system;

– *critical-evolutionary motivation*: the idea that the work evolves from one edition to another towards a better form is a false myth; the last editions are not always the best, and indeed the inherent value of a work can be better appreciated in the first edition, which 'normally represents the conclusion of the original creative process of a work and is therefore the result of the most intense creative period for the writer' (Stussi 2006: 192).

It is easy to see that, depending on the circumstances, these arguments can be applied both in favour of and against the adoption of the 'author's last will' as a criterion to establish which text we should publish. This can lead to what has been called a form of 'philological Pyrrhonism', if not to the 'agnosticism of the self-appointed New Philology' (Stussi 1994: 292), which can contribute to spreading a sense of annoyance at critical texts and apparatuses, often considered as 'accessory' elements of the text. In what follows, we will try to prove that that opinion is wrong. As Paolo Cherchi has noted about the debate sparked off by the New Philology, there are two matters at stake.

First of all, there is the dialectic between 'text' and 'work'. As Cherchi puts it, 'The authority of philology has ended up creating so much confusion between "text" and "work" that we feel uncomfortable when we read a work whose text features uncertain readings, although for centuries we have been doing nothing but reading "works"' (Cherchi 2001: 145). The second issue is the relationship between philology and Italian Studies. The prospect that (Romance) philology might develop in innovative ways into a form of cultural history, and that Italian Studies might grow into a form of comparative literature, has been regarded as an antidote to the crisis of philology. This prospect, however, is not borne out by the facts. On the contrary, such a notion has sometimes contributed to a process of trivialization of the discipline, which can be seen even in very prestigious editions. What is more, this issue has not fostered a general debate on the methods and aims of the philological discipline, especially beyond the field of Italian studies. As a matter of fact, there is no agreement within the scientific community on the terminology to be used and on how corrections and authorial variants should be represented. This has of course resulted in an anti-economic proliferation of signs and abbreviations. Each new critical edition forces the readers to learn a new system of representation (with new symbols, initials and abbreviations), thus complicating the debate even within the same community.

It is undeniable that reflecting on these issues, as well as on the reasonableness of any ecdotic choice, has far-reaching consequences for the reception of the text and therefore for its interpretation. Let us take as an example the case of the twentieth-century poet Giuseppe Ungaretti.

Ungaretti's poems offer an example where an author's last will only appears gradually, but has ultimately taken form in two editions that contain all the author's works. These two editions represent or have represented until now the unalterable standard, the *ne varietur* of Ungaretti's textual tradition. For Ungaretti, the Mondadori edition of 1942–1945, whose publication he sought and oversaw, concluded the long and tormented variantistic process of the two collections *L'Allegria* (we can now read this in a critical edition by Cristina Maggi Romano 1982) and *Sentimento del tempo* (in a critical edition by Rosanna Angelica and Cristina Maggi Romano 1988). The 1942–1945 Mondadori edition features three volumes: the first and the second contain the already mentioned *L'Allegria* and *Sentimento del tempo*; the third one is dedicated to the *Poesie disperse* and was published, at the behest of the author, with a dossier collecting the variants in print as commented on by Giuseppe De Robertis. This represents an exceptional case in which textual tradition and critics are connected by the author himself, who openly directs the entire operation.

The definitive edition of *Vita d'un uomo. Tutte le poesie* — edited in 1969 by Leone Piccioni while the author was still alive — gathers the two main collections in their 1942–1945 version (there were very few later authorial changes), together with the last final editions of *Il Dolore, La Terra Promessa, Un Grido e Paesaggi, Il Taccuino del vecchio, Dialogo, Nuove, Dernier Jours,* and the *Poesie disperse,* that is, the texts published between 1915–1927 and not included in the definitive editions of *Allegria* and *Sentimento del tempo*; another seven texts are grouped together in a separate section of the edition entitled *Altre poesie ritrovate*. The note to the text of *L'Allegria* — which was written by Ungaretti himself — significantly declares: 'As a leopard cannot change its spots, the author, who had defined the abovementioned editions as definitive, could not help introducing at each new time a few small changes of form' (Ungaretti 1969: 528).

The choice made by the editors of the two critical editions of 1982 (*L'Allegria*) and of 1988 (*Sentimento del tempo*) differs from the one made by Ungaretti in *Vita d'un uomo*. Cristina Maggi Romano and Rosanna Angelica did not choose the 1942–1945 Mondadori edition (reproduced in the three 'Meridiani') as base-text. They selected instead the second 1919 Vallecchi edition for *L'Allegria*, since this is more representative of the literary pathway of the work than the 1916 *princeps*, and they chose the initial version of each poem for *Sentimento del tempo*. In his 1990 'N.d.D.' ('[Nota del direttore]' published in *Studi di Filologia Italiana*), Domenico De Robertis has explained that the development of *Sentimento del tempo* essentially took place before the 1933 *princeps* (after which there would only be textual additions), so that the history of the book can be better understood 'through the thorough examination of the evolution of the single texts, until its 1933 definition' (De Robertis 1990: 306). The concept of 'author's last will' has been upset by the reasons put forward in favour of these choices and the objections that even very recently have been made.

The wide range of proposals which the critical editions have provoked exemplifies how delicate the choice made by the editor is. Let us just look at *L'Allegria*. One option would be to choose as copytext the text of V, that is, the 1919 Vallecchi edition: this is the choice taken by Maggi Romano. The alternative option would be to return to U, that is, *Il porto sepolto* published in Udine in 1916. The adoption of U is recommended by Carlo Ossola (Ungaretti 1990), who suggests making use of the evolutionary variants within the commentary to the text, thus, as Claudio Giunti remarks, 'putting the critical interpretation before the philological *esprit de système*' (Giunta 1997: 174). In a similar vein, Umberto Sereni and Carlo Ossola (1990) called for a critical edition taking into account the transmission in print only: this last solution was adopted in the 1945 Mondadori edition, which nevertheless 'cannot be called', as Claudio Vela reminds us, 'a critical edition' (Bembo 2001: 1276). A further option would be to stick to the 'last will' expressed in M (Mondadori 1942–1945), as proposed by Claudio Giunta (Giunta 1997: 175) on the basis of the 'historical prestige of the witness', 'related, on the one hand, to the exceptional "form" of the 1942 Mondadori print (M), and on the other to the repercussions that that form had on the subsequent work of Ungaretti'; this solution had already been adopted when Ungaretti was alive by the editors of the definitive edition of *Vita d'un uomo. Tutte le poesie* of 1969, but Giunta (1997: 183–84) proposes to also give 'the first version published in volume' of each witness, thus determining a 'multiplication of the textual items' of each witness. The existence of such opposite choices is a measure of the liveliness and importance of what is a still-open debate.

Before we start any critical-interpretative study, it will be necessary, as is now evident, to ask ourselves the following question: 'What text do we read when we read a text?'.

2.2 The apparatus

2.2.1 Genetic and evolutionary apparatus

If, as we have seen above, the apparatus is the concrete application of the hypothesis represented by the text, the kind of apparatus to be used in a critical edition will be determined by the choice we will have made about the text. That choice will especially depend on whether or not we stick to the author's last will; and on how we decide to represent the drafting process, either in a genetic or in an evolutionary way. According to a punctual definition by Dante Isella (2009a: 100), an apparatus can be genetic or evolutionary: what difference is there between one and the other?

1. A genetic apparatus is a graphical way to represent the corrections that have formed over time on a manuscript, or on a print with manuscript corrections, or on a typescript with manuscript corrections in the case of twentieth-century texts. The genetic apparatus is a synthetic and standardized system to represent the genesis of a text, from its first version to the

one thought to be its last complete form, that is, the one picked as copy-text. A genetic apparatus should not be considered as a photograph of the text: it is rather a hypothesis made by the scholar on the ways and chronological phases of the writing process.

2. The evolutionary apparatus collects the variants that are subsequent to the stage which we have decided to pick as copy-text: that is, variants which do not belong to a phase in the creation what is yet to become a text, but which rather belong to the evolution of what is already considered a text. Of course, the evolutionary apparatus is not an accurate reproduction of the status of a manuscript: it is an interpretation given by the editor of how the text evolved, from the phase which has been picked as copy-text to the last version which can be reconstructed from the manuscript.

The fact that an edition is provided with a genetic or an evolutionary apparatus depends exclusively on what the critical editor has decided to choose as copy-text (see Table 1 below). In short, if we decide to pick as copy-text the last version of a text, the apparatus collecting the corrections will be genetic. If, on the contrary, we choose as copy-text the first version of a text, the apparatus will be evolutionary. If we decide to choose an intermediary version as copy-text (e.g., the base-reading of the clean copy of a text immediately before further corrections were made on it), the apparatus will be both genetic and evolutionary. It will be genetic with regard to the corrections which have led to what has been selected as copy-text; and it will be evolutionary as concerns the corrections following the phase represented by the copy-text.

Table 1 Text and apparatus

Text	Apparatus
Last version which can be reconstructed	Genetic
First version which can be reconstructed	Evolutionary
Intermediary version	Genetic/Evolutionary

When we select as copy-text a version which is not the last one that we can reconstruct from a manuscript provided with further corrections, there are two possible scenarios: the variants persist or do not persist in the complete text. The second scenario (i.e., the variants do not persist) is offered by the eighteenth-century writer Giuseppe Parini's *Il mattino*, a work that was analyzed and edited by Isella. Parini's first and second versions of *Il mattino* follow a very different compositional logic. Between one and the other, there is an intermediate attempt to correct the first version. This attempt does not follow the logic that will subsequently characterize the second version; it rather belongs to a transitional, experimental phase, one soon abandoned by Parini. In this case, the editor has no choice: it is necessary to distinguish the different writing phases and to avoid any confusion. Thus, the variants concerning the intermediate and provisional phase must be collected in an evolutionary apparatus attached to the first version.

In general, however, corrections usually lead to some kind of a result, which is at least provisionally stable, and this can be achieved within the same witness (as with the case of an overall revision of the same writing phase), or on a different witness (when the corrections make it necessary for the author to rewrite the text). In this latter case, the choice between a genetic or an evolutionary apparatus is an open one, depending on the editorial criteria. Let us take as an example the manuscript of the most famous poem by Giacomo Leopardi, *L'infinito* (in the version of the so-called Naples notebook, housed in the Biblioteca Nazionale Vittorio Emanuele III of Naples, C.L.xiii.22). If we look carefully at the text, we see that a few lines have been corrected with a pen which looks different from the pen with which Leopardi wrote the base-version of the text (see Fig. 1). Should we want to publish the text of the manuscript, we would have two options:

1. we can publish the text which would better represent the 'author's last will': in this case, we should select as copy-text the transcription of the last reading which can be reconstructed on the manuscript;

2. we can publish the text in its first draft version: in this case, we should select as copy-text the transcription of the first complete reading which can be reconstructed on the manuscript.

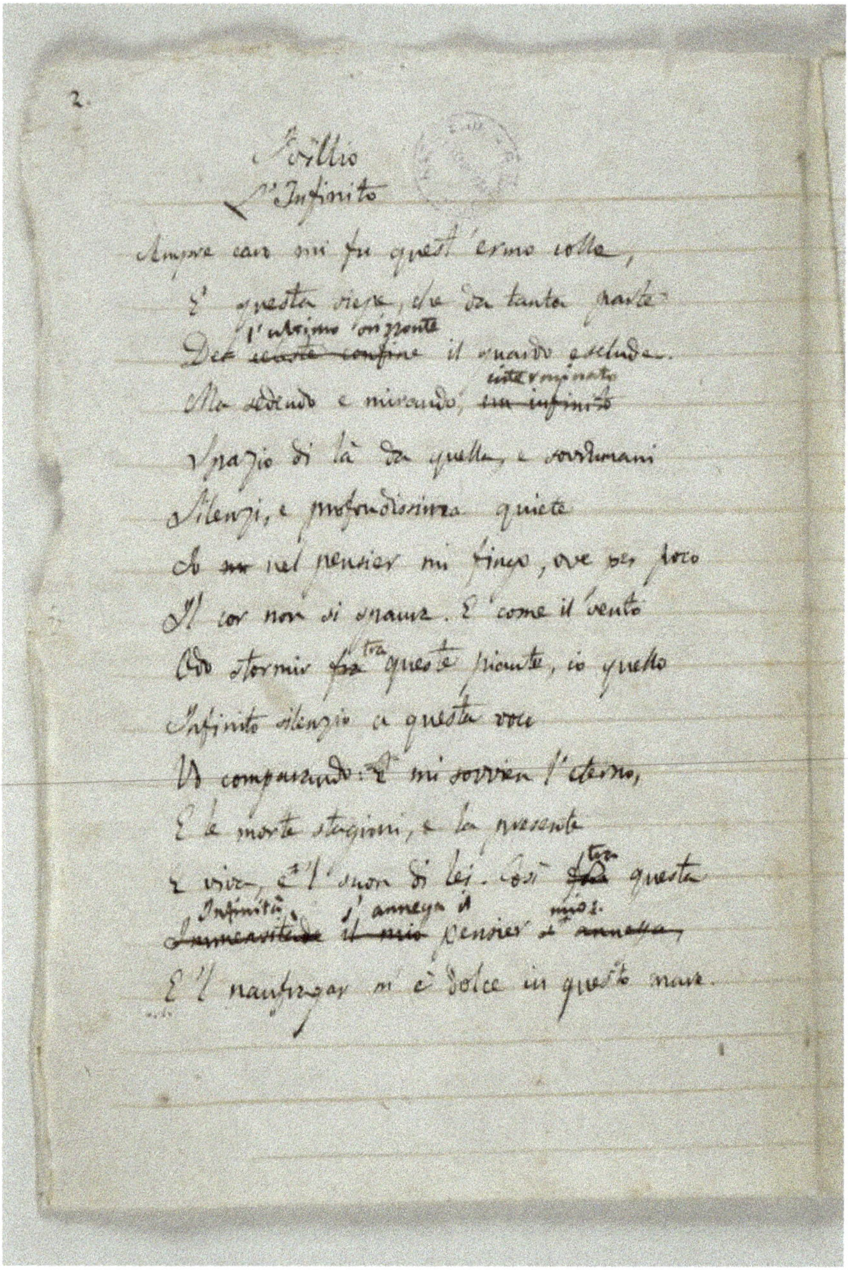

Idillio
L'Infinito

Sempre caro mi fu quest'ermo colle,
E questa siepe, che da tanta parte
Dell'ultimo orizzonte il guardo esclude.
Ma sedendo e mirando, interminato
Spazio di là da quella, e sovrumani
Silenzi, e profondissima quiete
Io nel pensier mi fingo; ove per poco
Il cor non si spaura. E come il vento
Odo stormir tra queste piante, io quello
Infinito silenzio a questa voce
Vo comparando: e mi sovvien l'eterno,
E le morte stagioni, e la presente
E viva, e 'l suon di lei. Così tra questa
Infinità s'annega il pensier mio:
E 'l naufragar m'è dolce in questo mare.

Fig. 1 Giacomo Leopardi, *L'Infinito*, 1819 (C.L.xiii.22, p. 2), https://www.wdl.org/en/item/10691/view/1/2/

Let us see the two solutions, and the consequences they have in terms of apparatus.

1. Text corresponding to the 'author's last will'

Idillio
L'Infinito

1   Sempre caro mi fu quest'ermo colle,
2   E questa siepe, che da tanta parte
3   **De l'ultimo orizzonte** il guardo esclude.
4   Ma sedendo e mirando, **interminato**
5   Spazio di là da quella, e sovrumani
6   Silenzi, e profondissima quiete
7   Io **nel** pensier mi fingo, ove per poco
8   Il cor non si spaura. E come il vento
9   Odo stormir **tra** queste piante, io quello
10 Infinito silenzio a questa voce
11 Vo comparando: **e** mi sovvien l'eterno,
12 E le morte stagioni, e la presente
13 E viva, **e 'l** suon di lei. Così **tra** questa
14 **Infinità s'annega il** pensier **mio:**
15 E 'l naufragar m'è dolce in questo mare.

The parts of text concerned with variants are here given in **bold** (both in the case of immediate and late variants, about which see section 2.3.1). As we have chosen as copy-text the last reading of the text, the apparatus will necessarily be genetic, and it will try to represent the corrections occurring from the first version to the last one.

2. Text corresponding to the base-version (first writing of the text)

Idillio
L'Infinito

1   Sempre caro mi fu quest'ermo colle,
2   E questa siepe, che da tanta parte
3   **Del celeste confine** il guardo esclude.
4   Ma sedendo e mirando, **un infinito**
5   Spazio di là da quella, e sovrumani
6   Silenzi, e profondissima quiete
7   Io **nel** pensier mi fingo, ove per poco
8   Il cor non si spaura. E come il vento
9   Odo stormir **fra** queste piante, io quello
10 Infinito silenzio a questa voce
11 Vo comparando. **E** mi sovvien l'eterno,
12 E le morte stagioni, e la presente
13 E viva, **e 'l** suon di lei. Così **fra** questa
14 **Immensitade il mio** pensier **s'annega,**
15 E 'l naufragar m'è dolce in questo mare.

As we have chosen as copy-text the first complete reading, the apparatus will necessarily be evolutionary, and it will try to represent the corrections concerning the base-version as far as the last reading which can be reconstructed on the manuscript.

Of course, the same set of issue applies in the case of different printed versions, or in the case of versions transmitted both by manuscripts and prints. When the versions can be compared with one another, so that we do not have to provide an edition for each version, we have once again two options: either we select as copy-text the last version and represent the preceding writing process in a genetic apparatus, or else we pick as copy-text the first version and collect the subsequent corrections in an evolutionary apparatus. We will later focus on how it is possible to represent variants and corrections in a synthetic way by the means of symbols and/or abbreviations referring to general categories of corrections, without having to provide extended explanations. We will see, in other words, how an editor concretely sets up an apparatus. For now, let us see the general criteria that regulate how variants are represented.

2.2.2 Vertical and horizontal apparatus

Variants can be represented in two ways: in a vertical apparatus (also called 'column representation', Stussi 2006: 187), or in a horizontal apparatus (also called 'linear representation', ibid.: 189).

Vertical or column representation

All the corrections from the first to the last that concern a line are put in columns. Deletions leading to the writing of a new reading and insertions of new readings are identified by using typographic markers such as italics or bold. The reference-text can be the last or the first as reconstructed from the manuscript. Sometimes it is identified with typographic markers such italics or bold; sometimes it is reproduced in full, either in the same page of the text put in columns, or at the beginning of the edition, where it can be read in full either as a starting or a finishing point. In the column representation, temporal succession is set out in vertical form. Lines or textual segments where variants are not found are not repeated, so that is easy to see where and how corrections occur. Clearly, this kind of apparatus can only be used for poetry because the line does not normally exceed a typographic line, so that the variants can be put in columns below it.

This kind of apparatus was adopted for the first time for Giacomo Leopardi's *Canti* in the 1927 edition by Francesco Moroncini. Since then, it has been used in several important editions of poetic texts. Its great advantage is that readers do not have to refer constantly to the apparatus in order to follow the genesis of the text, because text and apparatus are not divided, and they can visually reconstruct the writing process. The disadvantage is that readers cannot read the text in its entirety and free from the corrections, unless one form of the text is reproduced separately, either before the actual critical edition, as Moroncini did with Leopardi's *Canti*, or in the upper part of the page, as Emilio Peruzzi did

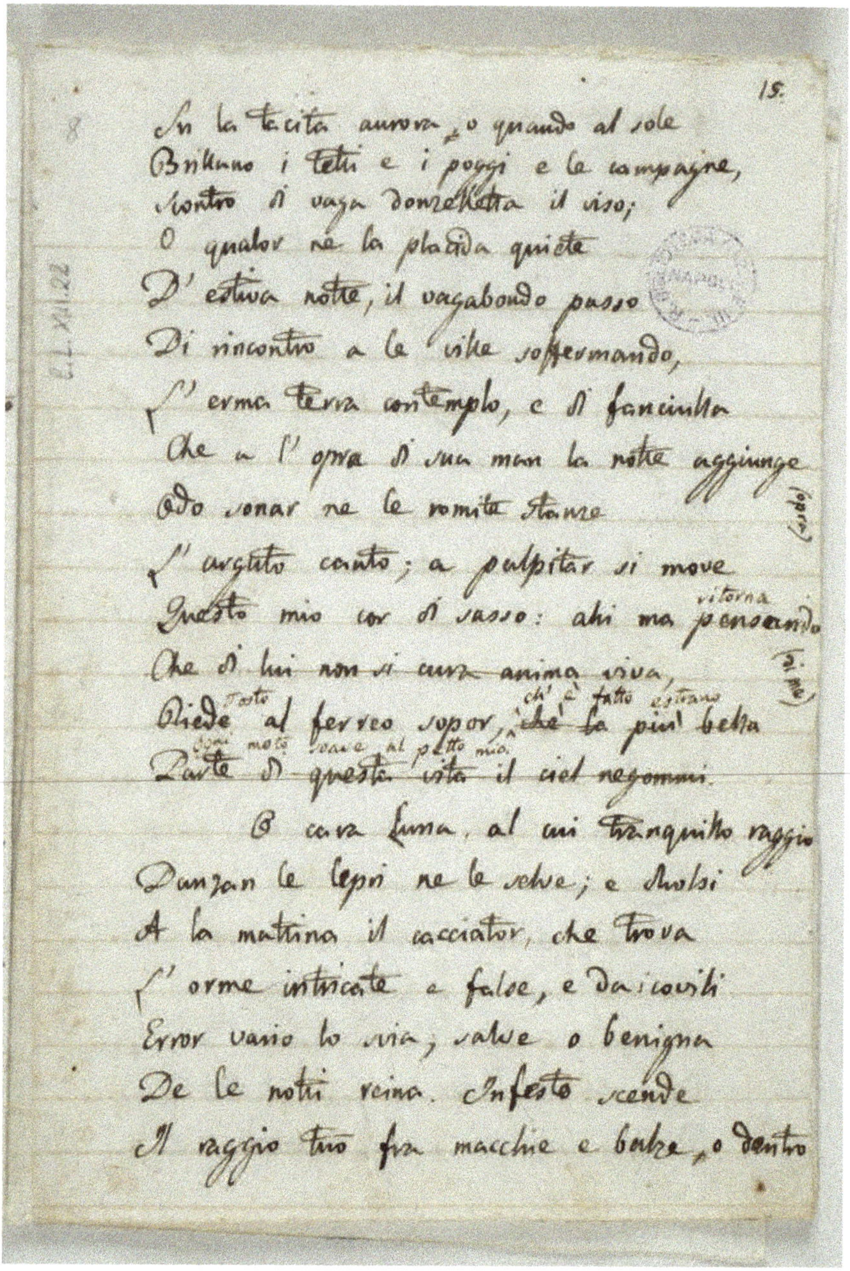

In la tacita aurora, o quando al sole
Brillano i tetti e i poggi e le campagne,
Mostro di vaga donzelletta il viso;
O qualor ne la placida quiete
D'estiva notte, il vagabondo passo
Di rincontro a le ville soffermando,
L'erma terra contemplo, e di fanciulla
Che a l'opra di sua man la notte aggiunge
Odo sonar ne le romite stanze
L'argutto canto; a palpitar si move
Questo mio cor di sasso: ahi ma pensando
                                        ritorna
Che di lui non si cura anima viva,
       tosto   ch'è fatto estraneo
Riede al ferreo sopor; chè la più bella
     ogni moto soave al petto mio
Parte di questa vita il ciel negommi.

       O cara luna, al cui tranquillo raggio
Danzan le lepri ne le selve; e duolsi
A la mattina il cacciator, che trova
L'orme intricate e false, e da i covili
Error vario lo svia; salve o benigna
De le notti reina. Infesto scende
Il raggio tuo fra macchie e balze, o dentro

Fig. 2 Giacomo Leopardi, *La vita solitaria*, 1918 (C.L.XIII.22, p. 15), https://www.wdl.org/en/item/10691/view/1/15/

in a subsequent critical edition of *Canti* (see section 3.5). Less obvious but just as significant is another drawback with this kind of apparatus, namely, that since corrections are grouped together according to the lines, this makes it difficult to see the connections between corrections that relate to bigger syntactic units and thus exceed the length of a verse. This often occurs in poetry, where syntactic and metric units do not necessarily coincide.

Let us now look at another example from the Naples notebook of Leopardi's *Idilli*: *La vita solitaria* (see Fig. 2).

Let us focus on lines 64–68 reproduced below. As per the column representation, corrections are given line-by-line. As can easily be seen, this does not help us to understand the syntactic connection underlying the real correction, which occurs between verses 66–67 (see 'ritorna' and 'riede', here marked in **bold**). At a first glance, the column representation can be misleading: 'pensando' ('thinking') seems to be corrected to 'ritorna' ('returns'), while 'riede' ('returns') seems to be corrected to 'tosto' ('quickly'). In fact, it is 'ritorna' that takes the place of 'riede' (in other words, 'ahi ma pensando / Che di lui non si cura anima viva, / Riede al ferreo sopor' is corrected to 'ahi ma ritorna / tosto al ferreo sopor'):

64 Odo sonar ne le romite stanze
65 L'arguto canto; a palpitar si move
66 Questo mio cor di sasso: ahi ma pensando
                            ritorna
67 Che di lui non si cura anima viva,

     Riede al ferreo sopor, chè la più bella
     Tosto   ch'è fatto estrano

68 Parte di questa vita il ciel negommi
    Ogni moto soave al petto mio.

Horizontal or linear apparatus

The horizontal apparatus is based on a clear distinction between text and apparatus, which are separated from one another and graphically distinguished. The text is located in the upper part of the page, while the apparatus is usually located immediately below it. Variants are collected in the apparatus one after the other. Whereas in the column representation temporal succession is set out in vertical form, in the linear representation temporality is represented by the means of horizontality. The part of text concerned with a variant is repeated in the apparatus and is followed by a square bracket. The variant is located immediately after the square bracket. In a horizontal apparatus we can also find numbers and/or letters which refer to various *phases of elaboration*; *abbreviations* which indicate the position of the variants; and *diacritic signs* or *different fonts* which distinguish the variants from a chronological viewpoint. The end of a series of corrections is marked with the letter T (Text), meaning that the series finishes with what we find in the copy-text (which in turn corresponds, of course, to what we find before the square bracket). We will focus on the meaning of the most commonly used abbreviations and diacritic signs in section 2.5.

The disadvantage of the horizontal apparatus is that, in order for readers to follow and appreciate the corrections, it is necessary for them to refer constantly to the text placed above. This becomes more problematic when the apparatus is located, due to editorial reasons, at the end of the book — and not, as would be preferable, immediately below the text. If the apparatus is overly complex, it can even be printed apart, in a separate volume. This was the case for the critical edition of *Fermo e Lucia*, that is, Manzoni's first draft of the novel *I promessi sposi* (see section 3.4). Most scholars are more familiar with a representation in which text and apparatus are separated. As well as this familiarity, another benefit of the horizontal apparatus is that it can be used for both poetry and prose. In poetry, the verse number is usually given immediately before the part of text in which the variants appear. In prose, the topographic reference is given with the number of the *carta* (*recto/verso*) or page (side of the page); or sometimes with the number of the paragraph when the text is divided into paragraphs made by the editor (this will then need to be explained in the Note to the text).

Let us see once again the lines 64–68 of *Vita solitaria*, now represented with a horizontal apparatus:

64	Odo sonar ne le romite stanze
65	L'arguto canto; a palpitar si move
66	Questo mio cor di sasso: ahi ma ritorna
67	Tosto al ferreo sopor, ch'è fatto estrano
68	Ogni moto soave al petto mio.

66–68 ritorna … mio.] **AN** ¹pensando | Che di lui (*see varia lectio*) non si cura anima viva, | Riede al ferreo sopor, chè la più bella | Parte di questa vita il ciel negommi. *from which* T (*with pen C*)

Further on, we will see in detail the meaning of numbers, letters, abbreviations and different fonts used in the apparatus.

2.3 Variants

2.3.1 Immediate and late variants

Let us now return to the manuscript of *L'infinito* (Fig. 1). If we look carefully at the text, we can easily notice that the corrections are not all of the same kind, since they have been made with different pens, and probably at different times.

- Let us focus for a moment on the correction concerning line 9, where the proposition 'fra' is corrected by Leopardi to 'tra'. It seems that the correction was made with a different pen from both the pen used for the base-text and the pen used for the other corrections: the colour of the ink is more reddish and the stroke of the pen is thinner.

- The text concerned with a variant in line 7 remains the same in both the final versions. Here, the correction was made at the time of the first draft of the text, and it is likely to have been caused by the anticipation of the pronoun 'mi' when writing the verse: 'Io **mi**' *is corrected to* 'nel pensier **mi** fingo'.

- Finally, let us examine line 13, where the punctuation mark of the apostrophe mistakenly referred to 'e' is corrected with the same pen used for the base-text: 'e' l' *is corrected to* 'e 'l'.

These examples show that variants cannot be regarded as an undifferentiated unified group. They should be rather understood as series, or layers, of corrections that are chronologically separate from one another. The term 'layer' and the geological image of the 'stratification' are extremely useful metaphors in order to better understand a manuscript as it appears to the eyes of a scholar: a document that will usually contain two kinds of variants, both immediate and late ones. Immediate variants are made at the time of the writing of the text, and can be recognized as such because they are normally located in the writing line. In the case of an immediate variant, the author has generally deleted a part of text which has just been written and has replaced it with something else; then, the author has kept writing on the same writing line. Coming back to *L'infinito*, the correction concerning line 7 ('Io mi' → 'nel pensier mi fingo') was undoubtedly made at the time of the writing of the verse. Had it not been made at that moment, the space between 'Io' and 'mi' would be difficult to explain.

Of course, a deletion on the writing line does not necessarily indicate an immediate variant. If a deletion concerns a part of text not necessary for the meaning, then it could have been made at a later time, too. In such a case, the text 'works' (that is, 'it makes sense'), regardless of the deleted part. On the contrary, in the presence of an immediate variant, the text usually makes no sense if we read it with the deleted part. Line 7 of *L'infinito*, for instance, should be read as follows: 'Io mi nel pensier mi fingo'. Such a reading would be problematic not only in terms of meaning, but also from a metrical viewpoint, since it would imply that Leopardi wrote a hypermetrical verse, and obviously the metrical aspect is to be carefully considered when the editor works on a manuscript of a poem.

In order to distinguish between immediate and late variants, it is very important to pay close attention to the way the page is set out. A part of text located in the external margin in place of a part of text deleted in the writing line is very likely to have been added later in time than the base-text. See, for instance, Figure 3.

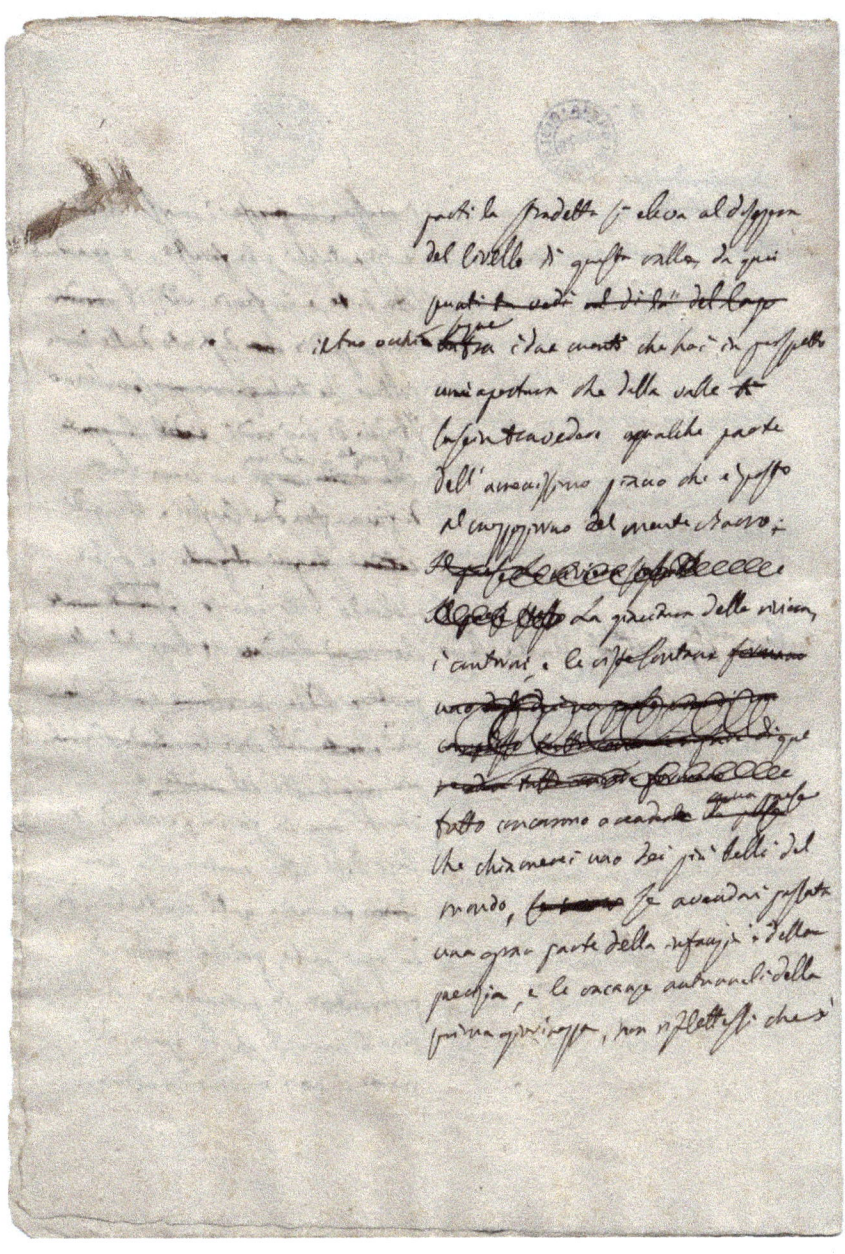

Fig. 3 Alessandro Manzoni, *Fermo e Lucia*, 1821–1823 (Manz.B.II, t. I, cap. I, f. 4b), http://www.alessandromanzoni.org/manoscritti/624/reader#page/24/mode/1up

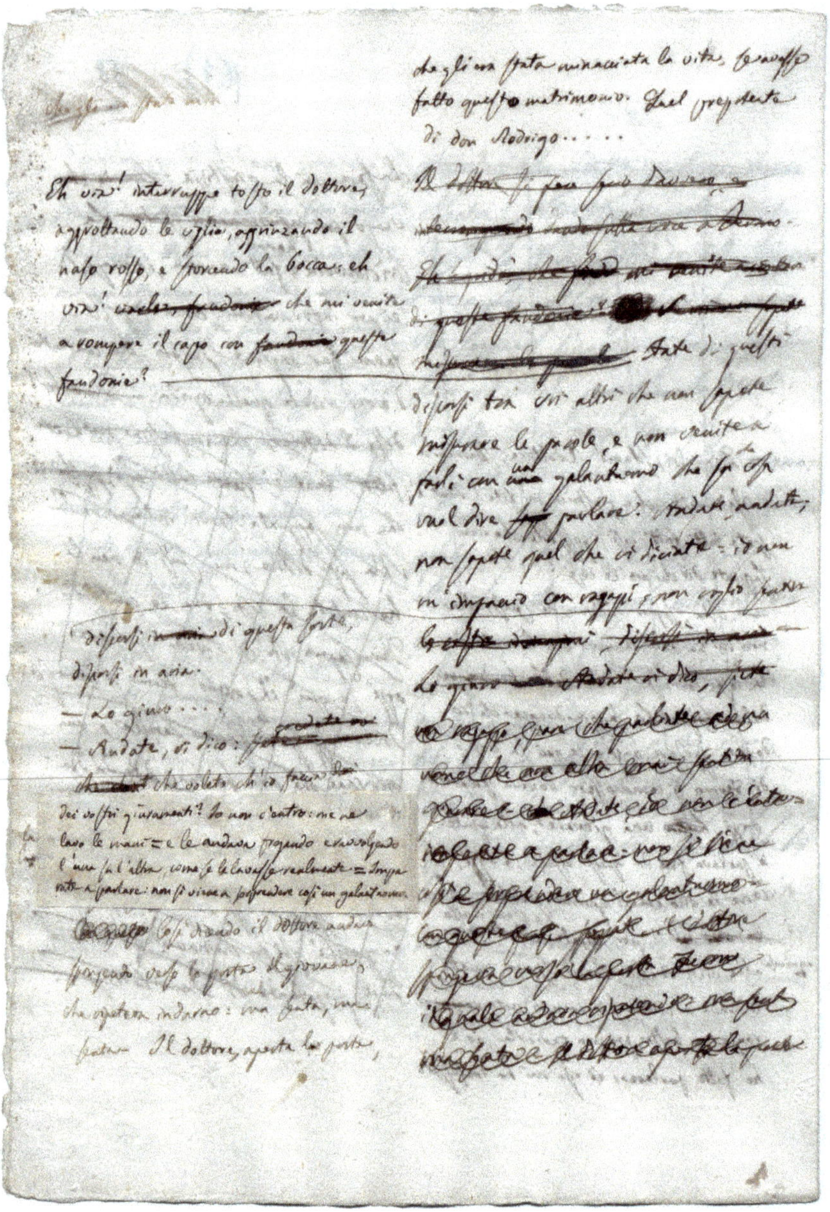

Fig. 4 Alessandro Manzoni, *Fermo e Lucia*, 1821–1823 (Manz,B.II., t. I, cap. III, f. 29d), http://www.alessandromanzoni.org/manoscritti/624/reader#page/125/mode/1up

A peculiar kind of immediate variant is represented by the *implicated variant*. This category includes all the corrections implicated in the meaning of what follows and that are *above-written, below-written*, or *aside-written* (that is, written beside the base-text, either on the right or on the left of it). The term *implication* refers to the connection between textual elements: it can be syntactic, as in the case of gender or number agreement, morphological, as in the case of verbal agreement, onomastic, toponymical and so on.

Let us consider the manuscript of Manzoni's *Fermo e Lucia* (Figure 4). Although it is written above, the correction 'una' → 'un' must be immediate (i.e., it took place at the time of the writing of the base-text), since it is grammatically implicated with the following masculine noun 'galantuomo'. On the contrary, the correction 'che' — which is located in the interline — cannot be considered immediate because the text retains its meaning even without the insertion: 'che cosa vuol dire parlare' → 'che sa che (*inserted*) cosa vuol dire parlare?'.

The corrections made after the first draft are called late variants. Strictly speaking, all the corrections not located in the writing line and not implicated with the following text should be regarded as late variants. Of course, a variant can be unmistakably acknowledged as late only in a few cases. One such case is when an author has used two different pens: one for the first writing of the text; the other for the following corrections. Another case is when a text has undergone systematic corrections which have something in common, such as an onomastic or toponymical change, or else when it is possible to identify within the text different graphic or lexical habits belonging to the author. It is therefore clear why it is fundamental for editors to have great familiarity with the language and style of the text on which they are working, and why philology, history of literature, and history of the language are always interdependent in the edition of a text. An author can sometimes come back to the text even shortly after writing a line, making an above-written, below-written, or aside-written correction. In such a case, if seen from a topographical standpoint, the variant could be considered late, while it is in fact immediate when understood in terms of chronology since it takes place at the same time as the writing of the base-text. How is it possible, then, to identify — amongst the many above-written and below-written variants that are not implicated — which variants are truly late, i.e., which variants were truly made in a subsequent moment of revision? How can we identify which variants belong to a layer of corrections later than the first writing?

In the absence of graphic markers, such as different pens or pencils with different colors, which could indicate different writing phases, it is necessary to take into account a number of factors: the *ductus* (that is, the stroke of the pen on the paper), the handwriting, the syntactic and lexical connections, the style of the author, as well as the author's habits in terms of corrections. Of course, none of these factors can give us certainty about whether a correction happened at the same time as the first drafting of the text. However, all of these elements can be taken into examination and contribute — especially if they are all in agreement with one another — to argue in favour of or against a hypothesis about the chronology of a correction. This is the case for the late variants that can be found in the so-called *Prima minuta*, that is, the manuscript of *Fermo e Lucia*, Manzoni's first draft of *I promessi sposi* (see section 3.4). Some of the variants are to be traced back to a late revision of the text of the *Prima minuta*. Others are to be traced back to an initial revision of the text of the so-called *Seconda minuta*, that is, the manuscript of the novel's revised version entitled *Gli sposi promessi*. For we now know, in the case of many chapters of the first tome and of a few papers of the fourth one, the *Seconda minuta/Gli sposi promessi* has been written on the same, thickly corrected papers of the *Prima minuta/Fermo e Lucia*.

Although authorial philology — like philology in general — is not an exact science, it works towards the interpretation of the given information with a precise scientific method, arguing for the most plausible hypothesis to explain a problem. When new elements emerge which cannot be explained by a given hypothesis, its validity is suspended.

2.3.2 Horizontal apparatus: Explicit or symbolic

Since corrections over time are represented by the position of variants vertically in the column, the vertical apparatus does not need abbreviations or symbols. On the contrary, in the horizontal apparatus, the use of markers and symbols keeps the editor from providing verbal and analytical explanations for each and every variant. An effective apparatus must be rational and synthetic, making use of a coherent and consistent system of representation of the same graphic phenomena with appropriate markers. The markers can be provided in an abbreviated form in a symbolic way. Hence, the distinction between:

- *explicit apparatus*: the apparatus is called explicit when it makes use of abbreviations in order to represent the same graphic phenomena;
- *symbolic apparatus*: the apparatus is called symbolic when it makes use of symbols for the same purpose.

In order to represent one of the most common cases in manuscript texts — the correction from one variant to another, Italian editions of authorial philology often make use of the generic abbreviation: *corr. in* (= *corretto in*, 'corrected to'), or of a directional arrow such as →. Different arrows may represent different kinds of variants: a simple arrow such as → may represent, for instance, an immediate variant, while a two-colour arrow such as ➤ may represent a late variant. If a variant is located in the interline, the explicit apparatus can make use of the abbreviation: *ins.* (= *inserito*, 'inserted'), which indicates that the text in the manuscript is inserted in the upper interline (in the rare case of a variant inserted in the lower interline, it is possible to further specify: *ins. nell'interl. inf.* = *inserito nell'interlinea inferiore*, 'inserted in the lower interline'). For this same kind of correction, the symbolic apparatus can make use of special markers such as a slash isolating the inserted word: \word/. *Mixed-type apparatuses*, explicit and symbolic at the same time, are very frequent: in order to represent in a synthetic and coherent way the corrections, the apparatus makes use of both abbreviations and symbols. Abbreviations are always italicized, so it is easy to distinguish the text of the editor from that of the author. Both abbreviations and symbols are usually explained in a Table, which is normally placed in the edition after the Note to the text.

2.3.3 Photographic apparatus and diachronic apparatus

We are starting to see that some apparatuses try to account for the dynamics of the corrections, while others try to provide a typographic transcription of the status of the manuscript. This is the fundamental difference which distinguishes the authorial philology practiced in Italy from the French *critique génétique* and the German *Editionswissenschaft*, all of which tend to represent the variants as they are found in a manuscript, without distinguishing between text and apparatus. In an attempt to respect the topography of the manuscript, above-written variants are reproduced in the upper interline, while the parts of text inserted in the margin of the manuscript are reproduced in the margin too, and so on.

Following on from the methods of representation used by Francesco Moroncini for Giacomo Leopardi's variants, techniques of formalization intended to reproduce the diachronic dynamics of the text have become more and more sophisticated. This has been possible especially thanks to Dante Isella and his students. A transition towards an apparatus understood in a diachronic and systemic way has gradually taken place over the last twenty years in Italy in the field of authorial philology, thus placing the Italian school at the forefront in the European philological context. Let us see a few examples.

At the outset, the intention of the philologist was — even in the first horizontal apparatuses — to represent typographically the complex phenomenology of the text. The idea was to provide a typographic transcription of the text by means of abbreviations and symbols. A particular effort was made attempting to provide the relevant explanations with appropriate symbols or exponents. In the edition of the Chigiano Codex of Torquato Tasso's *Rime* supervised by Franco Gavazzeni (Tasso 1993), for instance, the explanations concerning the variants are given with an alphabetic superscript that refers to where each variant is placed, depending on whether it is above-written (a), below-written (b), written on the right (c), or written on the left (d). This was a highly effective means for a better understanding of a manuscript that is difficult to decipher such as the one considered here (see section 3.3).

The same set of considerations applies for the most representative apparatuses of twentieth-century works, that is, the ones included in the editions of the works of Carlo Emilio Gadda. The fundamental 1983 critical edition of *Racconto italiano di ignoto del Novecento* by Isella adapted a triple-filter system in order to represent in a rational way all the textual materials which were not part of the copy-text: the apparatus, the marginalia (metatextual notes) and the alternative variants (see section 3.6). In fact, this edition marked for authorial philology the beginning of a new phase, one that was both more scientific and innovative in terms of methodology.

In the apparatuses produced from the end of the 1990s onwards, scholars have tried to represent — instead of the topographical location of the variants — the stages in the text's evolution as connected to one another in chronological terms. The focus has not been on the way in which a variant is graphically realized in relation to the base-text (above-written, below-written, inserted, aside-written, and so on), but rather on the chronological relation which a variant has with the base-text and the other variants too. The main difference — and the main difficulty when it comes to setting up the apparatus — lies in the possibility of comparing the different phases with the final text, as well as in identifying and grouping the variants in relation to a 'system': 'in the apparatus [...] the portion of text altered by a variant (i.e., the portion of text that comes before the square bracket) can always be directly compared with the variant, or the variants, that affect it, so that it can be studied directly and autonomously, without having recourse to the copy-text' ('Introduzione' to the critical edition of *Canti* supervised by Franco Gavazzeni, in Leopardi 2009a: XLIV).

The main advantage of this kind of apparatus is the autonomy it offers to readers in terms of following the genesis of the text, with no regard to its photographic representation. This possibility is even more facilitated when there is the opportunity to have high-definition digital reproductions, which allow us to distinguish — on the base of the *ductus* and of the hand — the different phases of correcting presented by the text. The apparatuses should not be designed to provide a better interpretation of the autograph; they themselves should be an interpretation of the autograph. Consequently, the reading of the autograph should be intended as a possibility to test and verify — in parallel — the work of philological interpretation and critical analysis carried out by the editor. It is undeniable that, in order to set up an apparatus of this kind, it is necessary to invest much more time than was previously allocated in analyzing the manuscript. It is necessary in fact to understand more deeply the 'mechanisms' underlying the correcting process as well as the linguistic construction, whether in prose or in poetry. It is one thing to provide a representation of the variants in a topographic way, but it is quite another to understand the variants in relation to a diachronic system and place them within it.

2.3.4 Horizontal apparatus: progressive or derivative

Another important difference concerns the distinction between progressive and derivative apparatuses. The part of text concerned with a variant, as we have said several times, is repeated in the apparatus and followed by a square bracket. The corrections following the square bracket can be represented in a progressive or derivative way, according to the order followed in the presentation of the chain of variants. In an evolutionary apparatus the corrections follow a progressive chronological order, from the first to the last. The passages from one correction to another can be explained with an arrow or, as happens in Italian editions, with the abbreviation *corr. in* (= *corretto in*). See the following example, where *corr. in* is translated and abbreviated in English as *corr. to* (= *corrected to*):

reading picked as copy-text] A *corr. to* B *corr. to* C *corr. to* D.

In a genetic apparatus, the corrections follow the exact opposite order: they are reproduced in the apparatus from the last to the first, i.e., in a derivative way. In Italian editions the chain of variants starts with the abbreviation *da* (translated as *from* in the example below), followed by the chronologically second to last correction, which means that the reading picked as copy-text is derived from the second to last, and that the second to last is derived from the third to last, and so on, until the oldest reading:

reading picked as copy-text] *from* D *from* C *from* B *from* A.

In a few cases, corrections can be represented both in a progressive and derivative way. The correcting phases, for instance, are always represented in a progressive way (e.g.: [1] *from which* [2] *from which* [3] etc.), while minor corrections encompassed within the same correcting phase are usually represented in a derivative way (e.g.: [1] *from which* [2] (*above-written to*[1]) *from which* [3] (*aside-written to*[1] *and* [2])).

2.4 Marginalia and alternative variants

The work of Dante Isella also forms an essential precedent for one of the major methodological innovations introduced over the last two decades in the use of apparatuses. In his aforementioned 1983 edition of Gadda's *Racconto italiano di ignoto del Novecento*, Isella successfully rationalized the representation of the different textual levels found in the manuscript with a triple-filter system distinguishing between apparatus, marginalia (metatextual notes) and alternative variants. Let us now examine these elements in their fundamental relation to the text, considered as it were as the fulcrum around which — unlike the methods adopted in French philology — the critical edition should pivot.

2.4.1 The apparatus

The term 'apparatus' refers to a part of text which has a relation of topographical and typographical subordination with the copy-text. The apparatus is usually located in the footer and is in a smaller font size. The apparatus may also be placed at the end of the volume. In this case, the relation between apparatus and copy-text may become an extreme subservient one. In a few cases, the apparatus occupies an entire volume and is in the same font size of the copy-text. One example of this is found in Isella's edition of *Fermo e Lucia* (Manzoni 2006).

2.4.2 Marginalia (metatextual notes)

Isella has given the most exhaustive definition for the term marginalia (Italian, 'postille') in the abovementioned edition of *Racconto italiano di ignoto del Novecento* (Gadda 1983: xxxiv–xxxv):

> [Marginalia refers to] the remarks provided by Gadda almost everywhere on the page, commenting on what he has already written or what he is about to write afterwards: the list includes statements of disappointment or satisfaction, as well as words of warning or advice directed towards himself; doubts (sometimes expressed with an interrogation mark), and references to different sections of his text; and sometimes also annotations which can be attributed to a later writing stage and are functional to the rewriting of single passages in a clean version, or to the reuse of single passages outside of the context of the *Cahier*.

As they are side annotations to the base-text, the marginalia should be ideally imagined in the margin of the page. In an edition, however, typographical and editorial reasons make it necessary to collect them in a separate section at the end of the text (ibid.):

> The interested reader is punctually informed at the occurrence of every marginalia by a conventional cross-reference mark located in the margin of the page in place of the marginalia itself (>): something like a graphic stylization of a hand with a pointed index finger which was frequent in former times.

The placement of the cross-reference mark in relation to the text is nothing more than a mere typographic and graphic arrangement to indicate the presence of the marginalia. This is all the more appropriate if we consider that the marginalia do not have the same status of the text, but should be considered as metatextual notes (that is, as part of the metatext).

2.4.3 The alternative variants

According to the definition given by Isella, alternative variants — which are not to be mistaken for genetic or evolutionary variants — are 'competing readings amongst which the author cannot choose, or amongst which he/she has not made it unequivocally clear whether or not he/she has chosen' (Gadda 1983: xxxv). In editions, alternative variants are located in the footer (below the copy-text) and are tagged with superscript alphabetic letters, whereas a superscript number is generally used for the notes of the author present in the text. Alternative variants have a relation of parity with the text, both in typographic and graphic terms, since they are in the same font size as the text. The idea underlying this presentational approach is that the editor does not know if the author — in a phase of further revision of the manuscript — would have chosen the alternative variant, or the reading that the editor has selected as copy-text. Consequently, from a theoretical point of view, the alternative variants have the same status and value of the text. The location in the footer and the use of the same font size as the copy-text are, in other words, a way of confirming that they are part of the text and not of the apparatus, i.e., that they have the same status and value of the text as they are potentially part of it.

Likewise, marginalia are separated from the actual critical apparatus, as we have seen above, as they do not have the same status and value of the materials therein collected.

The distinction between text, apparatus and metatext is not only very important in general terms, but it also has remarkable consequences for the editing of single-witness texts which, although they cannot be properly said to be 'critical', are nonetheless presented as 'scholarly', resembling in every aspect a critical edition with regard to what is found in the copy-text, despite not having an apparatus. These editions — which meet a need for philological precision and accuracy, as well as satisfying material and editorial requirements (the kind of readers they address, the cost of paper, and so on) — attempt to preserve the basic 'theoretical framework' we have just seen. They give an account to readers of the alternative variants (located in the footer) and of the marginalia (separately collected in an appendix or in the Note to the text), although they do not offer the genetic and/or evolutionary apparatus; or do not have the space for it. An example of the former case is offered by the works of Pier Paolo Pasolini as edited by Silvia de Laude and Walter Siti for the Mondadori series 'i Meridiani'.

This simple, straightforward distinction between different textual levels is the core premise of many critical editions by Isella and his students, editions which contributed to providing specific ecdotic solutions in several complex cases. It is particularly in these editions that took place over time a significant development towards a diachronic and systemic apparatus.

2.5 Diacritic signs and abbreviations

In order to represent the phenomena found on the manuscript, critical editions in the field of authorial philology have made use of the most diverse range of diacritic marks and systems of abbreviations. Even though the scholars have repeatedly expressed the need for homogenization, there are still no standard criteria. For this reason, readers find themselves forced to familiarize with the various systems adopted by the editor every time they encounter a new edition. Standard symbols are available only for a few corrections, and there is widespread confusion about most of the others. Sometimes, the same symbol can even be used by different editors to represent different, if not opposite, phenomena.

There is a certain agreement as for what concerns the most frequently used symbol: the square bracket [ ]. It is well known that square brackets are used to mark everything that is due to intervention of the editor, including: restoring letters missing in truncated words (e.g., wor[d]); the explanation of various phenomena; the filling in of *lacunae* and of punctuation in texts with no print tradition (although it would be preferable to explain how punctuation has been restored in the Note to the text). When we find square brackets, in other words, we should expect an editorial intervention on the text. In a few cases, editors can also make use of the angle brackets < > in order to represent the same phenomena.

There is some agreement on the use of the series of three dots or ellipsis within square brackets [...] or round ones (...) to indicate that part of the text is missing (the ellipsis is regularly used in this way in abbreviated quotations). A closing square bracket] marks in the apparatus the separation between text and variant. What comes before the bracket is the copy-text; what comes after it is the variant (which can be either manuscript or in print), including any symbols and/or abbreviations used to explain its topography and/or chronology. Inverted angle brackets > < generally refer to a deletion (e.g., >xxxxx<). A deletion can also be noted by the use of the *italics* (e.g., *xxxxx*). In several apparatuses, however, the italics can also be used to indicate what does not change (the 'invariant'), while square brackets are used to signal the deletion. Square brackets are often used, as we have seen, to restore parts of the text, or even when the reading of a word is doubtful: this is of course a very hazardous enterprise, because the use of the same symbols to represent different phenomena, as we are seeing, can cause great confusion.

Unlike the symbolic apparatus, the explicit apparatus makes use of several abbreviations in order to represent the phenomena found in the manuscripts. To distinguish them from the text (which is in a standard non-italic font), the abbreviations are usually *italicized*. Here below you may find a list of some of the most frequently used abbreviations found in Italian editions (an English abbreviation is suggested next to the English translation):

Table 2 Abbreviations and their meaning

Abbreviation	Complete Italian form	English translation	English abbreviation	Meaning
da		from	*from*	the reading is derived from a previous reading, with one or more letter being reused
da cui T	da cui il testo finale	from which the final text	*from which* T	the final reading (that is, the one chosen as copy-text) is derived from a previous reading, with letters and/or words being reused
corr. in	corretto in	corrected to	*corr. to*	the previous reading is corrected in the following reading
sps.	soprascritto	written above	*written above*	the final reading is written above a reading deleted in the writing line
sts.	sottoscritto	written below	*written below*	the final reading is written below a reading deleted in the writing line
ins.	inserito	inserted	*ins.*	the reading is inserted
prima		before	*before*	the final reading is preceded by a previous reading deleted in the writing line (there is no reuse of the words/letters)
dopo		after	*after*	the final reading is followed by a reading deleted in the writing line and then abandoned

In a symbolic apparatus, these abbreviations are replaced with diacritics that are understood in the same way. While the explicit apparatus usually gives us some details on the position of the variant such as whether it is written above, below or in the margin of the text, the symbolic apparatus cannot provide the same information, or must gather it in footnotes attached to the apparatus. This was the approach taken by Isabella Becherucci in her apparatus to Alessandro Manzoni's *Adelchi* (see Manzoni 1998).

In order to represent the diachronic relationship between the variants, the symbolic apparatus makes use of arrows:

- the direct arrow → represents a correction (and thus replaces the abbreviation *corr. in* 'corrected to');
- the inverted arrow ← represents a derivation (and thus replaces the abbreviation *da* 'from').

In a few cases, in order to represent the chronology of the variants, two kinds of arrows can be used: a simple arrow for an immediate evolutionary variant (→), a two-colour arrow for a late evolutionary variant (➤). In the case of a particularly extensive correcting phase, it can be useful to represent smaller corrections within the same phase.

Topographic and diachronic details are placed within italicized round brackets and are to be referred to the word that comes immediately before the opening brackets. When details are referred to more than one word, a reference mark is located at the beginning of the part of text concerned with the variant. This mark can have different forms: a black dot, a little star, an asterisk, or half of a square opening brackets (⌈). When on the same line of the apparatus there are more than one different variant, the variants are separated one from another with a fixed blank space (corresponding to the space of four or five characters), a small square figure □, or a tilde ~.

2.6 How to prepare a critical edition

Let us now see how an editor can prepare the critical edition of a manuscript that features various series of corrections. Let us examine the manuscript of Giacomo Leopardi's poem to the Moon *Alla luna* — titled in the manuscript (as we will now see) *La Ricordanza* — which helps us to understand, because of the number and types of corrections it presents, how an editor should proceed. Like the manuscript of *L'infinito* that we have discussed above, the manuscript of *Alla luna* (see Fig. 5) belongs to the so-called Naples notebook, which is housed at the Biblioteca Nazionale Vittorio Emanuele III of Naples (C.L.XIII.22) amongst other papers that belonged to Leopardi. As we have already noted, the manuscript is a clean copy, but still bears traces of interventions of different kinds. The question one might ask when facing such a document is: which textual version should be chosen as copy-text?

If we decide to document the last textual version of the manuscript, we will have to transcribe the text including in it all the corrections, no matter if they are immediate or come from later phases. We will have to include in the text, in other words, both the corrections made with the base-pen (the pen used for the first writing) and the corrections made at a later time. As we have decided to publish the last textual version, the apparatus will obviously be genetic, giving account of all the correcting phases tagged with superscript numbers. Any deletions made on the writing line will be represented in the apparatus in a smaller font size with a two-point difference from the rest of the apparatus. Further corrections will be indicated with round brackets, which will also be in a smaller font size to help the passage to be read easily and to assist the understanding of the compositional phases.

Let us see the corrections which interest the title of the poem, changing from [1]La Luna to [2]La Luna o la Ricordanza to [3]La Ricordanza. The phases are always indicated with a superscript number and separated by a double spacing. If a phase is derived from another with the conspicuous reuse of textual materials, such as one or more letters, that phase is introduced by the abbreviation *from which* (It. *da cui*), or by a direct arrow →. How can we understand that the original title was 'La Luna' and not 'La Luna o la Ricordanza'? Even though the *ductus* and the ink (which is identical in both phases) do not provide enough information, the placement of the text on the page provides useful orientation. If the original title had been 'La Luna o la Ricordanza', it is easy to imagine that the author would have placed it right at the center of the page — and not on the right, as the autograph clearly shows. Based on this, we can think that the title 'La Luna' was already written, and that, at a later time, Leopardi added on the right of it the second part 'o la Ricordanza', changing only at a third further stage the lowercase character 'l' (contained in the article 'la') to uppercase. This last correction does not seem contemporary to the base-writing, but bears some similarities with a few interlinear corrections in lines 2, 7–8 and 9, which were made at a further stage, and are contemporary to the writing of the texts which follow 'La Luna' in the Naples notebook, the so-called 'second time' of the *Idilli* (see Italia 2007b). This important observation gives us the possibility of identifying different levels of corrections in the text, corresponding to different pens, always indicated by the editor with capitalized alphabetical letters (A, B, C, D), which, alongside the superscript numbers, identify each correcting phase. In the case of smaller corrections, such as the one in line 5, the pen used is given within italicized round bracket and in a smaller font size. Further variants can indeed be found in the reconstruction of the same correcting phase, and, where present, they are represented in a smaller font size in a derivative from, such as in the case of line 4:

> (su quella selva) ^{1A}sopra quel bosco, *from which* ^{2A}sopra quel prato, (*with* prato *written over* bosco) ^{3A}su quella selva, (*written next to²*) *from which* ^{B}T

This example gives us the opportunity to go into more detail on the use of the abbreviations *from* (It. *da*), *from which* (It. *da cui*), and *from which* T (It. *da cui* T). The first one *from*/*da* is used to represent a correction in which the final text materially reuses one or more letters of a previous reading. The second one *from which*/*da cui*, which can be replaced by the arrow →, refers to the reuse, in a subsequent variant, of a major textual portion of a previous variant. When the subsequent variant corresponds to the copy-text, it is possible to use the abbreviation *from which* T/ *da cui* T, and this can be replaced with an arrow pointing to T: → T.

The representation of the variants in lines 7–8 illustrates what we meant when we introduced the notion of diachronic and systemic apparatus. The first definition — diachronic — stems from the fact that the apparatus does not focus on representing the placement of the corrections: for example, it does not indicate where the variants are located in the manuscript, that is, if above, below, or next to the text. It rather focuses on representing the chronology of the corrections, the evolution, that is, of the variants from an earlier to a later form, with each phase identified by a superscript number. Phases are here reconstructed as being four, including the last one, which corresponds to what has been chosen as copy-text. The second definition — systemic — refers to the fact that corrections are not represented individually and linked to the term (or terms) to which they refer from a topographic standpoint; corrections are instead represented in a system, including the variants and the final text too. The variant can obviously exceed the measure of a line and be related to the following line (this is the case of lines 7–8).

This example shows that it is very difficult, if not almost impossible, for the vertical apparatus — which parcels out every variant and connects it very strictly to the words that are positioned closer to it — to represent effectively the corrections which concern two or more lines (a detailed examination of this is found in section 3.5).

In the edition of the manuscript, immediately below the band occupied by the genetic apparatus, there is a box collecting the so-called *varia lectio*, that is, all the variants, quotations, linguistic and metatextual observations which Leopardi would annotate on his own manuscripts. We find them — albeit to a lesser extent than in other Neapolitan autographs — also in the manuscript of *Alla luna*. Leopardi penned a variant in the right margin of the page, in a position directly opposite to the written text of the poem, probably in a phase of later revision of the manuscript, as indicated by the reddish ink (here identified as *pen D*). Immediately below the box dedicated to the *varia lectio*, a further band accommodates the 'Philological notes', which are clearly distinguished from the apparatus by being italicized. When notes of this kind are instead included in the 'Note to the text', they are generally printed in a standard non-italic font. As these 'Philological notes' provide an analytical illustration of the makeup of the manuscript and its correcting dynamics, they serve a very useful function. Such notes also suggest various ways of interpreting the text, and report if and when the reading of one or more words is doubtful. More generally, the 'Philological notes' can include everything that editors might like to add in order to justify their choices in terms of apparatus, especially if such explanations cannot fit in the limited space underneath the text. A way to understand whether or not an ecdotic choice has been made judiciously is to reflect on the delicate balance between the need for analytical accuracy and the need for an economical form of representation. An apparatus is successful only when it represents the manuscript and its corrections in

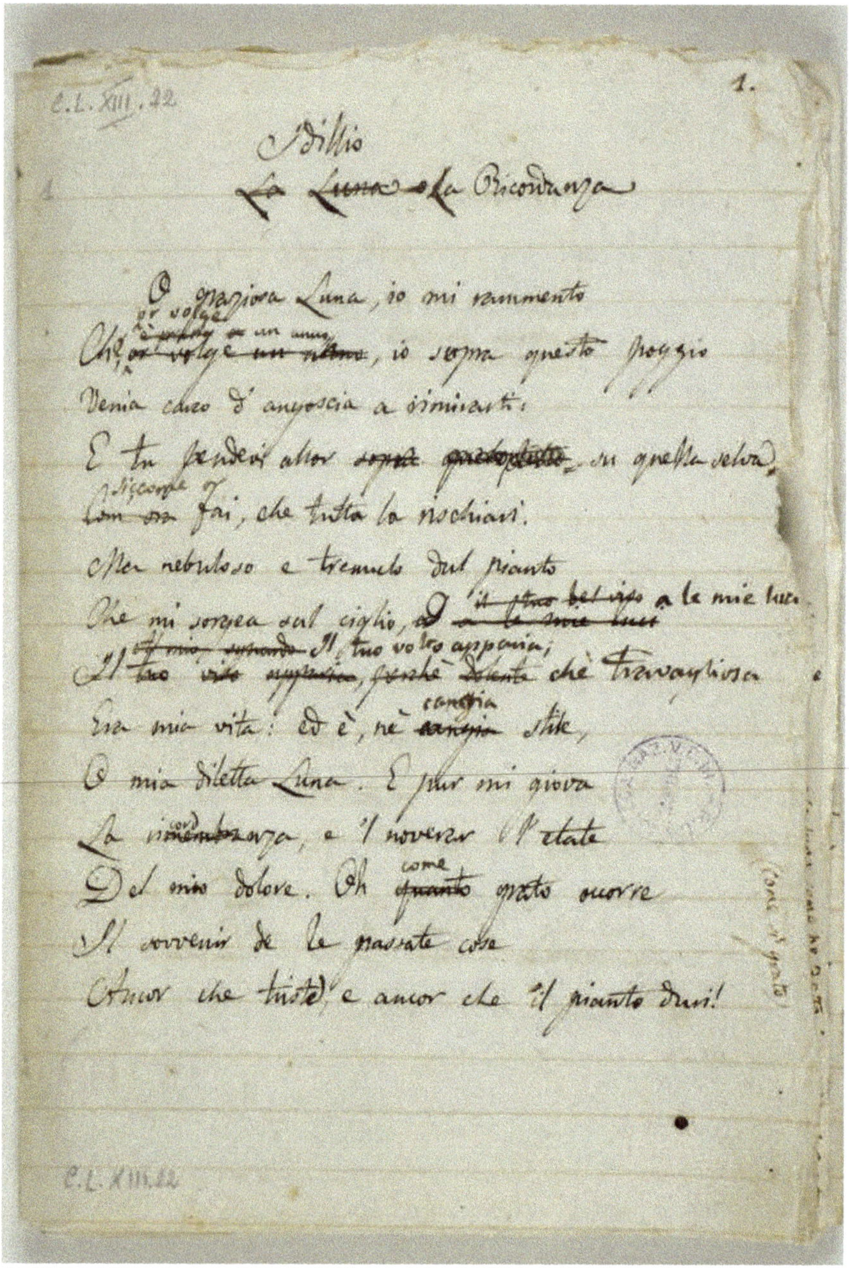

Fig. 5 Giacomo Leopardi, *Idillio | La Ricordanza*, 1819 (C.L.XIII.22, p. 1), https://www.wdl.org/en/item/10691/view/1/1/

the most precise, clear and synthetic way, turning what is at first visual and iconic into a dynamic text.

Let us now examine how the critical edition of the manuscript would look like. The abbreviations and expressions used in the 'Philological notes' have been translated in English as clearly as possible on the model of the abbreviations which would be used in an Italian apparatus (see sections 2.3.2, 2.3.4 and 2.5).

AN p. 1

Idillio
La Ricordanza

1   O graziosa Luna, io mi rammento
2   Che, or volge un anno, io sopra questo poggio
3   Venia carco d'angoscia a rimirarti:
4   E tu pendevi allor su quella selva
5   Siccome or fai, che tutta la rischiari.
6   Ma nebuloso e tremulo dal pianto
7   Che mi sorgea sul ciglio, a le mie luci
8   Il tuo volto apparia; ché travagliosa
9   Era mia vita: ed è, nè cangia stile,
10   O mia diletta Luna. E pur mi giova
11   La ricordanza, e 'l noverar l'etate
12   Del mio dolore. Oh come grato occorre
13   Il sovvenir de le passate cose
14   Ancor che triste, e ancor che il pianto duri!

tit.   La Luna o La Ricordanza] ^{1A}La Luna *from which* ^{2A}La Luna o la Ricordanza *from which* ^{3B}La Ricordanza (*with* L *over* l)

2   Che, or volge un anno,] ^{1A}Ch'or volge un anno, (*with an over* al) *from which* ^{2A}Ch'è presso a un anno, *from which* ^{3B}T   sopra] *from* su (*pen A*)

4   su quella selva] ^{1A}sopra quel bosco, *from which* ^{2A}sopra quel prato, (*with* prato *written over* bosco) ^{3A}su quella selva, (*written next to*^{2}) *from which* ^{B}T

5   Siccome or] *written above* Com'ora (*pen B*)

7–8 a le mie luci | Il tuo volto apparia; chè travagliosa] ¹ᴬa le *(before* al<le>*)* mie luci | Il tuo viso apparia, perché dolente *from which* ²ᴬil tuo bel viso | Al mio sguardo apparia, perché dolente ³ᴮa le mie luci | Il tuo volto apparia, che travagliosa *from which* ⁴ᴰT

9 cangia] ¹ᴬcangia ²ᴮcambia *(written above*¹*) from which* ³ᴰT

11 ricordanza] *from* rimembranza *(pen A)*

12 come] *written above* quanto *(pen B)*

14 triste] *from* tristi *(pen B)* il] *from* 'l *(pen C?)*

AN c. [1r]

right margin, directly opposite to the written text

(12) (come sì grato) *(pen D)*

---

tit. The text, initially only consisting in the title 'La Luna', is corrected to 'La Luna o la Ricordanza' with the same pen being used for the base-text (A); subsequently, it is corrected with pen B to 'La Ricordanza'. The two phases A in the writing of the title are identified thanks to Leopardi's customary practice of writing the title at the center, immediately below 'Idillio' (as in 'La sera del giorno festivo' and 'La vita solitaria').

2 The first correction ('Ch'è presso a un anno,') is made with pen A; the same applies for corrections in ll. 7–8 and 11.

4–5 The corrections made with thicker and heavier ink belong to phase B.

7–8 As already noted by Domenico De Robertis (in Leopardi 1984: II, 327), the correction of the comma to a semicolon after 'apparia' and the accentuation of 'che' seem to have been made with the pen with a reddish ink (here called D).

9 The correction of 'cambia' in 'cangia' was made at a later time (De Robertis in Leopardi 1984: II, 327) with pen D, the same pen which introduces in l. 8 the grave accent on 'che' and which Leopardi uses to write the variant in the right margin, directly opposite to the written text '(come sì grato'); in the edition 'come' is not in bold because the correction of l. 12 'quanto' → 'come', made with pen B (though Lucchesini (in Leopardi 2009: I, 278) thinks that the correction was made with pen A) is thought to have been made before the writing of the *varia lectio*.

14 The correction over 'tristi' obscures with the lower part of the 'e' the point of the 'i', creating an unusual upward swirl in the formation of this letter. If the correction of "l' to 'il' might belong to phase C, given the serial nature of the intervention, the *varia lectio* in the margin is closer to phase D, sharing with it the *ductus* and the reddish color (again De Robertis in Leopardi 1984: II, 327).

3. Italian Examples

Paola Italia and Giulia Raboni[1]

3.1 Petrarch: The *Codice degli abbozzi*

Petrarch's *Canzoniere*, also known as *Rerum vulgarium fragmenta*, is the earliest Italian work of which we have the original manuscript, which is partly autograph and partly idiograph (i.e., written by Petrarch's copyist under the author's direct supervision).

Codex Vatican Latin 3195 preserves the final redaction on which the poet worked until his death, but at the same time contains traces of multiple redactions in authorial interventions on the manuscript itself. Along with this fundamental document (now available online: https://digi.vatlib.it/view/MSS_Vat.lat.3195), we also possess other manuscripts (and their copies) that were derived from 3195 with the intention of making a gift to someone or simply meant for circulation. These copies represent intermediate forms in the elaboration of the *Rerum vulgarium fragmenta*. The three most important codices — Chigiano L V 176 (written by Giovanni Boccaccio), Laurenziano XLI 17 (a copy of a lost codex donated to the Lord of Rimini Pandolfo II Malatesta) and Queriniano D II 21 (a copy of another lost manuscript made for an unknown recipient) — were used to reconstruct the elaboration of the text in specific moments in time. As for the content of the lost intermediate redactions, this was reconstructed indirectly, through the testimony of letters and derived manuscripts, as well as through comparison with the extant manuscripts. Among these redactions, the most important is the so-called 'Pre-Chigi' or 'Correggio'-form (from the name of the recipient, the Lord of Parma Azzo da Correggio) that represents the first and central phase in the construction of the *Canzoniere*'s narrative.

---

[1] Paola Italia wrote sections 3.5, 3.6 and Giulia Raboni wrote sections 3.1-3.4.

Thanks to the sum of these testimonies, it was possible for modern scholars, beginning with Ernst Hatch Wilkins's studies in the 1950s (see Wilkins 1951), to analyze how the structure of Petrarch's work evolved. Wilkins identified nine forms (whose hierarchy was re-discussed by later scholarship), which allow us to connect the codex's structure, and the factors determining its internal cohesion, with specific variants in the individual poems. Wilkins justified this analysis partly on account of internal reasons and partly on account of their relationship with the rest of the poems.

Examining the individual variants of a single text can indeed reveal the internal motivations of its evolution, but their implications may remain unclear if their relationship (be it one of similarity or opposition) with the other poems is not also analyzed. It is precisely because of this need for broader analysis that much of the scholarship on variants in the *Canzoniere* is not focused on single texts but on groups of texts, whose genetic apparatuses sometimes reveal a tormented creative activity aimed at making the collection more coherent and at redistributing organically its contents and themes. The problem with giving a unitary representation of Vatican Latin 3195 using an apparatus of variants is therefore complex. One reason for this is that, while it is possible to create an apparatus for a single text, the text's position and function in the wider work may vary between different redactions of the *Canzoniere*, and this kind of representation might not do justice to the variants that are due to structural reasons. As a result, Petrarchan philology has in recent years explored two parallel paths. On the one hand, there has been a growth in studies about the constitution of the *Canzoniere* as a whole (see especially the work of Domenico De Robertis, Cesare Segre and Marco Santagata), its chronology, changes in the disposition of the texts, and new interpretations of its macro-structures; and on the other, multiple photographical and critical editions of the main witnesses have been produced.

Of particular interest among the Petrarchan codices is the autograph manuscript Vatican Latin 3196 (also available online: https://digi.vatlib.it/mss/detail/Vat.lat.3196) , which was already the object, as we have noted (see Chapter 1), of a ground-breaking edition by Federico Ubaldini (1652), who had rendered the variants using advanced typographical solutions, such as using a smaller print and italics for the rejected variants and a larger print for the definitive text. This edition, reprinted in 1750 and still employed by the eighteenth-century scholar Ludovico Antonio Muratori in his Petrarchan commentary, was used by scholars until Appel's 1891 diplomatic edition (which was in turn replaced by Romanò's 1955 edition). Laura Paolino's critical edition (Petrarca 2000) represents a fundamental advancement in our capacity to fully appreciate the readings found in the manuscript. Paolino devotes much space, in the introductory chapters, to the history of Petrarch's autographs, providing a reconstruction that also represents a significant contribution to the history of Petrarchan philology and of *petrarchismo* over the centuries. Her introductory chapters give a comparable amount of attention to the detailed description of the material characteristics of the manuscripts, as well as to discussing the criteria adopted in her edition (these are extremely conservative, and quite close to being diplomatic, extending even to the poet's graphical use, and they are justified by the peculiar nature of the object itself of the edition).

Paolino's edition also reconstructs the chronological order of the manuscript's leaves, allowing us to isolate significant moments in the elaboration, the earliest one being the group composed of fols 7–10, 11r, 15r, 16, datable to 1336–1337/8. Recent studies suggest that the first project of the narrative structure of the collection is to be dated to these same years, although this was significantly different from the definitive structure (Pancheri 2007). A peculiarity of this codex, which justifies the particular treatment it has received, as we will see, is that it is composite, i.e., containing leaves belonging to multiple moments in time. The codex includes, together with seventy-three poems — four of which are by correspondents of Petrarch, others in double or lacunose redactions —, two fragments of the *Triumphus Cupidinis* and of the *Triumphus Aeternitatis*, and one of *Fam.* xvi 6. Because of its composite nature, neither the order of the texts, nor the individual readings correspond to a single stage of the composition. The situation is made even more problematic by the fact that there may be later authorial interventions that cannot always be dated with certainty. In addition to this, in some instances, the texts are from a period later than the intermediate forms of the *Canzoniere* that we possess.

Adopting the usual praxis of authorial philology, namely, that of choosing as copy-text the final authorial intervention that the codex presents, would have led to privileging the most advanced state, which is not the same for every text in the codex, and is often closer to the other codices of the *Canzoniere*. Had this approach been adopted, the process of authorial re-elaboration would have been less noticeable. Paolino instead reproduces the oldest text as the copy-text and allows the reader to reconstruct the subsequent interventions from the apparatus, where they are dated on the basis of evidence of varying kinds, graphical (*ductus*, ink), topographical (the position of the variant in the manuscript), or chronological (in the case of marginalia where the date is reported).

Paolino justifies her 'heterodox' choice with two arguments, one 'internal' and the other 'external'. The first one is the authority of Domenico De Robertis, who chose the earliest redaction as copy-text when editing Leopardi's *Canti*, and therefore opted for an evolutionary apparatus, differently from Moroncini and his successors who instead opted for the author's last will. This is actually a bit of a forced parallelism, as Leopardi's *Canti* exist in multiple printed forms, and De Robertis's criteria, based on the meaningfulness of the first printed edition for the author and the public alike (see section 3.5), cannot be applied to Petrarch's private drafts, which were in no way 'definitive' and were never meant to be seen by the public. The second argument is more convincing: most texts are clean transcriptions, and the variants they present are not 'instaurative' (i.e., introducing new content to the text) but rather 'substitutive' (i.e., modifying an already stable form of the text). In cases of 'live' elaboration (variants applied during the process of the first writing, affecting the text that follows), Paolino uses a different form of representation by including the effaced passage in italics directly in the copy-text, before the version that replaces it. Consider an example in the following sonnet, https://digi.vatlib.it/mss/detail/Vat.lat.3196, c. 5v (the apparatus of the original Italian edition was translated by us):

36 [150]

c.5v	1	Che fai, Alma? che pe(n)si? aurem mai pace?
	2	Aurem mai tregua? od aurem guerra et(er)na?
	3	Che fia di noi? che dir? p(er) quel ch'io scerna,

	4	A' suoi begli occhi il mal nostro no(n) piace.
	5	Che pro, se co(n) quelli occhi ella ne face
	6	Ghiaccio di state (et) foco qua(n)do iuerna?
	7	Ella no(n), ma quel dio che gli gouern[a].
	8	Questo ch'è a noi, s'ella sel uede, et tace?
A	9	*Tace talor la li(n)gua, e 'l cor sospira*
	10	*E co(n) la uista asciutta i(n) duol si bagna*
	11	*Dentro doue mirando altri nol uede.*
	9	Talor tace la li(n)gua, e 'l cor si lagna
	10	Ad alta uoce, e 'n uista asciutta (et) lieta,
	11	Pia(n)ge doue mira(n)do altri nol uede.
	12	P(e)r tutto ciò la mente no(n) s'acqueta,
	13	Né ro(m)pe il duol che 'n lei s'aghiaccia (et) stagna,
	14	Ch'a gran sp(er)a(n)ça huom misero no(n) crede.

3. che dir p(er) > no(n) 'l so ma in: *correction written in left margin and referred with a cross-reference mark to the effaced text.* 6. Ghiaccio di state (et)> di state vn [g]hiaccio (Ghiaccio *effaced,* (et) *crossed out and the words* vn [g]hiaccio un *written above, between the lines; the* g- *of* [g]hiaccio *is hidden by an inkblot*) 7. Quel dio > coluj A 10. i(n) *preceded by an effaced letter, perhaps* n; *redaction A is erased by three oblique lines* 13. Né ro(m)pe > ro(m)pendo; s'aghiaccia > s'accoglie (*above the line*)

MARGINAL NOTES

1. *Above the sonnet, left:* tr(anscriptus)

A particular problem is that of variants made illegible by later interventions (such as heavy erasures). In this case the editor is forced to integrate the later variant in the text despite it being extremely likely to belong to a later phase — not unlike the variants that the author wrote in the margins or the interline, that are instead relegated to the apparatus, as they represent a later revision of the text than that found in the copy-text. See for example the first quatrain of sonnet 7 [191]. https://digi.vatlib.it/mss/detail/Vat.lat.3196, c.1v:

	1	Sicome eterna uita è ueder dio,
	2	Né più si brama, né bramar più lice,
	3	Così me, do(n)na, il uoi ueder, felice
A	4	Questo breue (et) fugace uiuer mio.
	4	Fa in q(ue)sto breue (et) fraile uiuer mio.

In this case, as the apparatus explains, 'me' on line 3 was written over an erasure, under which Angelo Romanò (Petrarca 1955) had deciphered a 'fa' — a reading that is grammatically well-coordinated with redaction A of line 4, in a construction later superceded by the complete rewriting of the final line of the quatrain. Because of the way the text is presented in Paolino's edition, this is not immediately clear to the reader.

It is therefore evident that an optimal solution cannot always be found. Choices often entail gains as well as losses and risks, so all factors must be taken into consideration in order to make the solution as compliant to one's theoretical objectives as possible. Other than the advantages and the minor problems that we have discussed, one can also argue that Paolino's edition could ideally be integrated into a progressive apparatus of the whole *Canzoniere*, where the earliest version will necessarily have to be picked as copy-text.

Paolino also edited the *Codice degli abbozzi* (before the proper critical edition was published) in Mondadori's *Meridiani* series (Petrarca 1996) as the second volume of Petrarch's rhymes, where, despite presenting essentially the same text and most of the apparatus of the critical edition, the spelling and punctuation have been notably modernized. In this way, Paolino offers us an example of an astute double edition of an autograph directed to different audiences.

3.2 Pietro Bembo: The *Prose della volgar lingua*

The first direct reference to the fact that Pietro Bembo was working on a dialogue on the vernacular language dates to April 1512, in a letter to Trifon Gabriele which was also directed to his other Venetian friends and primarily to Giovanni Battista Ramusio. In this letter, Bembo announces that he is going to send his friends two books ('and perhaps half the work'), asking for proofreading and suggestions on the revision of the text. However, there are no extant witnesses of this first redaction or of the discussions that followed. Similarly, although in a letter sent in 1525 to Cardinal Federigo Fregoso Bembo claims that there exists an earlier version of the dialogue dating to when he was at the Urbino court (after 1507), this is not proved by any extant document.

Bembo's statement must be taken with a grain of salt, as it was part of a strategy to claim the precedence of his work over the first Italian grammar to be printed, Francesco Fortunio's *Regole della volgar lingua* (1516); Bembo's dialogue itself also implicitly declares its own priority, given that it is set in 1502 and mentions Giuliano de' Medici (d. 1517) as alive. It is, however, also true that indirect traces might suggest the existence of at least a work of planning and grammatical classification at a quite early date. For not only is there a testimony by Lodovico Castelvetro documenting the circulation of the text before 1508 and an allusion by Bembo himself to some 'annotations on language' he had written in a letter to Maria Savorgnan in September 1500, but there are also still stronger hints in the so-called 'B Fascicle' added to the edition of Petrarch' *Canzoniere* printed by Aldo Manuzio, which Bembo curated (1501), which contains grammatical notes that re-appear in an almost identical form in the *Prose* (better known with the less accurate title *Prose della volgar lingua*; see Patota 1997), thereby proving the continuity of Bembo's project of linguistic reform since the time of the Manuzio editions of Dante and Petrarch.

By the time he sends the fascicle to his Venetian friends, Bembo has already been present for a few months in Rome at the court of Pope Leo X, who would later, in March 1513, take him as his secretary. It is likely that this role, together with his irritation for the existence of Fortunio's aforementioned *Regole* (which also implied the necessity to update his work), and the particular complexity of the third book of the dialogue (which is essentially a grammar of literary Italian language in dialogue form) kept him for some time from completing the work. It is nevertheless true that the *Prose* is not mentioned again until the letter to Fregoso of January 1525, where he says that he has already given a manuscript copy of the text to Clement VII in November 1524, and claims that he intends to publish it in Venice. Since Clement's copy is now lost, the *Prose*'s extant witnesses are limited to the three printed editions (Tacuino 1525, Marcolino 1538 and the posthumous Torrentino 1549, edited by Carlo Gualteruzzi) and the autograph Vatican Latin 3210 (known as V), preserved at the Vatican Library and composed in 1521–1522, at a time when Bembo, dissatisfied with the papal court, had retired to his villa in Padua, devoting himself to the cultivation of literary pursuits. On account of the importance of the dialogue in the Italian literary tradition, all of these redactions have lately been the object of a particular attention, allowing us to closely follow the process of their elaboration.

The most important recent contributions are those on the stop-press corrections of the Torrentino 1549 edition (discussed first by Bongrani (1982) and more recently closely analyzed by Sorella (2008)), which has allowed us to identify interventions made by Benedetto Varchi meant to normalize the text's language, even going in some cases against Bembo's own precepts. This will lead in the long run to a critical edition of the final text innovating on Dionisotti and Martelli's current 'vulgate' editions. The earliest redaction of the text has also received special attention, giving new insights into the times and processes of its composition, with two critical editions, one centred on manuscript V and another on the *princeps*, respectively produced by Mirko Tavosanis (Bembo 2002) and Claudio Vela (Bembo 2001).

Despite being based on the same witnesses, these two editions are radically different not only because both authors had to take into account the existence of the other's work (Vela, despite having published his one year before Tavosanis, does cite Tavosanis's 1996 PhD thesis), but also because of a partially different critical approach.

Tavosanis's editon is indeed focused on the sources employed by Bembo, specifically the manuscripts that he used to exemplify and define his vernacular grammar, including the medieval lyric chansonniers, Dante's poems and Boccaccio's works, specifically the *Decameron*, for which Tavosanis proves that the Hamilton autograph was used. The adoption of this 'critical focus' obviously did not prevent Tavosanis from discussing the dating of V and its relationship with the *princeps*, and often but not always his findings fit with Vela's conclusions. However, such an approach led Tavosanis to privilege the manuscript's earliest redaction (which he calls 'phase A'), relegating to the apparatus both the genesis (on the first part of the apparatus) and the text's following evolutions as found in later interventions on the manuscript, as well as in the Tacuino print (P) (on the second part).

The key advantage of this structure is that it isolates the earliest redaction from Bembo's later interventions on the manuscript, which were meant, on the one hand, to add more examples, especially in the third book, and, on the other, to normalize the text itself to his own grammatical rules, which were not originally applied systematically and might have been fully elaborated only at a later stage, as can be seen from the evolutionary apparatus. What the apparatus cannot instead attest is the difference between V's final redaction and P, a difference that is at times quite considerable, and which suggests the existence of a copy of V with corrections, probably lost precisely because of its use by the printer. The evolutionary part of the apparatus does not indeed distinguish V's later reading from P, just as it does not represent the genesis of the interventions on the manuscript; instead, this part of the apparatus substantially limits itself to two moments of the elaboration, that of base reading and that of the *princeps*, thereby making the apparatus extremely easy to read.

The critical edition produced by Vela is more complex, but also more analytical and exhaustive, and it is based on two fundamental choices. First, the 1525 *princeps* was selected as the copy-text. Despite not being the author's final will, the *princeps* indeed represents the point of arrival for the 'imposition across Italy of a language learned on books, which only in the most cultured environments overlaps to some extent with everyday language, but is nevertheless spoken and written as though it was a living language' (Dionisotti 1966: 47), a linguistic norm adopted by the new literature which ultimately replaces the form of Italian cultivated in the courtly tradition that precedes it. Furthermore, the adoption of P as copy-text also allowed for the use of extremely conservative criteria in the text's linguistic and graphic usage, extending as far as the use of punctuation and accents, and thereby underlining the importance of Bembo's choices in defining linguistic norms in all these domains, as well as highlighting the Tacuino edition's pursuit of elegance, which is symptomatic of the treatise's 'noble' implied readership. As far as representation is concerned, the identification of a specific phenomenology of correction both for the later interventions on V and for the passage from V to P has led, in this edition, to an unprecedented 'dialogue' between text and apparatus, one in which much information, rather than being delegated to the apparatus, can be inferred from the text thanks to the use of particular indicators that allow instant visualization of the various phases by which the text has been elaborated according to the following analytical representation:

1. *Editorial strata in V*

a) when V's final reading coincides with P and is the result of a process of an internal correction of V, the segment is signalled in the text by two interpuncts (·text·), and the genesis can be found in the first part of the apparatus;

b) when in V a segment is erased without being replaced by anything, this is signalled by a single interpunct (·) in the text, and the deleted content can be found in the apparatus between > and <;

c) if instead the segment is erased without being replaced, but it is rewritten in a substantially identical form elsewhere in V, the same symbol is used in the text, while the apparatus will report the erased text between ↑↑> and <↑↑ or ↓↓> and <↓↓, depending on whether the new collocation, indicated in brackets, is before or after in the text;

d) a passage which was originally written in a substantially identical form but was collocated elsewhere in V (in other words: what we have called 'the new collocation' at 1c) will be delimitated in the copy-text by ↓↓ or ↑↑ depending on whether the original collocation was before or after the new one, with the first band of the apparatus reporting the original collocation (see par. 28 of the example reported below);

e) text added while revising V is isolated by two asterisks (with smaller asterisks indicating further additions); in the case of longer additions that are adjacent, or are one within the other, superscript letters are instead used (in bold if the addition happened on extra leaves that were physically added).

2. *Passage from V to P*

a) P's additions are signalled by two superscript 'P' letters at the beginning and end of the section in the text (^{P}text^P);

b) where P suppresses a segment that was in V's final reading, this is signalled by ∧ in the text, with the second band of the apparatus reporting the removed section;

c) segments that changed their collocation from V's final reading to P are marked out by two single downwards or upwards arrows in the text (↓text↓ or ↑text↑), with the original collocation given in the second band of the apparatus;

d) if P's reading is different from V, it is underlined in the text: the manuscript's final reading is in the second band of the apparatus;

e) purely paragraphematic or minor graphic variants are in a third band of the apparatus at the bottom of the page, written in a smaller font.

3. *P's errors*

a) when the correction appears in the print's *Errata corrige*, the text will incorporate the correction, with the segment being marked out by two superscript E's (^{E}text^E), and the substituted text can be found in the third band, which is marked by [E];

b) where Vela has corrected the text, this is not reported in the text itself, and can instead be found in the table of P's corrected readings at the end of the volume.

The three-band apparatus thus reports, where applicable, the segments as follows: 1. a), b), c), d) in the first band; 2. b), c), d) in the second band, e) at the bottom of the second band; 3. a) in the 'E-band'.

Here is, as an example, the passage corresponding to I XI 24–31 (pp. 28–29 in the Vela edition):

$^{24+}$Et come che il dire IN HISPAGNA paia dal latino esser detto: egli non è così; percioche quando questa voce alcuna vocale dinanzi da se ha, ·SPAGNA· *le più volte*: et non *Hispagna* si dice. ∧ $^+$ ^{25}Il-qual uso tanto innanzi procedette; che anchora in molte di quelle voci, le-quali comunalmente ·parlandosi· hanno la E. dinanzi la detta .s. ·quella .E. pure nella .I. si cangiò· bene spesso. ISTIMARE, ISTRANO, et somiglianti. ²⁶Oltra che alla voce NUDO ·s'aggiunse· non solamente la .I. ma la G. anchora, et ·fecesene· IGNUDO; *non mutandovisi percio il sentimento di lei in parte alcuna: ²⁷il-quale in quest'altra voce ·IGNAVO· ·si muta nel contrario di quello della primiera sua voce; che nel latino solamente è ad usanza: la-qual voce nondimeno · Italiana è più tosto, si come dal Latino tolta; che Thoscana. * ²⁸††Ne solamente molte voci, come si vede; o pure alquanti modi del dire presero dalla Provenza i Thoscani.††ᵃ|²⁹Anzi essi anchora ·molte figure· del ·parlare·, molte sentenze, molti argomenti di Canzoni, molti versi medesimi le furarono: et piu ne furaron quelli; che maggiori stati sono et miglior poeti riputati. ³⁰Il che agevolmente vedera; chiunque le Provenzali rime pigliera fatica di leggere: senza che io; a cui sovenire di ciascuno essempio non puo: tutti e tre ᴾvoiᴾ gravi hora recitandolevi. ³¹Per le-quali cose *quello* estimar si ·puo·; che io M. Hercole rispondendo vi dissi; che il verseggiare et rimare da quella natione, piu che da altra s'è preso.

---

24 ⁺... ⁺] *transcribed in the last charta. In the final text the corresponding text is added in margin and is elaborated as:* >Spag< SPAGNA

25 >favellandosi< parlandosi   >essi< quella .E. pure nella .I. °si *ins.* cangiò (*from* cangiarono *with* -ò *over* -a- *and* >rono<)

26 >si giunse< s'aggiunse   fecesene] -se- *ins.*

27 IGNAVO] -AVO *over* –ORANTE   >et peraventura in altro< si muta   >voce< Italiana

28 ††...††] *cf.* x, *apparatus of* §§ 36–38

29 molte (e *over* i) >modi et< figure   >dire< parlare *written above*

31 puo *rewritten* istimar

---

24 ∧] NELLA SPAGNA: PER LA SPAGNA.

---

24 detto;   cosi: volte,   *Hispagna*,   dice:
26 IGNUDO. Non   27 Latino   30 Ilche   31 Perlequali   altra,

This structure has the advantage of being highly analytical and compact, and the understanding of its complex system of signs is also helped by the inclusion of an extremely useful bookmark containing the legend of the symbols. However, it is only useful for a text such as this one, in which most interventions are additions, and it would not fit cases in which the witnesses bear very different redactions or the elaboration of the single witnesses is more convoluted.

Likewise, it is evident that such an 'invasive' structuring is justified by its critical function, and the text is nonetheless usable, after removing the symbols, for an edition aimed at a broad public.

3.3 Tasso: The *Rime d'amore*

The editorial history of Torquato Tasso's works is connected to a sort of legend, one particularly nurtured in the Romantic age as in, for example, Goethe's eponymous tragedy, and generated by the dramatic, true-life vicissitudes of the poet, who was locked up in the *Sant'Anna* asylum in Ferrara for having allegedly attempted to assault with a knife a servant at the court of the Duke. Probably, behind his imprisonment there lurks too the suspicion aroused by the poet's restless behaviour towards religion, which was particularly inconvenient in Duke Alfonso II Este's court, as his duchy was under the constant threat of being annexed to the Papal state, and this made the Duke particularly zealous in dealing with any suspicion of heresy.

The news of the poet's madness aroused during his lifetime an immediate and morbid interest for his texts, which began circulating in editions that were mostly derived from his autographs, which the publishers obtained from the poet himself. Tasso himself indeed encouraged these editions in the hope that his fame might win him freedom, although afterwards he was very dissatisfied with their hasty and slapdash editorial choices which involved including apocryphal texts and adopting incoherent or contaminated readings.

The poet's confined and deprived living conditions also had their consequences on the times and modes of his production. On the one hand, the need for protection abnormally nourished his creativity, especially for encomiastic poetry; and, on the other, Tasso finds himself forced to work on the manuscript leaves and the printed editions to which he has access, and this makes it even more difficult to reconstruct the ways in which his work was composed and revised in the years of his seclusion. In this period, Tasso also organizes his poetry according to a tripartite structure divided into *love rhymes*, *encomiastic rhymes* and *holy rhymes*, with the *holy rhymes* also including encomiastic poems sent to members of the clergy. This three-fold division represents an attempt to move beyond the Petrarchan 'unitarian' model of the *Canzoniere* towards a more 'parcelled out' mode of organization which would become particularly popular among the poets of the Baroque age.

The project only found partial realization with the publishing of the *Parte prima* (containing the love poetry) in 1591 by Francesco Osanna in Mantua, and that of the encomiastic rhymes by Pietro Maria Marchetti in Brescia in 1593. As for the third part, it was destined to remain unpublished, and its intended outline has been recently reconstructed by Luigi Poma on the basis of the manuscript Vatican Latin 10980, copied by Marcantonio Foppa from a holograph, and edited in 2006 by Franco Gavazzeni and Vercingetorige Martignone. Before this edition, the situation was muddled and almost unsolvable because of the arbitrariness of the printed editions that the author could not personally supervise. Tasso's often overly dramatic declarations on the situation also led many scholars to consider a reliable reconstruction of these texts impossible. This is evident in the first edition with some scholarly ambitions, produced at the beginning of the twentieth century by Angelo Solerti (Tasso 1902), which contains 1708 texts but admittedly gives up on reconstructing the author's will, even ignoring some undeniably authorial attempts at systematization, and instead employing a chronological order reconstructed on the basis of the poet's biography. What Solerti keeps of Tasso's project is only the thematic tripartition, albeit redistributing its contents and significantly altering its form by changing the order of the poems and also including ones that the author later excluded, especially the madrigals. In this way Solerti effaced Tasso's design, regardless of the fact that this can be reconstructed through the short expositions that he wrote for each of the published poems in line with this aim of giving both a narrative and exegesis to his own poems. Tasso's texts are further altered in Solerti's edition by the contamination of individual readings from different redactions, and worsened by the choice to only include in the apparatus the readings that the editor deemed meaningful.

Despite the undeniable merit of being the first edition to list the manuscripts and give them a siglum, Solerti's edition is unsatisfying for modern philologists. All the same, Solerti's work was, for a long time, the basis of both scholarly editions and editions for a general public, as well as for critical works on Tasso. For this reason, many scholars ended up ignoring Tasso in works that deal with more technical aspects of poetic practice and that require a solid philological basis, as Valeria de Maldé (1999) noticed in commenting upon Aldo Menichetti's monumental monograph on Italian poetic metres.

A first rigorous examination of the problem of editing Tasso's *Rime* came in Lanfranco Caretti's *Studi sulle Rime del Tasso*, a collection of essays published in 1950. After having analyzed in detail the history of the poems and having classified the main manuscripts and printed editions, Caretti reviewed Solerti's edition in detail, underlined its shortcomings, and proposed a systematization based on the author's final will. Thus, Caretti claimed that in editing the poems, the Osanna edition had to be used for the first part, the Marchetti edition for the second and the codex Ravelli of the Angelo Mai library in Bergamo for the third part, as Caretti considers it the witness closest to the author's final will for the holy rhymes. Rhymes excluded from this authorial systematization had to be placed in a separate section instead. The entire previous process of correction would have to be represented as well, including the first authorial attempts to structure the collection as attested by the autographs. These guidelines were used for multiple researches promoted by Caretti himself at the University of Pavia and now form the basis for the National Edition of Tasso's works. We thus now know — as already mentioned — which manuscript, namely, Vatican Latin 10980, contains the most advanced version of the third part. Different forms for the second part have been identified as well: one is found in the manuscript F1 of the communal library of Ferrara and in the Parisian codex Pt, while another, earlier, systematization (which will soon be published) has been found in manuscripts E1 and E2 at the Biblioteca Estense in Modena.

The most important contribution on the love lyrics instead came from Dante Isella's studies (collected in 2009a: 51–114). What makes Isella's work innovative is not so much the way he pinpoints the importance of the autograph Chigiano L VIII 302, known as C and datable to 1583–1584 (which contains the earliest systematization of the love lyrics and was already known to earlier scholars), but rather the fact that he clarified how it was composed, leading him to theorise a new edition, different from the one Caretti imagined. Isella indeed proved the direct derivation of the readings found in the Chigiano from two annotated prints: Ts1 (an exemplar of the *Prima parte delle rime* published by Vittorio Baldini in 1582, known with the siglum 11), and Ts2 (an exemplar of the *Terza parte*, published by Vasalini in 1583, also known as 22), both published in Ferrara and both harshly criticized by the poet despite his involvement in their production. The derivation proposed by Isella demonstrates how, although one should always use them with some circumspection, these editions actually contain heretofore unattested redactions. When re-elaborating his texts, the poet, deprived of his own autographs, found himself forced to use these editions, somewhat 'authorizing' them regardless of their reliability.

The detailed analysis of the genesis of the Chigiano manuscript also underlines the originality of the collection it contains. This autograph has an individual character, based on the revision of the printed texts, but altered to make the collection as a whole more coherent. Such a character is significantly different from that of the collection ultimately published in the Osanna edition. From this difference came Isella's proposal to subdivide further this theoretical edition so as to present both systematizations. The apparatus of this ideal edition would therefore have to represent the respective genesis of each of the two different copy-texts, while the earliest attempt at an authorial systematization, dating to 1567 and known as *silloge degli Eterei*, would go in an appendix. The reason for this is that this version precedes the thematic subdivision and is therefore radically different from both later forms in terms of structure (see Gavazzeni 2003). As in Caretti, a separate volume would then contain all poems that do not belong to any of the collections.

The 1993 edition of the *Rime d'amore (secondo il cod. Chigiano L VIII 302)* by Gavazzeni, Leva and Martignone therefore presents, in accordance to this plan, the rhymes of the collection with the final readings as the copy-text and an apparatus divided in three bands (see the example) containing:

- a first band with the internal evolution of the manuscript;
- a second band with the readings of the printed editions known as 11 and 22 and the two annotated exemplars, where used (with the addition, for a few poems, of the testimony of later prints);
- a third band with extra observations (for instance, material details of the manuscript).

The apparatus, placed at the bottom of the page, is linear and somewhat 'photographic', as the *varia lectio* found in the printed editions and annotated exemplars is separate from that belonging to the Chigiano. The apparatus clearly divides the two phases of the work, but requires the reader to look at both bands in order to get a conspectus of the whole; at the same time, the part dedicated to the manuscript is rich with topographical indications (using superscript letters) where the authors deemed such information relevant to defining the manuscript's chronology, but again requiring the reader to make his deductions (Gavazzeni himself would later prefer other ways of presenting the *varia lectio*, see his edition of Leopardi's *Canti* in section 3.5). Here is how sonnet XXI of the Chigiano appears in the edition:

XXI c. 13r

Appressandosi a la sua donna, dice a' suoi pensieri et a' suoi affanni che si partano da lui.

Fuggite, egre mie cure, miei aspri martiri,
Sotto il cui peso giacque oppresso il core,
Ché per albergo hor mi destina Amore
Di nova speme e di più bei desiri.   4

Sapete pur che quando avien ch'io miri
Gli occhi infiammati di celeste ardore,
Non sostenete voi l'alto splendore
Né 'l fiammeggiar di que' cortesi giri,   8

Ma ve 'n fuggite qual notturno e fosco
Stormo d'Augelli inanzi al dì che torna

A rischiarar questa terrena chiostra. 11

E già, s'a certi segni il ver conosco,
Vicino è il sol che le mie notti aggiorna,
E veggio Amor che me l'addita e mostra. 14

2 mi^a] >lo< 4 Di nova speme di più bei^a] >A le sue gioie, a' suoi dolci<
5 pur^a] >ben<

11 (I, 3)
Ts1 (lines 2, 5, 6a, *6b*, 8, 9)

Arg. Appressandosi ... lui] Sonetto nel ritorno   2 il cui peso] 'l cui >pondo<
3 mi] lo   4 Di nova ... bei] A le sue gioie, a' suoi dolci   5 pur] >ben< /
quando] quand'   6 Gli occhi infiammati] >Que' Soli accesi<□*I lumi accesi*   8
que'] >duo<   9 ve 'n] >via<   13 il] 'l

In this example, only the first two bands can be found (the second one being divided, as we will see, in two parts). In the first band, the angled brackets (><) indicate an effaced passage, while the superscript letters indicate the position of a correction (in the example, ^a stands for a correction found in the interline above).

The second band is divided in two parts: the first part contains, in bold, the indication of the print witnesses: in this case, the poem can be found in 11 (the aforementioned 1582 edition printed by Vittorio Baldini) and in Ts1, an exemplar of 11 annotated by Tasso himself. The brackets following the sigla contain, for 11, the volume and page containing the text (I, 3), and for Ts1 the list of the lines that the author altered in this exemplar (2, 5, 6a, 6b, 8, 9); the line number is in italics if the correction makes the line coincide with the one in the copy-text: when this happens, the text of the correction is omitted from the second band of the apparatus, as it can easily be read in the copy-text. In the second part of the second band, the forward slash (/) at line 5 separates two corrections belonging to the same line, while the square □ at line 8 separates two subsequent interventions on the same portion of text.

The critical edition of the Osanna version, carried out by Vania de Maldé (Tasso 2016), allows us to better understand the process of Tasso's elaboration, both in terms of narrative and of form, as already shown by Colussi 2011 which examines the Chigiano's evolution from the points of view of syntax, phono-morphology, lexis and rhetorical style. Colussi's study enriches and confirms our perception of the importance of the collection in Tasso's development of a new poetic, and shows how it differs from the one of his youth in two different ways: the progressive abandonment of the poetic model offered by Giovanni Della Casa (this is indicated by the way Tasso limits *enjambements*, that is, Della Casa's most signature stylistic feature) and the pursuit of a 'middle' lyric style, eliminating the more popular elements (as evident from the removal of the madrigals) but at the same time reducing the *gravitas*, which becomes confined instead to his heroic poem *Gerusalemme liberata*.

3.4 Alessandro Manzoni: *Fermo e Lucia* and the *seconda minuta*

The beginning of Manzoni's long work on his novel (*I promessi sposi*) can be dated with precision to 24 April 1821, thanks to a note written by the author on the first sheet of the initial chapter of the earliest draft of the work (conventionally called *Fermo e Lucia* after the main characters). After having written poems, plays and essays, Manzoni attempted a novel. In doing so, he at the same time addressed both the complaint made by contemporary romantics about the absence of the novel as a genre in the Italian high culture tradition and the call of the pre-unitarian nationalist movement for a national language that might assist the realization of cultural unification. The work was composed over two years, and reached its conclusion in September 1823 in a form where, while the narrative is mostly complete, the linguistic problem — that is, which of the vernacular languages, employed both in the past and present, in Italy to use — is consciously ignored for the moment. We know, however, from a letter to Claude Fauriel that Manzoni was aware of this issue and already convinced of the need to find a solution.

The only form of national language that existed in Manzoni's time was the hyper-literary language of lyric poetry. This begged the question regarding which language one should adopt in writing a novel that strived to be popular (both in terms of public and of narrative) and understandable for the entirety of the nation. After having been set aside, the linguistic problem re-emerged once the first draft was complete, when the author started revising his text to prepare a manuscript for which a copyist would make a fair copy so as to send it to the censor. After correcting a few chapters, roughly until the end of the first volume, Manzoni seems to be increasingly convinced that he was able surpass the language of that rough draft, one he himself defines as 'an indigestible mixture made of sentences that are part Lombard, part Tuscan, part French, and even part Latin, as well as of sentences not belonging to any of these groups but rather derived through analogy and extension from one or the other'.

By gaining experience from the process of writing itself and from reading Tuscan works and dictionaries, as well as perhaps through discussions with his friends, Manzoni soon grew convinced that he could reach a less 'subjective' unitary language, based on chiefly comic Tuscan authors and the *Vocabolario degli Accademici della Crusca*, a dictionary characterized by a heavy linguistic conservativism. After a few chapters had been revised on the same paper as the first draft (Manzoni had intentionally only used one vertical half of the page in order to leave the other half for corrections), and after the copyist had transcribed them in fair copy, Manzoni began a much deeper revision which would in the long run lead to the first print of the *Promessi sposi*, produced in Milan by Vincenzo Ferrario in instalments from 1824 to 1827. Since the beginning of this revision in spring 1824, the new text progressively distances itself from the earlier drafts, not only because it is done on other leaves of paper, but also because the narrative is entirely restructured, with many episodes being shortened and the 'montage' of the events being altered. Whereas in the earlier version the adventures of the two separated lovers were told separately (first everything that happens to Lucia, and then the vicissitudes affecting Fermo), in the later form the episodes are 'interlaced', leading to what amounts to an almost complete rewriting of the novel. From the documentary point of view, these are the witnesses from the first draft to the Ferrario edition:

- *Prima minuta* ('first draft'): the autograph dossier of *Fermo e Lucia*, which survives in its entirety with the exception of a few leaves. The leaves are numbered on the first page and folded vertically so as to use the right column for the text and the left one for corrections;

- *Seconda minuta* ('second draft'): the autograph of the revised version, which for the earlier chapters reuses some leaves from the *Prima minuta*;
- Censor's copy: drafted by the copyist, it contains interventions, some quite major, by Manzoni dating to the period before it was sent to the censor and the printer;
- Printing proof: only a few extant pages;
- The 1824–1827 print (known as the *Ventisettana*): two stop-press corrections were found by Neil Harris and Emanuela Sartorelli (2016) only on two of the sixty-eight examined exemplars, while the analysis of the watermarks indicates that fifteen pages were replaced during the long print of the three volumes.

All these autographs can now be directly consulted online on the website www.alessandromanzoni.org, a database that collects all the manuscripts conserved in the Braidense Library of Milan and the books of the writer, together with their description and the critical bibliography on Manzoni's works.

Due to the first draft's structural difference from the *Ventisettana*, the editors had to publish it separately from the manuscript versions, as Chiari and Ghisalberti (Manzoni 1954) already did when first editing the full work as part of the 'Classici Mondadori' series. This edition, while accurate and commendable, is not exhaustive and is unsystematic in the presentation of the variants that are relegated to notes at the end of the book. The 2006 edition directed by Dante Isella attempts to address this issue, by adopting more accurate and efficient criteria for the representation.

First of all, the apparatus, which is too extensive to fit in the footer, is in a separate volume, written in the same font size as the text to facilitate the comparison and underline its importance. In this way, the reader is able to appreciate the phases of the correction over the longest textual segments possible. In other words, where there are multiple corrections over a single segment, the interventions are presented in a systemic apparatus which attempts to highlight the 'direction' of the corrections as a whole rather than indicate where each individual correction is found on the manuscript page — a choice that comes with the risks implied in such a bold interpretative effort.

See this example of the apparatus, from vol. 1, chapter 1, f. 5a, paragraph 20 (see Fig. 6):

20 [osservando come aveva fatto tante altre volte] sul monte i riflessi del sole già nascosto, ma che mandava ancora la sua luce sulle alture, distendendo sulle rupi e sui massi sporgenti come larghi strati di porpora.

5a   20 sul monte ... porpora] (reading 1 and part of 2 are on f.4d) ¹i massi sporgenti e le rupi sporgenti illuminate ᵃdagli ultimi raggi del sole ᵇ(*above*) dai rifle<ssi> che riflettevano quà e là → ²sui massi e sulle rupi sporgenti ᵃl< > ᵇil sole già tramontato ᶜil sole già nascosto ᵃper chi ʰai suoi occhi, e la luce sparsa quà e là come a grandi strati di porpora ᵈla luce ᵉil riflesso del so<le> i riflessi del sole già nascosto, ma che ³sull'alto del monte i riflessi del sole già nascosto, ma che splendeva ancora mandava ancora la sua luce sulle alture, distendendo sulle rupi e sui massi sporgenti come larghi strati di porpora. → T

The evolution of this segment is schematized in three phases (corresponding to the superscript numbers ¹ ² ³): the second phase materially reuses elements of the first (hence the use of the symbol →), while the final one, which is the copy-text (here indicated as T), partially reuses the third phase (the process is therefore represented as → T). There is no reusage of materials from phase 2 to 3, as the absence of arrows signals: this means that Manzoni completely effaced the sentence he had written in phase 2 and rewrote it from scratch (phase 3), then altered it to the form found in the copy-text. Where there are more evolutions internal to a single phase, this is represented with superscript letters, first in roman, then in italic and, where there is a further development, this is marked in bold. The final formulation for each phase is in the regular font size, while the 'accidents', that is, minor changes within a phase, are in smaller print, so that the final reading for each phase is always immediately evident. Topographical indications are minimal: the arrow signals reuse of materials, but the way this happens (whether the new material is inserted in an empty space or written above or below, etc.) is

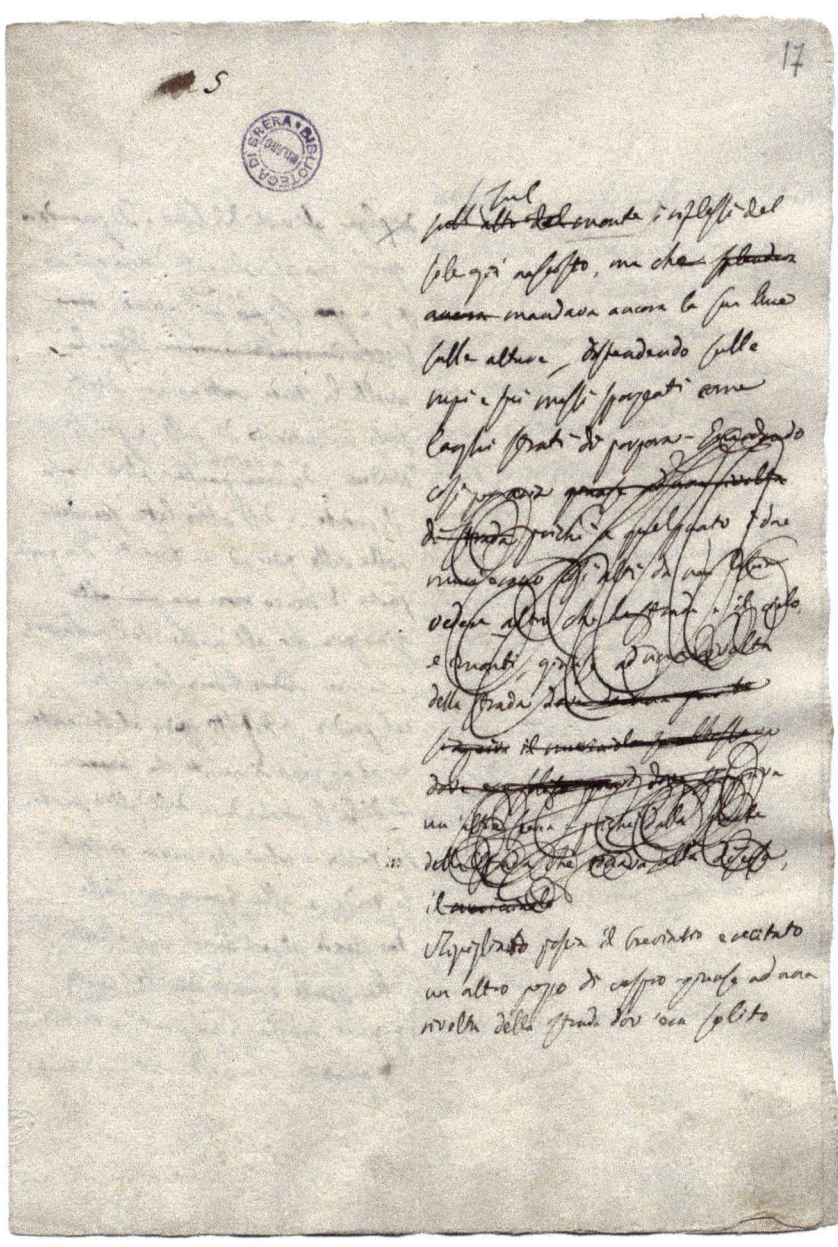

Fig. 6 Alessandro Manzoni, *Fermo e Lucia*, 1821–1824 (Biblioteca Nazionale Braidense, Manz.B.II, t. I, cap. I, f. 5a), http://www.alessandromanzoni.org/manoscritti/624/reader#page/28/mode/1up

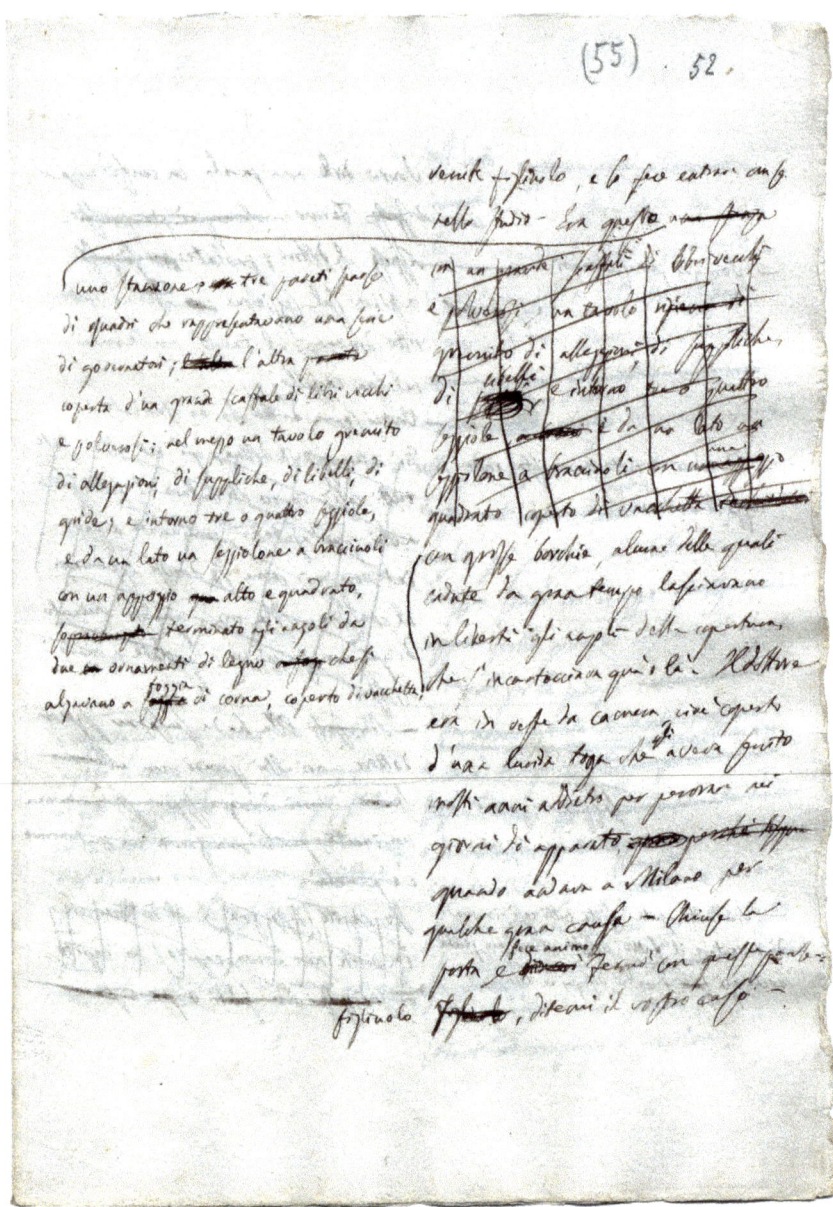

Fig. 7 Alessandro Manzoni, *Fermo e Lucia*, 1821–1824 (Biblioteca Nazionale Braidense Manz.B.II, t. I, cap. III, f. 26c), http://www.alessandromanzoni.org/manoscritti/624/reader#page/112/mode/1up

not specified unless it holds chronological significance (i.e., it suggests that an individual intervention is from a later time compared to the rest of the segment). This solution clearly obliges the editor to determine what to consider an autonomous phase and what not, and to attribute each correction a relative chronology.

From the chronological point of view, the greatest difficulty stems from the re-use of leaves from the first draft in the second, which requires the distinction of the readings belonging to the second draft from those of the first so as not to confuse two different moments in the elaborative process. While this distinction can be made on the basis of graphical usage, language, and content, it is impossible to make with absolute certainty. In uncertain cases, a footer is added to both the text and the apparatus, with the uncertain reading preceded by a bicuspid arrow (↔), thereby signifying that the reading might belong to either form, while the copy-text reports the earlier reading. In the text, these uncertain readings are signalled by superscript numbers. See for instance vol. 1, chapter 3, leaf 26c (Fig. 7), where the description of the lawyer's office is effaced during the revision and completely rewritten in the left-hand column only after a first attempt at reusing the first version as attested by an aborted correction (un] una *above*). Two variants are instead uncertain (and these are numbered 7 and 8, implying that six other uncertain variants precede in that same chapter), as they might belong to the genesis of the second draft as much as to the revision of *Fermo e Lucia*. Here is the text and apparatus relative to leaf 26c:

venite figliuolo, e lo fece entrare con se nello studio. Era questa una stanza con un grande scaffale di libri vecchj e polverosi, un tavolo gremito di allegazioni, di suppliche, di papiri[7], e intorno tre o quattro seggiole, e da un lato un seggiolone a bracciuoli con un appoggio quadrato coperto di évacchetta inchiodatavi[8] con grosse borchie, alcune delle quali cadute da gran tempo lasciavano in libertà gli angoli della copertura, che s'incartocciava quà e là. Il dottore era in veste da camera, cioè coperto d'una lurida toga che gli aveva servito molti anni addietro per perorare nei giorni di apparato, quando andava a Milano per qualche gran causa. Chiuse la porta e rincorò Fermo con queste parole: Figliuolo, ditemi il vostro caso.

↔ [7]libelli [8]vacchetta

26c   21 venite] *before* (*on f.* 26b) addio   22 libri vecchj] libri *written over* v<
> gremito di] *before* ripieno di   e da un lato ... bracciuoli] ¹a bracci<uoli>
²T {e} *over* i}   23 gli aveva] gli *ins.*   apparato, quando] *from* apparato =
quan<do> perchè bisogna   rincorò] r- *on* d

↔ 22 papiri] libelli *above*   vacchetta inchiodatavi] *corr. to* vacchetta

The problem of representing the later steps in the elaboration of the novel is even more complex. Unlike what happens between the two drafts, in the passage from the *Seconda minuta* to the Ferrario editon (that is the *Ventisettana*) the narrative remains almost identical. As a result, it would be theoretically possible to edit the *Ventisettana* by putting the *Seconda minuta*'s readings in the apparatus. However, the *Seconda minuta* underwent an extensive work of internal revision, with entire pages being rewritten or eliminated, so that a single apparatus would be illegible. It was therefore decided to edit the *Seconda minuta* autonomously (Manzoni 2012), while the edition of the *Ventisettana* only reports in the apparatus the changes that happened between the *Seconda minuta*'s final reading and the *Ventisettana*'s reading (through the censor's copy and, when available, the printing proof). The apparatus follows the same rules as that of the *Fermo*, while the paragraph division is that established by Caretti in his 1971 edition of the *Ventisettana* (Manzoni 1971) and still adopted by most later editors, so as to make the comparison easier.

Of course, particular attention was paid to the re-used leaves from *Fermo*. They are signalled by a grey background, and in the cases where Manzoni had originally attempted a correction of the text from the *Fermo* but then decided to rewrite the entire passage instead, the apparatus indicates the corresponding paragraph of the *Fermo*, marking any case of a dubious reading with a bicuspid arrow. This solution is not without some issues. The main one is that the *Seconda minuta* is a work in progress and not a complete, organic text. Manzoni actually worked at the same time at rewriting the text from the *Fermo* and at printing the already-rewritten parts, so that, in short, we cannot read the second tome of the *Seconda minuta* as continuous with the first one, since between these parts there is the entire work on the censor's copy and the replacement of some of the already-printed leaves with new, revised ones (which Manzoni used to call 'cartons'). The decision made, then, was taken both to prevent the apparatus from becoming unwieldy and to underline the most critical moment of Manzoni's linguistic elaboration from the mixture of languages found in *Fermo* to the ever-more Tuscan-centric solution of the following versions. In this way, the edition proposes itself as a tool to reconstruct the process that brought the text to its final version through much more complex steps than was previously recognized.

This edition constitutes perhaps one of the most advanced solutions so far from the point of view of interpretation, leaving aside photographic representation in favour of a diachronic structure that allows for the comparison of long segments, with recourse to appendixes only when the elaboration is too complex to be represented in the apparatus.

This is nowadays a common tendency in authorial philology and it undoubtedly has many advantages, especially for prose texts, since it allows us to see the evolution of variants in its totality even in terms of syntax and style; this approach does not, however, come without disadvantages, especially from the linguistic point of view. Indeed, if on the one hand, the organization of the apparatus in phases makes it easier to perceive the evolution of a segment, it is actually harder, on the other hand, to notice the substitution of single words, which would aid lexicological and morphological research. If one made this kind of objection, one could answer that: 1) often the replacement of a word is the consequence of changes in the wider structure; 2) in the case of the systematic application of a linguistic norm, the replacement is likely to also happen in isolation (that is, it is not always within a wider re-worked segment) and can be immediately noticeable; 3) it is true that comparing single words is more difficult in this way, but the lexical change is nevertheless registered by the apparatus, while one could not pinpoint major changes from a word-for-word apparatus without having to look at the autograph; 4) one can always find a way to give representation to single variants while privileging the phase of the correction.

3.5 Giacomo Leopardi's *Canti*

The importance of Giacomo Leopardi's collection of poetry, the *Canti*, lies not only in their being a fundamental poetic work of the first half of the nineteenth century, but also in their particular editorial history, which will be worth retracing here before speaking about the technical problems connected with their multiple critical editions. The *Canti* are in fact the only case in Italian literature where four critical editions have followed one another, with each featuring a different structure. This case also deserves a longer discussion compared to the previous ones, because the history of authorial philology begins with Moroncini's 1927 critical edition, which, by highlighting the extraordinary writerly dynamics of Leopardi's texts, helped to inspire Contini in founding criticism of variants.

Even leaving aside the editions, the history itself of the *Canti*, with their long and often non-linear evolution, justifies the particular philological attention they have received. The relevant witnesses are:

- The first edition of the two patriotic *canzoni* 'All'Italia' and 'Sopra il monumento di Dante', printed in Rome in 1818 (R18);
- The 'Ode ad Angelo Mai', printed in Bologna in 1820 (B20);
- The first collection, *Canzoni*, printed in Bologna in 1824 accompanied by the *Annotazioni* ('Commentary') (B24);
- The collection *Versi*, printed in Bologna in 1826 (B26);
- The first proper edition of *Canti*, printed in Florence in 1831 (F31);
- Another edition of the *Canti*, printed in Naples in 1835 (N35), with its *errata corrige* (N35err);
- An exemplar of N35 with the addition of the author's corrections, in part autograph and in part written under his dictation by his friend Antonio Ranieri (*Starita corretta* or N35c).

One must also add other intermediary stages, namely the publications of one or more poems in journals, such as the *Nuovo ricoglitore*, which between 1825 and 1826 hosted the author's earliest idylls and re-published the aforementioned *Annotazioni* as well as the poem 'Alla sua donna' (these editions are known as NR25 and NR26). A similar case is that of the 1825 publication of the idyll 'Il sogno' on the journal *Il Caffè di Petronio* (CP). The chronological series of the main witnesses therefore is R18, B20, B24, NR25–26, B26, F31, N35, N35c.

As well as the printed editions, multiple autographs survive. In analysing them, one must however take into consideration that they are not drafts, but rather revised fair copies (Gavazzeni 2006: 409), which contain corrections in the interline, in margins, or occasionally on separate slips of paper physically added to the page. For the first three *canzoni* ('All'Italia', 'Sopra il monumento di Dante', 'Ad Angelo Mai'), Leopardi sometimes adds variants to the printed versions, while for the others they can only be found in manuscripts. The marginal space of the manuscripts is also used for the *varia lectio* (the sum of 'genetic variants, alternative readings, glosses and lists of synonyms meant to "authorize" the language', ibid.). The *varia lectio* therefore does not only include proper variants (be they genetic or alternative), but also footnotes which are functional to the text and at times pre-exist parts of it, even though they cannot be properly considered part of the text itself of the poems. One such case is provided by the linguistic glosses (sometimes in the added slips), indications of sources, authorial commentaries, and other elements that should be represented separately from genetic, alternative and evolutionary variants. Therefore, the analysis of how the text was formalized leads the critic to understand more fully the layers of its elaboration, and ultimately the compositional strategy lying behind it and the authorial poetics inspiring it.

Starting with the *canzone* 'Bruto minore', Leopardi becomes his own copyist, writing a stanza per page while filling the lower, left, and (rarely) right margins with the *varia lectio*, surrounding the text in a way that is visually reminiscent of classical and humanistic commentaries. The *varia lectio* is especially used in B24. This is perhaps due to the young poet's need to justify to himself and to the literary world a series of linguistic choices, which were often perceived as heterodox, despite being rooted in the Italian canonical literary tradition. In the manuscripts written after the *Canzoni*, such as those containing the 'Epistola al conte Carlo Pepoli', 'Il Risorgimento', and 'A Silvia', there are fewer variants, and these are always reported on the left or right margins. For 'Le ricordanze', 'La quiete dopo la tempesta', 'Il Sabato del villaggio', 'Canto notturno di un pastore errante dell'Asia', the situation changes, and 'the variants are included between round brackets in the text (in the case of 'Le ricordanze' there are also square brackets indicating rejection)' (Gavazzeni 2006: 410). By examining the manuscripts, the *modus operandi* of the poet can be reconstructed. As Gavazzeni puts it (ibid.: 410–11):

> After having copied what at the time he considered the final reading, Leopardi continues copying from that same source — a now-lost dossier from which he transcribed the provisionally final text together with its genetic materials and alternative readings. These genetic variants and alternative readings, together with other materials, were included in the *varia lectio* that the author used for interlinear corrections and, more rarely, for changes to prints following the *princeps*. From this, one can deduce that normally Leopardi would first transcribe the text, then report the variants in the footer (or occasionally in the lateral margins or the header), and then started altering his base-text.

Let us therefore start our examination of the critical editions with Moroncini's (Leopardi 1927), which Folena called, in the 1978 reprint, 'a happy encounter of knowledgeable empiricism and dogged scrupulousness' (Leopardi 1978: n.p.). As for the copy-text, Moroncini (later followed by Peruzzi and Gavazzeni in their editions) opts to reproduce the texts and order of the *Starita corretta* (N3c), the printed edition with corrections written under Leopardi's dictation, considering this as representative of the author's final will. The apparatus is vertical and covers the manuscript and printed tradition without distinction. Invariants are given in square brackets, variants in italics (though this can be confusing since Leopardi himself largely employed italics in his manuscripts), and the final text is in bold. Variants are separated by single spacing when in a single witness, while they are double spaced when more than one witness is noted. Moroncini also distinguishes substantial from interpunctive variants by putting them in two different bands of the apparatus. The authorial *varia lectio* is reproduced in smaller print and included in a box in the lower margin of the page; when the text is abbreviated or incomplete, the editor completes the word or sentence himself.

Innovative and scientific in its way of representing the manuscripts, especially for that time, the Moroncini edition was also strongly interpretative in transcribing and in ordering the variants. Nevertheless, it remained essential for more than half a century, being the basis on which all studies on the *Canti* were built for a considerable period.

The critical edition that followed, curated by Emilio Peruzzi and published in 1981, had the merit of printing for the first time the facsimiles of all of the poet's manuscripts together with the critical edition itself (though Peruzzi's edition does not include notes, prefaces and dedications). In this way, the 1981 edition allowed the reader to double-check the philologist's work for every text. Despite agreeing with Moroncini on the importance of using the author's final will (the *Starita corretta*) as copy-text and on presenting together manuscript and printed tradition, Peruzzi differs from his predecessor on two fundamental points. First, he does not separate interpunctive and formal variants from the substantial ones on the grounds that 'often a comma is enough to change the meaning of a sentence, and even more so in poetry, where punctuation also defines pauses, scans the rhythm, and traces the melodic curve, bringing about specific meanings' (Leopardi 1981: vi). Moreover, Peruzzi's transcription of the variants is significantly less interpretative, compared to Moroncini who used to 'develop hemistichs or even entire lines from single words' (ibid.) without signalling such integrations in the apparatus. The representation of the variants is based on the same principles as Moroncini's, as they are put in a column, with each phase occupying a different typographic line. Peruzzi, however, reports the final readings of each verse in the header of each page and gives their genesis below, with Greek letters indicating different phases of a single witness. If a line remains unchanged from the first version to the final one, the line is given with the specification of the earliest witness, without any other indication. N35's final readings are repeated only where there have been elaborations, as the point of arrival of a chain of variants. When the reading of a witness does not change in the following witnesses, the sigla of the following ones are not reported, thereby implying the identity of the readings.

Greek letters indicate the different phases of the elaboration of a line in a specific redaction. This of course only applies for manuscripts that may present different phases of elaboration: AR (the autographs preserved in Recanati), AN (the ones at the Biblioteca Nazionale Vittorio Emanuele III in Naples), AV (preserved in Visso, near Recanati). Effaced portions of the text are reported between square brackets, and italics indicate invariant portions, unlike most apparatuses, where italics either indicate text that is underlined in the original or effacement. Words that are underlined in the autograph or in italics in the printed edition are rendered using small capitals, while upper-case italic indicates a double underlining. There is a similar 'switch' of signs in the case of words that Leopardi wrote in brackets, which are rendered in double square brackets, because single brackets are already used for erasures. Incomplete letters are indicated by a dot below each letter, while an X with a dot below it indicates an unreadable character. Peruzzi's edition, which was reprinted in a less costly version in 1998, is still widely used by scholars, but its main shortcoming is the limitation of the vertical apparatus (which presents variants line by line) to represent corrections that affect more than one line, as often happens in Leopardi's elaboration (see the example at section 2.6 of this volume).

As its very title suggests, the *Edizione critica delle stampe e dei manoscritti* (*Critical edition of the prints and manuscripts*), the critical edition produced by Domenico De Robertis in 1984, is completely different for its way of representing variants and the solutions adopted. De Robertis indeed separates the manuscript tradition from the prints, editing the printed editions in the first volume and publishing very high-quality reproductions of the manuscripts in the second. The real innovation lies, however, in De Robertis's choice of *the first printed edition* as copy-text for each poem, with the apparatus containing the entirety of its evolution until its latest printed version in N35. For instance, the *Ode ad Angelo Mai* is published according to the first print (B20), while the apparatus presents the evolutionary variants of the printed tradition: B24, B26, F31, N35. If the reading of a printed edition is based on the manuscripts AR or AN, it is signalled in a separate apparatus of footnotes with superscript letters. The text is in the upper half of the page, and the apparatus in the lower one. For each witness, all the variants are given, in columns, with the number of the line to which the variant refers.

The edition, as already noted, does not represent the genesis of the autographs. This is both for practical and theoretical reasons. For, according to De Robertis, not only would such a representation 'require an extremely refined editorial technique, whose costs are at the moment unaffordable' (Leopardi 1984: xxii), but as editor he wanted to underline — rather than the genetic process — the 'crystallization' of the poem, 'the moment [...] in which the poetic endeavour, no matter how complex, has reached a fully-defined aspect, and the text breaks free of the author's control, at least until the following reprint' (ibid.: xxi). The reader is therefore presented with the entirety of Leopardi's manuscripts, which are considered autonomous and not in need of an apparatus. Nevertheless, the philologist adds, in the introductions to the reproductions of each manuscript in the second volume, a useful comparative apparatus so as to show that manuscript's final reading and the printed edition to which it is connected.

De Robertis's edition presents itself as 'a new methodological hypothesis, based on a different philology and aiming for a different way of representing the text so as to obtain full legibility both for the text and its history, in order to organically present to the "user" the moment of "production"' (ibid.: xvii). To use the author's own metaphor, the 'history of the text's vicissitudes is privileged over its final form, so that, rather than the ultimate *plot* (Starita), the reader can appreciate its long and complex *fabula*' (ibid.: xviii).

A different solution is instead found in the new critical edition directed by Gavazzeni and published in 2006 by the *Accademia della Crusca* (with the addition, in the 2009 reprint, of a third volume of *Poesie disperse*). The Gavazzeni edition uses, like those by Moroncini and Peruzzi, the author's final will as copy-text (N35c), but follows De Robertis in the choice of recognizing the importance and individuality of the two elaborative moments (manuscripts vs printed editions) of the text, without nevertheless giving up on representing the manuscripts' genesis. The result is an edition that presents the final reading of the *Canti*, and documents its genesis by reconstructing its manuscript and printed tradition, but also separately represents, as a tool for scholars, the most advanced manuscript reading. This is particularly useful (perhaps necessary) for particularly complex manuscripts such as those connected to B24, for which the full transcription of the manuscript and printed variants would have made the study of the autographs more difficult. We are able to see the manuscript's final reading with the possibility of analysing the phases of the corrections thanks to the integral reproduction of the text means that one can distinguish chronologically interventions, different inks and the textual stratification. This is very clear in the example of *La Ricordanza*, reproduced in Figure 5.

This is not *strictu senso* a second critical edition, but rather a tool for scholars to be read together with the final print, to which it is connected by the comparative apparatus. The manuscript's final reading, if different from the first print, is presented in round brackets in N35c's apparatus. This 'bridges' the gap between the two texts and apparatuses, allowing us to retrace the author's intervention in the passage from manuscript to *princeps*. Isolating the manuscript text also allows an evaluation of how much of it survives in the printed editions (the manuscript variants that are used in the printed text are in bold).

Let us look at the two (both genetic) apparatuses from up close. The apparatus for the manuscripts is horizontal and explicit, and represents all corrections on the manuscript in relation to the final reading, which is the one found in the copy-text. The collocation on the page and the chronological ordering of each variant are specified in italics. Depending on the kind of correction, these variants might be presented derivatively (X *over* Y, X *written below* Y etc.), or progressively (^{1}X *from which* ^{2}Y *from which* T, or simply X *from which* T). In the case of minor corrections, it is more 'agile' to represent the correction derivatively: X *written above* Y.

Where there are instead wider corrections, or variants in complex order, the progression is more useful than the derivation (^{1}X *from which* ^{2}Y *from which* T or X *from which* T) so as to make the process clearer. Minor corrections within a phase, as already seen in the previous chapters, are better represented derivatively, so as not to obscure the understanding of the longer segment.

The apparatus pertaining to the manuscripts is therefore always diachronic and not synchronic, as the chronological order of the variants is privileged over their position in the text (unless the position gives information relevant to chronology), obliging those who want to know where a correction can be found on the manuscript page to check the manuscripts themselves. It is also a *systemic* apparatus, as the portion of text affected by the variant (the one before the square bracket) is always directly comparable with the variant itself and re-written entirely in the apparatus. In this way, the reader can see it immediately without having to go back to the text. The apparatus of the prints is positive for the variants, negative for the invariants. The presence of a reading preceded by the siglum **B26**, for instance, implies that all testimonies older than B26 report the reading that precedes, while all the later ones have the same reading as B26, unless another siglum informs us that from another edition onwards the reading changes again. The last siglum indicates the first print to present the final reading. The prints whose sigla are omitted because of this solution can be found on the top left corner of every page, which for each poem lists in chronological order all the prints that contain it.

The *varia lectio* is instead isolated in a box (like in Moroncini's edition) and transcribed with absolute fidelity to the autograph, down to its position in the page and its graphic peculiarities. The number of the line to which the varia lectio refers in the text is indicated within brackets and in bold, preceding the portion of text itself. To make critical study of the text easier, different typographic characteristics correspond to different kinds of *varia lectio*. Thus, for instance, a grey background indicates self-commentaries and linguistic sources, so as not to confuse them with alternative variants.

AN c. [1r] (p.1)   AV c. [4r] (p.7)

La Ricordanza
Idillio III

1   O graziosa Luna, io mi rammento
2   Che, or volge un anno, io sopra questo poggio
3   Venia carco d'angoscia a rimirarti:
4   E tu pendevi allor su quella selva
5   Siccome or fai, che tutta la rischiari.
6   Ma nebuloso e tremulo dal pianto
7   Che mi sorgea sul ciglio, a le mie luci
8   Il tuo volto apparia; chè travagliosa
9   Era mia vita: ed è, nè cangia stile,
10 O mia diletta Luna. E pur mi giova
11 La ricordanza, e 'l noverar l'etate
12 Del mio dolore. Oh come grato occorre
13 Il sovvenir de le passate cose
14 Ancor che triste, e ancor che il pianto duri!

title   La Ricordanza | Idillio III] **AN** ¹Idillio | La Luna *from which* ²Idillio | La Luna o la Ricordanza *from which* ³Idillio | La Ricordanza (*in pen B, with L on I*)

1   O] **AV** *from* Oh

2   Che, or volge un anno,] **AN** ¹Ch'or volge un anno, (*with* an *on* al) *from which* ²Ch'è presso a un anno, *from which* T (*in pen C*)   Che, or] **AV** Ch'or *from which* T   sopra] **AN** *from* su (*see* Philological Notes)

4   su quella selva] **AN** ¹sopra quel prato, (*with* prato *rewritten on* bosco) ²su quella selva, *from which* T (*in pen C*).

5   Siccome or] **AN** *written above* Com'ora (*in pen C*)

7–8   a le mie luci | Il tuo volto apparia; chè travagliosa] **AN** ¹a le (*before* al<le>) mie luci | Il tuo viso appariva, perchè dolente *from which* ²il tuo bel viso | Al mio sguardo appariva, perchè dolente ³a le mie luci | Il tuo volto apparia; che travagliosa (*in pen B*) *from which* T (*in pen C*)

9   cangia] **AN** ¹cangia ²cambia (*in pen B, written above* ¹) *from which* T (*in pen C*)

11   ricordanza] **AN** *from* rimembranza

12   come] **AN** *written above* quanto (*in pen B*)

13   de le] **AV** *from* delle

14   triste] **AN** *from* tristi   il] **AN** *from* 'l (*in pen C*)

AN c. [1r]

right margin, transversal

(**12**) (**come** sì grato) (*in pen C*)

(*AV*) NR26 B26 F31 N35 (N35err) N35c

XIV

ALLA LUNA.

1   O graziosa luna, io mi rammento

2   Che, or volge l'anno, sovra questo colle

3   Io venia pien d'angoscia a rimirarti:

4   E tu pendevi allor su quella selva

5   Siccome or fai, che tutta la rischiari.
6   Ma neuboloso e tremulo dal pianto
7   Che mi sorgea sul ciglio, alle mie luci
8   Il tuo volto apparia, che travagliosa
9   Era mia vita: ed è, nè cangia stile,
10 O mia diletta luna. E pur mi giova
11 La ricordanza, e il noverar l'etate
12 Del mio dolore. Oh come grato occorre
13 Nel tempo giovanil, quando ancor lungo
14 La speme e breve ha la memoria il corso,
15 Il rimembrar delle passate cose,
16 Ancor che triste, e che l'affanno duri!

title   xiv | ALLA LUNA.] **NR26** LA RICORDANZA. | Idillio iii.   **B26** LA RICORDANZA|IDILLIO iii   **F31** XIII. | ALLA LUNA.   **N35**

1   luna] **NR26** Luna   **F31**
2   l'anno, sovra questo colle] **NR26** un anno, io sopra questo poggio   **F31** l'anno, io sovra questo colle   **N35**
3   Io venia pien] **NR26** Venia carco   **N35** Venia pieno   **N35err**
7   alle] **NR26** a le   **N35**
8   apparia, che] **NR26** apparia; chè   **N35**
10   luna] **NR26** Luna   **F31**
11   il] **NR26** 'l   **N35**
13–17 Nel tempo ... duri!] (AV Il sovvenir ... duri!)   **NR26** Il sovvenir ... duri!   **B26** Il sovvenir ... duri.   **N35c**
(15)   rimembrar] **NR26** sovvenir   **N35c** delle]   **NR26** de le   **N35** cose,]   **NR26** cose   **B26**
(16)   e che l'affanno duri!] **NR26** ancor che il pianto duri!   **B26** ancor che il pianto duri.   **N35c**

3.6. Carlo Emilio Gadda's work

What has been called the 'Gadda case' has dominated twentieth-century Italian philology. This has been due to two main factors. First, the particular conditions of his production, one in which only part of his works were printed, while many others remained unfinished. And second, the writer's habit of keeping in his 'legendary vaults' all the documentation relating to his literary activity. The publication of all of Gadda's works in the 'Libri della Spiga' series by Garzanti began in 1988 and finished five years after. This edition was — as the director of the series called it — 'a well-meditated philological proposal' that was based on 'a general project for a critical edition' ('Presentazione' by Dante Isella in Gadda 1988: xviii). Isella and his students published a rigorously-established text for each work without an apparatus, with the exception, as we will see, of *La meccanica*, and this represented the first attempt to give an order to a particularly intricate textual situation. Isella summarized this state of affairs in the introduction to the first volume (ibid.: xx):

> The first problem we had to face while organizing this edition was the aforementioned gap between public and private, i.e., between what Gadda wrote but kept in his legendary vaults and what he managed to publish during his tormented and often desperate life. We did not fear the mixture of completed and unfinished works: the 'non finito' is a constitutive, ontological, element of Gadda's creativity. Nevertheless, from the outset, it was apparent that it would have been absurd [...] to organize this edition as a strictly chronological succession of edited and unedited works. Even by distinguishing and grouping separately different genres of texts (as much as possible with a writer for whom the *pastiche* is a fundamental feature), it would nevertheless be evident (and irritating even for the most well-disposed reader) that there is an inconsistency between the texts that underwent the final revision and those that (even after philological scrutiny) remain fluid both in terms of reading and structure.

As curator of a posthumous work whose author had not left a precise editorial plan, Isella opted for the historical reconstruction of the authorial project that emerged from the letters the author exchanged in the mid-1950 with Giulio Einaudi (publisher of Gadda's masterpiece, *La cognizione del dolore*), and particularly that which is contained in the letter written on 14 December 1954, from which it is possible to deduce that Gadda wanted to organize his works by separating narrative texts from essays. Gadda's proverbial reticence to 'almost posthumously' publish texts written many years before is another reason why Isella did not want, in transmitting Gadda's work to readers in the new millennium, to mix the edited works with the rich and extremely important unedited material (see Italia 2007c; Italia and Pinotti 2008).

It is, however, undeniable that the two characteristics of Gadda's work, namely its 'complex system of communicating vessels' and its 'textual metamorphosis' (Isella in Gadda 1988: xx) over time, have made it a particularly fertile field for study and have led to new developments in authorial philology in general. Beginning in 1983, with the edition of the *Racconto italiano di ignoto del Novecento*, a new method of representing manuscripts was established, distinguishing apparatus, marginalia, and alternative variants (see sections 2.3–2.4), thereby allowing us to identify and separately represent multiple textual levels (Isella in Gadda 1983 and in Gadda 1993: 1267–1268). As Isella put it:

> This model is based on the double need to represent fully the complexity of Gadda's page while at the same time to rationalize its many components, freeing them from the threads in which they are entangled. It is indeed first of all necessary to distinguish the text from the marginalia, the latter being the series of the writer's interventions, written in margins or in the interline of the text proper, that report indications, doubts, self-commentaries, etc. It is also necessary to distinguish readings that by succeeding one another constitute the phases of the established (*i.e.* most advanced, but not necessarily definitive) text from the readings that are meant as possible variants (the so-called alternative variants), that virtually open it up towards new solutions.

This model was the basis for the main critical editions of Gadda's texts in the nineties, from the *Disegni milanesi* (1995) to *La meccanica* (published in 1989 in the *Opere* in a complete edition with apparatus), to *Un fulmine sul 220* (Gadda 2002). These editions were witness to an important evolution of the apparatus towards an ever more diachronic and systemic structure.

In fact, the earlier apparatuses, for reasons of clarity and simplicity, presented each correction by itself regardless of whether it was implied with others or not, and preferred a synchronic approach in which the physical characters of the page were preferred over the interpretation of the chronology of the corrections. The more recent ones instead try to connect variants that might be related and to present, whenever possible, their chronological order using superscript numbers that identify the different phases of a single segment.

We are thus moving from synchronic and photographic apparatuses, which are useful tools to help read manuscripts, towards diachronic apparatuses that attempt to put the complex genesis of the text into a timeline, and from apparatuses containing single variants to systemic ones that distinguish single phases that include other, appropriately represented, phases within them. One must also add to the above the necessity, since the early nineties, to pay more attention to the reconstruction of how the text is laid out, through the identification and chronological ordering of the various corrections within the wider genetic phase (see Italia 2007c, and Italia and Pinotti 2008: 28–34), so as to overcome the technical and theoretical obstacles that Gadda's manuscripts pose (on this, see Terzoli 1993).

If we have gained a better knowledge of the autographs and of the different types of texts (fiction, essays, poems), this does not change our perception of the dynamics of Gadda's corrections as consisting in a process of progressive insertions rather than substitutions, with the result that we find an ever-growing expansion of an initial segment with marginal, linear and interlinear additions, as well as with footnotes or even entire portions written elsewhere and recalled by the use of marginalia. Such features allow us to engage in deeper study of manuscripts by representing the different series of corrections and distinguishing immediate and late variants. Real, immediate variants are limited to those of the first redaction, on which during one or more subsequent moments, the author intervened with insertions (i.e., late variants). In this perspective, it might be useful, in some cases, to change the point of view from which we look at the genesis of the text by not taking over the final reading that the manuscript contains, but rather by adopting instead the first complete redaction, the one to which all the insertions are added later. This solution may not be helpful for unedited manuscripts, where it is better to choose the final reading as copy-text, as we see in the example that is based on the first draft of the *pamphlet* titled *Eros e Priapo*, which Gadda wrote in 1944–1945 but was only published in 1967 (see Italia and Pinotti 2008). However, it is a good solution for manuscript redactions of texts that were later published in journals and/or in volumes. In these cases, choosing as copy-text the earliest version which can be reconstructed on the manuscript would allow one to distinguish easily between immediate and late variants in a two-part apparatus, both genetic and evolutionary, especially when we consider that the final reading found in the manuscripts is often almost identical to that of the first print.

As a result of these observations, which future editions might confirm or disprove, the principle of the author's last will is being put into discussion in these specific cases. For the printed tradition, this is relevant because of the importance that the first editions have (especially when we look at Gadda as a 'twentieth-century classic', with everything that this implies for his tradition), compared to later or, so to speak, 'final' re-publications. In the case of the manuscripts, this approach is useful because of the importance of publishing the first complete reading (instead of the final one), i.e., the base-text on which Gadda developed his pyrotechnical linguistic virtuosity. In this way, the editor can make the entire process of correcting and of creating variants more understandable for the reader.

Eros e Priapo

'A' Redaction

Chapter I

[Ri 18] Dimando interpetrare e perscrutare certi moventi del delinquere non dichiarati nel comune discorso, le secrete vie della libidine camuffata da papessa onoranda, inorpellata dei nomi della patria, della giustizia, del dovere, del sacrificio: (della pelle degli altri.) Mi propongo vedere[a] ed esprimere, e non per ambage ma per chiaro latino, ciò che a pena è travisto e sempre e canonicamente è taciuto ne' nobili cicalari delle persone da bene: que' modi e que' procedimenti oscuri dell'essere che pertengono alla zona dell'inconscio, quegli impulsi animali a non dire anim<al>eschi da i' Plato topicizzati nell'epiθumetikon cioè nel pacco addominale, nel vaso delle [19] trippe: i | quali hanno tanta e talora preminente parte nella bieca storia degli omini, in quella dell'omo individuo, come in quella d'ogni aggregazione di omini. Non palese o meglio non accetto alla sublime dialessi di alcuni storici de' miei stivali, pure un merdoso lezzo redole su dal calderone della istoria, al rabido al livido, allo spettrale dipanarsi della tesi: dell'antitesi: della sintesi.[b] Tesi ladra, antitesi maiala, e ruffiana sintesi. Che ci ballano la loro ossitona zoccolante giga d'attorno, d'attorno al sangue, alla vergogna e al dolore, come le tre streghe shakespeariane da torno la pentola de' loro malefizî:

double double toil and trouble:
fire, burn and cauldron bubble.

'Italiani! vi esorto alle istorie'. Tra
le quali ci guazza dimolto dolore e
dimolto sangue, mi pare a me. 'Vi
esorto alle istorie'.

[Ri 18] interpetrare e perscrutare] ¹interp<retare> ²scrutare → T   e] *inserted in interline* canonicamente] *written above* regolarmente   impulsi animali a non dire animaleschi] ¹animaleschi impulsi → T (animaleschi *from* animalesche)   da i' Plato topicizzati] che Plato topicizzava → T   cioè] *written above* ossia   nel vaso] *written under* calderone [19] palese o meglio non accetto] palesi o meglio non accetti → T   alla] *rewritten without effacing*   alcuni] ¹alcuni ²taluni ³taluni → T   calderone] ¹tripposo calderone ²calderone tripposo → T   al rabido al livido, allo spettrale dipanarsi] ¹fra il → lo rabido dipan<arsi> ²allo livido, al rabido, allo (*from* al) spettrale dipanarsi → T   tesi: dell'antitesi: della sintesi] *from* tesi, dell'antitesi e della sintesi   al sangue, alla vergogna] al *from* all< >   da torno] *written above* dattorno   pentola] *written above* pignatta (la pignatta] *before* il)   dolore e di molto sangue] *written above* sterco

---

ªannotare
ᵇdi tesi, antitesi, sintesi.

4. European Examples

4.1 Lope de Vega's *La Dama Boba*
Marco Presotto and Sònia Boadas

Lope de Vega's vast theatrical oeuvre is one of the most expansive bodies of texts from early modernity in Spain, and, for some time now, his more than four hundred plays have been the focus of the methodical analysis of philologists attempting to create a complete critical edition. The PROLOPE Project was founded by Alberto Blecua in 1989 to tackle this monumental undertaking, along with numerous efforts to improve the philological understanding of his literary legacy (http://prolope.uab.cat/). The textual tradition consists of forty-four autograph comedies, many editions authorized by the playwright as part of his own project to publish his work, and also a wide selection of single editions and copies of all types, which drastically complicate the task of the editor. In addition to this, any plan to provide a critical edition must also consider the peculiarity of theatrical works of the Spanish Golden Age, intended primarily to be performed rather than read.

According to the conventions of the time, the playwright, called *poeta* or *ingenio*, sold his *original* to the owner of the theatre company, who bought all rights to its use and could change the text at will to suit a performance in a given context. Once the theatrical run was over, the play's manuscript could be sold to an editor to be printed, inevitably including all the changes implemented that the text had undergone 'on stage' during its life, including corrections by the theatre company manager, censor or others connected to the performing arts. The increased popularity of theatre and the rise in demand for plays made it necessary to develop an organized theatrical text editing system, especially for an acclaimed writer such as Lope de Vega, so that manuscripts could be produced quickly and according to the needs of the moment. Even if the documentation in this regard is unfortunately scarce, given the ephemeral nature of the intermediary steps, we can assume that the author generally composed his dramatic works with the following step-by-step writing method:

1. script in prose, which tended to already be divided into acts;
2. draft in verse, in which Lope de Vega transported the contents of the prose version, developed the poetic compositions (at least partially), and organized the polymetric structure of the work;
3. clean copy destined for sale.

However, this method resulted in numerous variants, especially because of the incessant changes brought about by the author, who was never satisfied with his results and always ready to update his texts, regardless of whether they were drafts or 'final' versions.

The autograph manuscript of *La Dama Boba*, dated 28 April 1613 and now in the collection of the Biblioteca Nacional de España (Madrid) with shelfmark Vitr/7/5 (http://bdh-rd.bne.es/viewer.vm?id=0000051826), is an interesting example of the playwright's creative process. Despite being a carefully drafted copy, destined for a prestigious theatre company very close to Lope, many of its pages show the corrections and changes of the author. These markings often make it possible to reconstruct different phases of his writing process, even if they were added mainly while revising the final text. Lope perhaps had a script in prose, or more likely a draft in verse, and, in the act of making a clean copy, he re-wrote entire sequences from a structural and chiefly poetic and stylistic point of view, testifying to the author's tireless creativity and constant perfectionism. In other words, Lope did not stop at copying what presumably appeared in the draft, but spent time improving and building upon the text even while transcribing it into a version fit for sale. It is thus interesting to reconstruct those changes in an attempt to retrace the steps taken in creating the text.

The play came to be known over the following centuries exclusively via the text published by Lope de Vega himself in 1617, which is quite different from the autograph version because the author, by his own admission, could not use it while preparing the edition, having to fall back on a copy that evidently was flawed. Rudolph Schevill can be credited with publishing the first edition of the autograph manuscript. Schevill provided a diplomatic transcription in his *The Dramatic Art of Lope de Vega, together with 'La Dama Boba'* (1918) with an apparatus of variants and ample room dedicated to the changes made by the author. To do so, he included the 'deleted' fragments in the autograph that represent different creative phases, inserting them in parentheses in the edition. Starting from this publication, the autograph manuscript has always been used as a base-text for subsequent editions. A focus on the creative process is also seen in the text edited by Eduardo Juliá Martínez in 1935 (Lope De Vega 1935: 283–449), which includes a diplomatic transcription of crossed-out verses, without comments. Recent editions destined for the general public within popular series of Spanish classics often refer to this peculiarity of the textual tradition, even if it is a secondary aspect of the editorial project.

The most up-to-date modern printed edition in terms of textual criticism is that by Marco Presotto, published as part of the PROLOPE Project (in Lope de Vega 2007: 1293–466). In the criteria of selection, Presotto has included a description of the characteristics of the manuscripts if considered important for the textual tradition. The system adopted is a symbolic one that refers to François Masai's model (Masai 1950: 177–93), albeit with a few minor changes. Similar to previous academic editions, this criterion only makes it possible to report that which appears in the manuscript, and does not offer indications on the genesis of the corrections and the various writing phases. Although the diplomatic transcription of the corrections based on Masai's system is reliable in that it leaves little room for interpretive errors, offering a direct description of what appears in the document, it ends up being an approach that is too cautious and out of tune with the work of a textual critic. After all, the job of a textual critic is to create a working hypothesis that connects all the information, as Gianfranco Contini's definition reminds us. To overcome these limits and propose various hypotheses about the writing process, the same research group published a digital edition of the play in 2015 (http://damaboba.unibo.it/), as part of the creation of a digital archive for the textual tradition of the work. The transcription of the autograph manuscript includes an attempt to represent the corrections through different colours, the chronological numbering of individual phases and, where possible, interactive annotations that display the times the text was edited, listing them chronologically according to the editors' hypothesis. In the end, the digital edition is undoubtedly an improvement compared to static printed texts, and XML-TEI encoding is a solid base for further developments. However, as the time of writing, it should be considered only partially adequate in terms of the way complex sequences are displayed. Indeed, the changes and corrections are not always easy to read or understand due to overlapping colours and a lack of uniformity in the display across different browsers, producing undesired issues even in the graphic layout. In this sense, Paola Italia and Giulia Raboni's *filologia d'autore* model offers a rather interesting tool due to its greater stability.

The example included here comes from the second act of *La Dama Boba* (Fig. 8), containing comic dialogue between the two main leading ladies.

Only the hand of Lope de Vega appears and the ink is always the same, demonstrating that the text was largely conceived in its final version directly on the pages of the definitive copy. For comparison, the modernized version and the diplomatic notation apparatus using the system included in the PROLOPE edition appear below (for the digital edition: http://damaboba.unibo.it/aplicacion.html#). The same apparatus, but this time relating the genesis of the text according to the *filologia d'autore* model comes next, offering a detailed account of the creative process just as it appears in the manuscript. Given the complexity of the corrections described, however, philological notes are still necessary to provide readers with more information about the textual critic's hypothesis. The result is quite satisfactory and undoubtedly innovative compared to previous models.

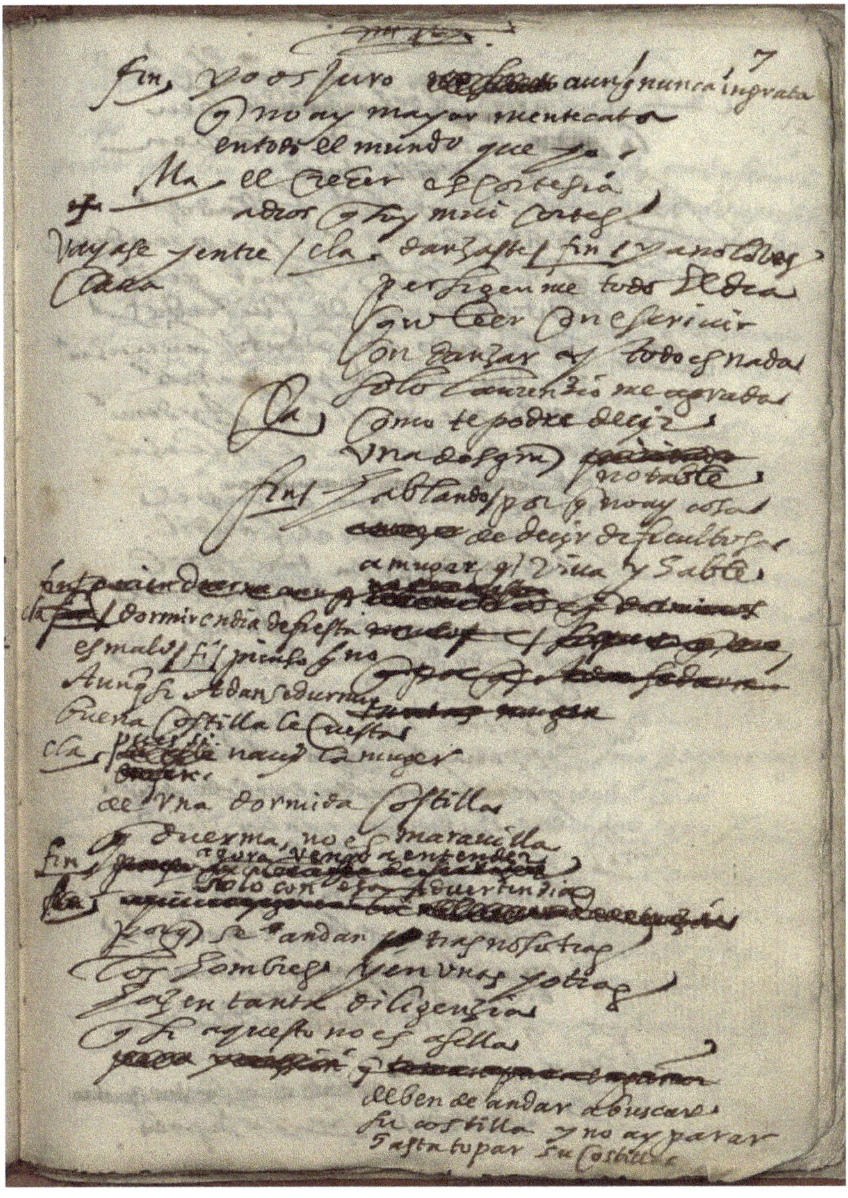

Fig. 8 *La Dama Boba*, 1613 (Vitr/7/5, f. 29r, num. 7, vv. 1422–1452), http://bdh-rd.bne.es/viewer.vm?id=0000051826

FINEA	Yo os juro, aunque nunca ingrata, que no hay mayor mentecata en todo el mundo que yo.		FINEA	I swear to you, though never ungrateful, that there is no greater fool in the entire world than I.	
MAESTRO	El creer es cortesía; adiós, que soy muy cortés.	1425	MAESTRO	To believe is a courtesy; farewell, as I am quite courteous.	1425
	Váyase y entre Clara			*He leaves and Clara enters*	
CLARA	¿Danzaste?		CLARA	Did you dance?	
FINEA	¿Ya no lo ves? Persíguenme todo el día con leer, con escribir, con danzar, ¡y todo es nada! Sólo Laurencio me agrada.	1430	FINEA	Can't you see? They pursue me all day with reading, writing, and dancing, and all for nothing! Only Laurencio pleases me.	1430
CLARA	¿Cómo te podré decir una desgracia notable?		CLARA	How can I tell you a notable misfortune?	
FINEA	Hablando; porque no hay cosa de decir dificultosa	1435	FINEA	By talking; for there is nothing difficult to say	1435

	a mujer que viva y hable.			to a woman who lives and talks.	
CLARA	Dormir en día de fiesta,		CLARA	To sleep late on a feast day,	
	¿es malo?			is it bad?	
FINEA	Pienso que no;		FINEA	I don't think so;	
	aunque si Adán se durmió,	1440		though Adam oversleeping,	1440
	buena costilla le cuesta.			cost him his rib.	
CLARA	Pues si nació la mujer		CLARA	Well, if woman was born	
	de una dormida costilla,			of a sleeping rib,	
	que duerma no es maravilla.			it's no wonder she likes to slumber.	
FINEA	Agora vengo a entender		FINEA	Now I understand	
	sólo con esa advertencia,	1445		only with this warning,	1445
	por qué se andan tras nosotras			why they go after us,	
	los hombres, y en unas y otras			men, and why some	
	hacen tanta diligencia;			are so diligent;	
	que, si aquesto no es asilla,	1450		as, if there isn't an occasion,	1450
	deben de andar a buscar			they have to go and look for	
	su costilla, y no hay parar			that rib, and there is no stopping	
	hasta topar su costilla.			until stumbling onto it.	

APPARATUS WITH DIPLOMATIC TRANSCRIPTIONS:

1422	aunque : <-no siendo> aunque O	
1433	notable : <-parecida / notable> O	
1435	de decir : <-a muger> de decir O	
1436	a mujer... hable : *followed by* <-pecamos los q dormimos \\ -Fin. quien duerme aunq no se acueste> O	
1437*Char*	Clara : <-Fin.\\ Cla> O	
1437	dormir... fiesta : <-mucho. Sospecho q no \\ dormir en dia de fiesta> O	
1438	es... no : <-q porq Adan se durmio \\ es malo Fi. pienso q no> O	
1439	aunque... durmió : <-tantas mujer \\ Aunq si Adan se durmio> O	
1441	Pues si : <-De este / en fin \ pues si> O	
1444	Agora vengo a entender : <-porq ... \ agora vengo a entender> O	
1445	solo con esa advertencia : <-a quien ... \ solo con esa advertenzia> O	
1446	tras : <-y> tras O	
1449	que... asilla : *followed by a deleted verse* <-para y ocassion q tiene para engañar> O	

GENETIC APPARATUS:

1422	aunque nunca ingrata] *before* no siendo
1433	notable] [1]parecida [2]T (*subscript of* [1])
1435	de decir] *before* a mujer
1437–1440	CLARA Dormir en día de fiesta, | ¿es malo? FINEA Pienso que no; | aunque si Adán se durmió, | buena costilla le cuesta.] [1]¿Pecamos los que dormimos | mucho? Sospecho que no, | que porque Adán se durmió, | tantas mujer | [2]FINEA Quien duerme aunque no se acueste [3]T
1437	CLARA] *before* FINEA
1441	Pues si] [1]De este [2]En fin *subscript of* [3]T (*superscript of* [1])
1444	Agora vengo a entender] *superscript of* porque <...> <...>
1445	solo con esa advertencia] [1]CLARA a quien <...> [2]<...> <advertencia> [3]T (*superscript of* [1] and [2])
1446	tras] *before* y
1450	deben de andar a buscar] [1]para [2]y ocasión [3]que tiene para engañar [4]T (*subscript of* [3])

Philological notes:

1422 *The intervention seems to be stylistic; probably the author's original intention was* Yo os juro, no siendo ingrata, *not completed to avoid the repetition of* no *that would have occurred in the following verse.*

1426 *Note how the annotation of the direction* Váyase y entre Clara *requires a shift in the text column.*

1433 *The change creates a new rhyme for the strophe, and thus was presumably implemented when the main text was written. The correction was placed on the line below, causing the verses to be farther apart than usual.*

1435 *The deletion may be to correct a copying error (a skipped verse), or, most likely, it may reflect the creative process of organizing the phrase. The author may have at first thought to write the octosyllabic phrase* a mujer dificultosa *but then changed it to simplify the syntax of the two verses.*

1437–1440 *The author re-wrote the entire strophe in the left margin, after various corrections around v. 1437; the following strophes are all in the same column, until the next* in itinere *correction in v. 1450.*

1437 *Note, in the deletion, the blank space separated quite clearly by two diagonal lines, left by the author around the abbreviated name of the character who will say the line. This may reflect a writing practice that involved inserting the name after the verse had been written.*

1441 *In the first draft, the author wrote* De este nació la mujer *but then decided to change it to* En fin nació la mujer, *with a correction placed in the line below, making it necessary to increase the spacing between lines. Not satisfied by this second solution, the author decided to change once again the verse to* Pues si nació la mujer, *a concessive phrase that he coherently connected with the following verse.*

1450 *The changes once again demonstrate the phases of verse creation that determined the following ones within the strophe. At first the author wanted to reinforce the aside that began in the previous verse and, in particular, the meaning of* asilla *('occasion', 'opportunity',* [1] *and* [2]*) until developing a relative completed phrase that created the rhyme (*[3]*). He then changed his mind and went directly to the reference to Adam's rib in the three verses available in the strophe, in which he concluded the concept and the words of Finea, reducing the size of the text to be able to use the little space available on the page without having to start a new one.*

4.2 Percy Bysshe Shelley's *Poems*

Margherita Centenari

The vast majority of Percy Bysshe Shelley's poems were published posthumously, or at least without his direct supervision, a fact that has complicated the work of critics and experts who study and publish the author's texts, and continues to have a notable impact on Shelleyan philology. Of the more than 400 compositions that are found in complete collections today, only about 70 or so were printed in Shelley's lifetime. These can be subdivided into verses found in editions and anthologies overseen by the poet (such as, in addition to the *juvenilia*, the 1813–1816 editions of *Queen Mab*; *Alastor*; *Laon and Cythna*, 1817 and 1818; *The Cenci*, 1819; *Oedipus Tyrannus*, 1820; *Epipsychidion*, 1821 and *Adonais*, the pastoral elegy composed upon the death of John Keats and edited in 1821, too), and those published in editions which Shelley did not so supervise, as they circulated during the long periods in which he was abroad (such as the collection *Rosalind and Helen*, 1819; *Hellas*, 1822; and the famous drama in verse, *Prometheus Unbound*, published first in 1820 with the addition of other poems, among which was the *Ode to the West Wind*).

The gradual constitution of the author's poetic canon is thus made up of different phases, and its complexity can be explained not only in relation to the adventurous lifestyle of Shelley and his circle, but also in light of the fluctuating critical appraisal of his writings throughout the nineteenth and twentieth centuries (Rossington and Schmid 2008) and in terms of the evolution of philology as a discipline across the Channel (Reiman 1972; Everest 1989; Fraistat 2000).

Proceeding in order, the first such phase is the work done by the author's second wife, Mary Wollstonecraft Shelley, on the unpublished autograph manuscripts left by the poet upon his sudden death (Shelley died in a shipwreck in the summer of 1822 off the coast of Viareggio, Italy). Despite the unwavering hostility of his family members, especially his father Sir Timothy Shelley, Mary Shelley immediately put her expertise to work on her husband's tangled manuscripts, in preparation for the 1824 publication of *Posthumous Poems of Percy Bysshe Shelley*. Though printed in a 500-copy edition by John and Henry L. Hunt in London, it was partially withdrawn from the market upon the insistence of the author's father. Later, Mary's collaboration during the preparation of *The Poetical Works of Coleridge, Shelley, and Keats*, the first anthology published in Paris by the Galignani brothers in 1829, was not enough to stop other people from following in their footsteps, and for at least fifteen years, numerous pirated editions of the poems were published. After 1838, when some of those restrictions were withdrawn, Mary was decidedly freer to dedicate her time to the publication of her husband's work. As such, in 1839 Edward Moxon managed to publish the four-volume *Poetical Works of Percy Bysshe Shelley* (dedicated to Percy Florence, the couple's young son), enriched by Mary's insightful editorial Notes and followed by two volumes of unpublished prose works in the same year.

This 1839 edition (which strengthened the results of the one before it but which also inherited its alterations, such as changes to its form and organization, promotion to text of fragmentary lyric poems, etc.) was so successful that it became the starting point for almost all subsequent anthologies of Shelley's poetry up until the twentieth century, with just two exceptions: *Shelley Memorials* (1859), published in London by Smith, Elder and in Boston by Ticknor and Fields, and *Relics of Shelley* edited by Richard Garnett (1862), both of which added new texts to the canon.

In the meantime, the marriage of Sir Percy Florence Shelley and Jane Gibson St John resulted in the transfer of the family archive (guarded over by Mary Shelley until then) to Boscombe Manor, purchased by Percy Florence for his mother in 1849. It then became the home of Lady Jane, who — in particular after the death of her mother-in-law — dedicated herself at length and with authentic devotion to the memory (or rather worship) of her famous relative. She issued a series of biographies and memoirs, and perhaps most importantly managed the author's papers, later even donating some of them to the Bodleian Library at Oxford.

The new availability of some of the manuscripts originating from the family's collection at the end of the century thus sparked a fresh wave of publications, which were, in a way, the continuation of those of Mary Shelley and the numerous projects that Lady Jane had worked on. The Victorian editions of the *Poetical Works* by William Michael Rossetti, brother of Dante Gabriel Rossetti and one of Garnett's collaborators, and by Harry Buxton Forman are prime examples. The Rossetti edition came out in 1870, only to be re-edited with corrections in 1878, with extensive changes to the metre, diction, grammar and punctuation of the texts. The Buxton Forman edition, which appeared in 1876–1877, offered a significantly more conservative approach. It was, in essence, the first scholarly publication of Shelley's poetry, not just because it scrubbed the verses of the numerous typographical/editorial corruptions accumulated over decades of unchecked dissemination and proposed a return to the author's original versions, but also because it was based on an advanced knowledge of Shelley's style and linguistic working methods (Buxton Forman 1876).

However, even this effort was still limited by the lack of exploration of a large quantity of autograph materials — materials that, up to the post-war period, were almost hidden from the public. As a result, the quality of the collections and comments released throughout the first half of the twentieth century was negatively impacted (like the 1911 edition from Charles D. Locock, who had nevertheless access to some of the Boscombe originals in 1903, extracting many new readings that were gathered in Thomas Hutchinson's Oxford Standard Authors Edition, the latter becoming the reference text for Shelley's poems for quite a long time). The *Julian Edition* by Roger Ingpen and Walter E. Peck came next, the only one collecting all prose, poetry and letters together, released in ten volumes between 1926 and 1930. It became almost immediately obsolete due to the excessively eclectic choices made by the editors and the broader access to the manuscripts that had become possible in the meantime. For the first time since Mary Shelley's efforts, the handwritten documents finally returned as the true protagonists in the 'third phase' of Shelleyan philology.

Indeed, Lady Jane's donation to the Bodleian Library (1893–1894) was followed by that of other materials, including some important notebooks, by Sir John Shelley-Rolls (in 1946), a direct descendant of the family upon the heirless passing of Percy Florence. More recently, in 2004, the library acquired the Abinger papers, which include many of Mary Shelley's manuscripts and most of the author's correspondence, thereby reuniting the entire Boscombe collection at Oxford. Today, these documents are available to researchers, as are the less numerous but no less significant papers scattered in collections outside of the United Kingdom, including those in the Huntington Library (California), the Library of Congress (Washington, DC), and the New York Public Library (where the rich Pforzheimer Collection is held).

Given the ease of access to the sources in more recent years, textual criticism of Shelley's work has seen rapid growth since the 1960s, all while in the absence of a complete critical edition of Shelley's poetry (Rossington 2013; Rognoni 2018: cxxxvi-cxxxvii). The main reason for such a state of affairs is to be found in the very nature of the author's manuscripts and in the complexity of the compositional mechanisms that Shelley's papers reveal.

In particular, the poet's notebooks, about thirty in total, contain drafts and re-writings that constitute different editorial states of the same works, often incomplete, or developed alongside other compositions, or even dating back to moments that are difficult to determine because they were so far apart. One further problem then concerns the speed and conditions with which the very writing of the texts took place: Shelley mostly wrote while travelling, indoors and outdoors, sitting still or even in movement, perhaps on a boat or in a carriage. The result is a notable sense of compositional disorder expressed on pages handwritten with cursive ductus and penmanship that is so broken down it is almost indecipherable, with numerous erasures, corrections, interlinear insertions or re-writings of portions of the text, one overlapping the other. And because notebooks were his favourite place to jot down ideas, they often intermingle with poetic fragments or glosses, comments, titles, quotes, calculations or even sketches of trees, mountains, buildings and faces. Moreover, the sheets of the notebooks, bound along the upper margin, were used by the author from both ends, without apparent regard for their material proximity. Quite often, different drafts of the same composition, including some clean copies, are spread across one or more different writing supports. Lastly, these issues are compounded by those deriving from the mass dispersion (or destruction) of many of the indicator-links that would have connected the first drafts or revisions of the poems to their definitive publication in printed volumes as arranged by Shelley (autograph or apograph copies, corrected drafts, etc.); not to mention that the author's practices included the frequent use of loose sheets of paper, many of which are now lost (Everest 1989: xxii–xxvi).

Faced with such a complex situation, the greatest and longest lasting effort by Anglo-American scholars has therefore consisted in providing the public with facsimiles of Shelley's manuscripts (and now, in many cases, digital scans, like those that can be found on https://digitalcollections.nypl.org/divisions/carl-h-pforzheimer-collection-of-shelley-and-his-circle, or https://hdl.huntington.org/digital/collection/p15150coll7/search/searchterm/percy%20shelley). A robust forty-one volumes containing images, transcriptions and commentaries on specific parts of the text (though selective and based on widely differing standards) make up the three main diplomatic editions currently available to philologists (Shelley 1985–1997; Shelley 1986–2002; Shelley 1961–), almost all thanks to the efforts of Donald H. Reiman. These tools certainly facilitate the work to be done, as they make it possible for the reader to check the hypotheses formulated by critics for each text. However, for obvious reasons, they cannot be considered the result of a systematic, genetic-reconstructive study.

Also dating to the 1960s, at least in its original conception coming from Geoffrey Matthews, is the first veritable critical edition, in the modern sense, of the writer's poetry, *The Poems of Shelley*, a collection that was published as part of the Longman Annotated English Poets (1989–) series. Originally divided into three volumes, today it has reached five total, though the last has yet to be released. The collection is actually one of two complete editions of Shelley's poems currently being worked on: other than the Longman edition, another series has been ongoing since 2000, *The Complete Poetry of Percy Bysshe Shelley* (*CPPBS*), published by Johns Hopkins University Press and divided into eight volumes, with only the first three having been printed.

These editions deserve a closer look. However, at least a brief mention must also be made of the Norton, the Oxford World's Classics and the Penguin Classics anthologies, alongside the Italian publication edited by Francesco Rognoni for Meridiani Mondadori (the largest selection of texts to date). Despite not being critical editions, they do constitute the main vehicles of the widespread dissemination of Shelley's work in recent years (often complete with optimal philological information resulting from a round of manuscript verifications).

In the Longman publication, the poems are published starting with a close-up examination of the handwritten and printed versions, and providing a systematic modernization of Shelley's spellings. The texts are arranged in chronological order according to the first writings, thereby abandoning the order imposed by Mary Shelley's *Poetical Works*. Each poem is preceded by a short introduction, which provides indications on the dates and the occasions of the drafts, up to the work's publication, information on the available sources (bibliographic and otherwise) and, where necessary, on the work's reception. The text is then printed and accompanied, at the bottom of the page, by an apparatus that includes both explanatory notes and comments and minimal lists of substantial variations taken from the autograph manuscripts and the most important printed publications (or re-issues). Contrary to that printed in the introduction to Volume 1 of the series (Everest 1989: xxvi), it should be mentioned that manuscript readings are not 'given in full'. Instead, they mainly correspond to the last developmental stages that can be deduced from the work carried out by the author on the drafts. Formal and punctuation variants appear here and there, but only when deemed relevant to the way the text is understood. Thus, a large number of the variants found in the originals are missing. In addition, the intermingling of critical and philological levels certainly does not help the legibility of the apparatus, and the chronological order, the true innovation of the Longman version, obviously has its own set of issues: Shelley often worked on multiple texts at the same time, interspersing long compositional pauses (weeks, even months) with corrections made to that same text. Meanwhile, the fragments are, by their very nature, very difficult to date and the writings revised later on are placed in conventional positions, seeing as they are established only by their editorial forms.

CPPBS, on the other hand, is quite different in its layout and textual criticism solutions, more clearly separating the handwritten text from the printed version, while reserving limited space for the former. Even the criteria that determine the presentation of the texts are different: here, the poems are first of all distinguished between published and unpublished. The published works are arranged in collections, according to the sequence of the author's editions, while the unpublished works, private because they never went beyond the draft stage, or because they were circulated exclusively within a close circle of friends and never meant to be printed, are mostly grouped according to the moments in which the poet's life can be sub-divided, spanning from 1803, the year of his lyrical poetry debut, to 1822. Within each section, then, the series follows either the desire of the author as shown by the reference editions, or a more generic chronological order of composition, particularly reliable when deduced from the available correspondence. However, the element that is actually new here is the base-text, which is a snapshot of one of its editions, conceived by the poet to be submitted to readers in a certain moment in time, and reworked as little as possible by the collection's philologists who, unlike those at Longman, opted for strictly conservative criteria in regards to linguistic form and punctuation. The result is a four-level structure: text; apparatus at the bottom of the page, limited to the different printed versions and used to justify any corrections to the text; Primary Collations with the selective annotation of authorial variants and those found in printed editions (identified through the comparison with other Shelleyan editions or with Mary Shelley's collections, which are supposed to preserve authorial variants); and Historical Collations including the variants that can be inferred from the most important nineteenth and twentieth century editions of poetry, helpful in tracing the historic fate of the texts. The picture is completed by a few supplementary sections, or proper appendices, where different materials appear occasionally: revisions for reprints, lists of *errata*, alternative versions of the same composition (as is the case, for instance, of the *Mont Blanc* poem, 1816, and others), or partial transcriptions of autograph fragments, including vertical apparatuses which are helpful for examination of the texts. As the American edition treats the poems published during Shelley's life in Volumes 1–3, it has the benefit of systematically documenting the printed versions, though it does not handle the manuscripts in the same way. For this reason, the Longman version is still in the lead, though the supplements to the edition remain indispensable.

The last twenty-five years seem to have marked a new era in the study of Shelley's poetry. On the one hand, the current state of Shelleyan philology is firmly rooted in the belief that a close examination of the originals is an indispensable premise for each attempt at a critical study of the texts and, because of this the large diplomatic undertakings mentioned above are favourably received, as are those that today are multiplying in the landscape of the Digital Humanities, such as the http://shelleygodwinarchive.org/ online platform developed in 2015 by Neil Fraistat, Elizabeth Denlinger and Raffaele Viglianti, which will host the complete digitized versions of the manuscripts of both Mary and Percy Shelley in the future, in addition to those of her father, William Godwin, and her mother, Mary Wollstonecraft. On the other hand, it seems that the manuscripts struggle to become part of the apparatuses of the reference editions, both for practical (space and problems with finding a system of representation) and theorical reasons. The traditional dilemma (which Mary Shelley herself grappled with) between the need to respect the author's last wishes, reflecting, in a 'historical' edition, the intentions that guided Shelley during each step of textual composition and revision, and the importance of guaranteeing readers a text that is comprehensible. The outcome is twofold: offering excessive freedom in altering mostly unfinished texts, and placing the available records in a hierarchal order which clearly prioritises the printed versions, thereby confirming a choice that is not exclusive to Shelley's texts, but generally applied to Anglo-Saxon textual criticism practices, in which the field of Textual Bibliography and the critical models offered by Greg (Greg 1950) and Tanselle (Tanselle 1998) seem to dominate.

To correct that situation, for some years now, especially among the scholars connected to the *CPPBS*, there have been a few attempts at *filologia d'autore* editions. It is worth mentioning them in conclusion: in 2012, an appendix to the third volume of the series was published, containing the genetic edition of the longest of Shelley's poems, *Laon and Cythna* (1817, later revised and reprinted in 1818 with the title *The Revolt of Islam*). The text presented on paper, accompanied by printed variants and the main collations, is followed by a supplement relative to the corrections handed down by seven Bodleian autographs, plus other rough drafts and copies that make up the history of the work (six fragments from the Pforzheimer Collection and another six from the British Library, National Library of Scotland, Trinity College in Cambridge, Texas Christian University and the University of Texas, Austin; with the addition of six more prints), even if the introduction specifies: 'this is not a complete record of draft variants; it does not include every repeated cancellation, stray letter, or indecipherable word or phrase in these MSS. But it does reproduce large sections of Shelley's draft material for *L&C* in an attempt to trace his thought process and the evolution of his language, imagery, and political, social, and philosophical ideas' (Neth 2012: https://romantic-circles.org/reference/laon_cythna/introduction.html).

The online edition, explicitly meant to have an ancillary function with respect to the paper version does not reproduce the text of the poem, to which it refers only by adopting the same numbering of the cantos, stanzas and lines. The apparatus is vertical and explicit: the explanatory editorial interventions, in italics, are frequent, alternating with the record of the variants, mostly described topographically and followed by the complete list of the record abbreviations involved. Brackets indicate the portion of the text involved in the variant, but also conjectural transcriptions (with the addition of question marks for the indecipherable readings); underlining and deletions are rendered via marks respecting those of the author. Going from top to bottom corresponds to the passage between references, or they identify correcting phases within the manuscript itself (though here and there the apparatus is synthetic and implicit).

The following example (in which the text has been taken from *CPPBS*: III, 133–34) is the ninth stanza of canto I (verses 73–81, containing the representation of an eagle and a serpent engaged in an allegorical struggle between revolution and oppression). It accounts for a solid argument for a panorama of research that is more developed than in the past and finally aimed at recovering the workshop-like aspect of the compositional process that, until now, has been partially overshadowed in the field of textual criticism.

IX

A shaft of light upon its wings descended,
And every golden feather gleamed therein—
Feather and scale inextricably blended.   75
The Serpent's mailed and many-coloured skin
Shone thro' the plumes its coils were twined within
By many a swollen and knotted fold, and high
And far, the neck receding lithe and thin,
Sustained a crested head, which warily   80
Shifted and glanced before the Eagle's stedfast eye.

73   *entire line canceled in pencil* Bod2
     shaft] *written above* ~~gleam~~ *and* ~~beam~~ Bod2
     its] it's Bod4
     descended,] ~~descended~~ Bod2
                 descended Bod4

74   *line preceded by* ~~From that~~ T *above* [?The]~~things~~ Bod2
     therein—] therein Bod2

75   Feather] *after* ~~The eagles~~ Bod2
     scale] scale, Bod4

77   thro'] thro Bod2
             through *1839 1840*
     plumes] wings Bod2
             plumes; *1834 1839 1840*
     twined] *below* ~~wreathed~~ Bod2

78   *entire line preceded by* ~~Voluminously Even as a waterfall among the woods~~ Bod2
     By] In Bod2
     swoln and] swoln & *in pencil below* ~~fold voluminous~~ *canceled in pencil* Bod2
     knotted fold,] knotted fold *below* ~~gathered fold~~ *all in pencil* Bod2
     and high] & ~~wide~~ high Bod2

81   stedfast] steadfast *above* [?——ing] Bod2
              steadfast *1839 1840*

82   Around,] Around Bod4
     around,] around Bod2 Bod4
     circles] ~~revolutions~~ *above* ~~circles~~ Bod2

83   clang] ing *of* clanging *written over separate word of*
     scream,] shrieks *above* ~~scream~~ Bod2
     Eagle] eagle Bod2

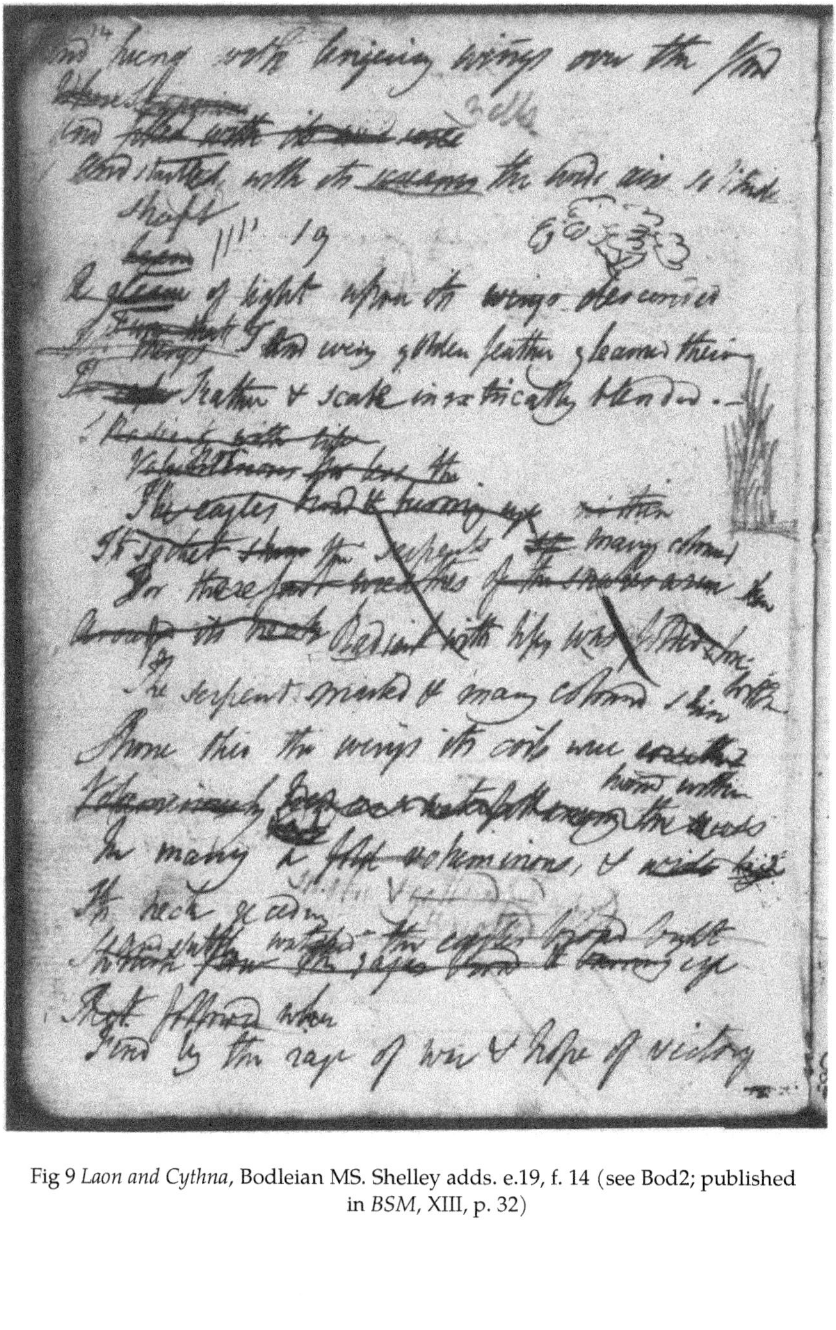

Fig 9 *Laon and Cythna*, Bodleian MS. Shelley adds. e.19, f. 14 (see Bod2; published in *BSM*, XIII, p. 32)

4.3 Jane Austen's *The Watsons*

Francesco Feriozzi[1]

Jane Austen's fiction manuscripts represent one of the earliest surviving conspicuous *dossiers* of materials for a British novelist, covering a large time span in Austen's life, roughly from 1787, when she was eleven, to 1817. Since all these manuscripts, be they drafts or fair copies, testify to works that were never published (and in the case of *Persuasion* to an alternative, unpublished, ending), it is widely believed that the author routinely destroyed the manuscripts of her published novels once they were printed, as was common practice in the period. Austen's manuscripts underwent two major dispersals, one in 1845 when at the death of the author's sister they were dispersed among surviving family members, and another in the 1920s when they began to enter auction houses to be divided among multiple British public and private collections.

These manuscripts have been the object of a digital edition directed by Professor Kathryn Sutherland, *Jane Austen's Fiction Manuscripts* (https://janeausten.ac.uk/), designed to reunite, order and preserve the materials. The website edits all the manuscripts respecting the author's use down to her graphic usage, with only minor normalization as regards punctuation. The reproduction of all the manuscript pages can be seen side-by-side with the corresponding transcription, so that the user can at all times double-check the readings of the edition or recover those graphic elements that inevitably get lost in the transcription. While the edition is strongly diplomatic, the chronological succession of the corrections is included as well. The transcription is indeed faithful to the page, reproducing erasures, interlinear corrections and carets as they are on the page; however, in cases of particularly complex, multi-layered corrections, the user can hover with the cursor on the relevant correction to 'reveal' the earlier phases, and many of the corrections are accompanied by footnotes that reconstruct particularly difficult elaborations of the manuscript in a fashion akin to that of authorial philology. Sutherland's team indeed included individuals with an

---

[1] Unless otherwise stated, all the information found in this chapter is from the *Jane Austen's Fiction Manuscripts* website. I would like to thank Kathryn Sutherland for her help with writing this chapter, and Carmela Marranchino for helping with the sample edition.

Italian/European philological background, and she herself cultivates philological interests, and therefore produced an edition in which material data and interpretation are productively intertwined.

This interpretative element is even more apparent in the printed version of the same edition (Austen 2018), where a number of new textual notes have been added. The printed edition was later incorporated in the *Oxford Scholarly Editions Online* (OSEO) portal. OSEO brings the edition back to the digital realm and overcomes a technical limit of the original *Fiction Manuscripts* website, now ten years old and partially reliant on discontinued Adobe Flash software, with the consequence that parts of it might soon become inaccessible. While this edition is extremely commendable and is from many points of view superior to the original *Fiction Manuscripts*, the passage to a physical edition sacrificed much of the astute interactive presentation of the original project, reverting it to a more 'classic' edition, despite preserving the synoptic presentation of the website. The evolution of technology is indeed a problem that one should keep in mind when working on digital editions, as all technical solutions used are bound to become dated. Because of this, one either has to keep their project constantly updated from the technical point of view (which can however be quite difficult and costly), or to also publish a physical edition to ensure its long-term usability at the cost of the benefits of the digital form. However, this should not discourage one from attempting digital editions altogether, especially considering how newer technologies such as HTML5 were conceived with the specific intention of avoiding drastic changes such as the discontinuation of Flash software.

Both the original *Fiction Manuscripts* and the *Scholarly Editions Online* version are nevertheless an excellent example of the multiplicity of perspectives offered by a digital edition. Editions such as this have been defined as 'paradigmatic' by Elena Pierazzo, Technical Research Associate of the project (2014: 4–5), with reference to the 'paradigmatic axis' of possible views from which the user is able to choose.

For this example, we are examining a draft to which Austen had not given a title, and which was named *The Watsons* by one of its first editors, James Edward Austen-Leigh. The 17,500-words long fragment was written around 1804–1805 in Bath, after *Pride and Prejudice, Sense and Sensibility* and *Northanger Abbey* had already been drafted. *The Watsons* is a case of *codex unicus*: the only witness of the work is a sequence of forty-four-leaves distributed across twelve small homemade booklets which were split into two parts in 1915 when the first six leaves were sold at a charity sale. The first six leaves are now held in New York (Morgan Library & Museum MS. MA 1034), while the rest is in Oxford (Bodleian Library MS. Eng. e. 3764). Some time after 2005, while still in private ownership, the second booklet of the manuscript (eight pages) went missing, so that the pictures found on the *Fiction Manuscripts* website and on its printed equivalent remain the only witnesses of those pages (Austen 2018: 1).

The manuscript pages are written in a neat hand covering the entirety of the page and leaving little room for large-scale revision other than lines of extra text crammed into narrow interlinear spaces. For more extensive revision (occurring in three parts of the manuscript), probably as part of a single correctional campaign, Austen applied separate 'patches' of a different paper which she carefully cut and pinned to the sheets where the correction/addition was intended to be placed.

The text is the beginning of a story, either a novella or, more likely, a longer novel, which was never finished, but whose narrative outline was known to Austen's sister (Austen 2018: 5–6). The author perhaps anticipated later division into chapters. As it stands, the text is separated in the draft only by lines or by wider spacing. Virginia Woolf considered *The Watsons* a model of Austen's writing strategy, believing its dry style to be due to her habit of writing the text in a bare, factual fashion, and revising the sentences later to 'cover them with flesh and atmosphere', not unlike what Gadda used to do (see section 3.6). According to Sutherland, Woolf's remark is true, but in *The Watsons*' case, Austen also did the opposite — when reviewing the text, she used to 'remove the flesh and on occasion expose the bones', not unlike what she later did when revising *Sanditon* (Sutherland 2005: 140). It might be that it was the almost cynical tone adopted in the draft that led Austen to interrupt her work on the novel. Other theories have however been proposed. According to her niece, Fanny Caroline, the reason for giving up on *The Watsons* was the sudden death of the writer's father; Austen-Leigh instead believes that it was due to disgust for the excess of social degeneracy that the continuation of the novel would have depicted; and Sutherland also advances the hypothesis that the cause might simply have been discouragement for the fact that despite having sent *Northanger Abbey* to the publisher more than a year before, it had not been printed yet (Sutherland 2005: 129–30). However, *The Watsons* was not disowned in its entirety, as materials from it were re-used in later novels (Sutherland 2005: 147).

The Watsons has been edited as part of longer literary works twice. Austen's niece Catherine Hubback indeed based the first five chapters of her novel *The Younger Sister* (1850) on the incomplete novel, while an apocryphal completion, which included the entirety of Austen's text with reworked punctuation, was written and published in 1928 by Hubback's granddaughter Edith Brown in association with her husband. The text was instead published by itself in the second edition of James Edward Austen-Leigh's *Memoir of Jane Austen* (1871: 297–364), and was edited again by the scholar Robert William Chapman in 1927. Both editions however normalized spellings and did not account for the corrections, with only Chapman giving a brief explanation of the characteristics of the manuscript in an appendix (Pierazzo 2016: 14–15).

A good example of how Austen worked in revision is in the evolution of the description of Mr Edwards's townhouse. Here is how it appears in the *Fiction Manuscripts* website (https://janeausen.ac.uk/manuscripts/qmwats/b2-3.html).

The diplomatic nature of the edition is clear from the example, where one can find even purely graphical characteristics such as the long s (ſ) that was a normal feature of handwriting at the time. An element of interpretation can however be found in the second note, where the editors give an account of the order of the overlapping corrections within the same sentence.

Here we will propose a *specimen* of how the same passage would look in an edition that follows the principles of authorial philology, to produce which we will also use the information found in the footnotes of the 2018 edition, using the latest text as base-text and preserving its graphic particularities even down to grammatical errors (cf. 'Mr. Es House' instead of 'Mr. E.'s House'). We will follow the representational criteria detailed in sections 2.5 and 2.6, but to make it easier for the reader to identify the many implicated variants found in the passage, I will represent them using a smaller font, as the Colli-Italia-Raboni edition of Manzoni's *Fermo e Lucia* does (see section 3.4):

[b 2-2] The old Mare trotted heavily on, wanting no direction of the reins to take the right Turning, & making only one Blunder, in proposing to stop at the Milleners [b 2-3] before she drew up towards Mʳ. Edward's door. — Mʳ. E. lived in the best house in the Street, & the best in the place, if Mʳ. Tomlinson the Banker might be indulged in calling his newly erected House at the end of the Town with a shrubbery & sweep in the Country. — Mʳ. E.s House was higher than most of its neighbours with windows on each side the door, the windows guarded by posts & chain the door approached by a flight of stone steps. — "Here we are — said Eliz: — as the Carriage ceased moving — safely arrived; – & by the Market Clock, we have been only five & thirty minutes coming. —which I think is doing pretty well, tho' it would be nothing for Penelope. — Is not it a nice Town? — The Edwards' have a noble house you see, & They live quite in stile. The door will be opened by a Man in Livery with a powder'd head, I can tell you."

[b 2-2] heavily] *written over* stupidly   [b 2-3] the place ... Banker] ¹the town, if the Banker *from which* ²T   his ... Country.] ¹his new House at the end of the Town in the Country, which however was not often granted. *from which* ²T {newly ... House] *from* newly erected one House}   was higher ... steps.] ¹was of a dull brick colour, & an high Elevation – ᵃa flight of stone steps to the Door, & two windows ᵇa flight of stone steps with white posts, & a chain, divided by a flight of stone steps. ²was higher than most of its neighbours with two windows on each side the door, & five the windows guarded by a chain & green posts & chain, the door approached by a flight of stone steps. *from which* T   nice] *written over* prett<y>   They live ... in stile.] *from* They live quite in stile I assure you   with] *written over* &

The edition that we have attempted here gives an idea of the advantages and disadvantages of editing the text using the methods of authorial philology — the chronological information that can be derived from the manuscript is made explicit at the cost of most information on topography, while a readable text is established without the arbitrariness of the old editions, and without sacrificing the strata of corrections that the manuscript attests. Thanks to the possibilities offered by paradigmatic (digital) editions, the reader could potentially be able to determine the level of interpretation s/he desires to see on his/her screen, from a minimum (photographs), to the genetic edition of the manuscript page, to a philologically-established text with apparatus. In this way, the materiality and spatiality of the page is both preserved and transcended at the same time.

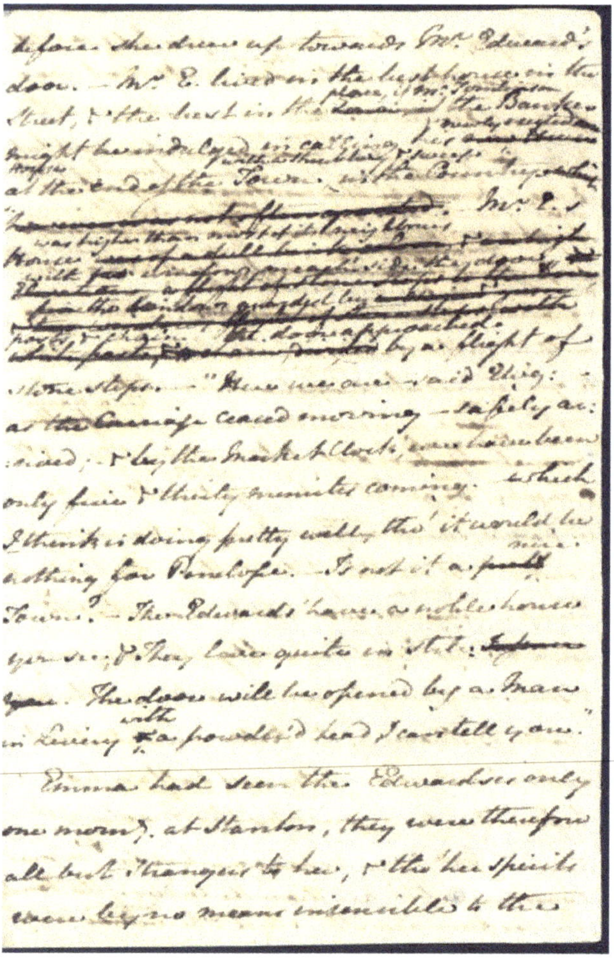

Fig. 10 Jane Austen, *The Watsons*, 1804–1805 (Oxford, Bodleian Library, MS. Eng. e. 3764, b.2-3), https://janeausten.ac.uk/manuscripts/qmwats/b2-3.html

4.4 Marcel Proust's À la recherche du temps perdu
Carmela Marranchino

The analysis of Proust's manuscripts, which has steadily increased since 1962 (when the Bibliothèque nationale de France (BnF) purchased a few autographs that had been in the possession of his heirs for years), is an exemplary case of French *critique génétique* (see section 1.4) in action. At the same time, the reconstruction of the history of the text of *À la recherche du temps perdu* has resulted in a fruitful, constant, theoretical and methodological reflection within the discipline, including recent digital developments. It is exemplary due to the complexity of Proust's *modus operandi*; the centrifugal structure of the novel that takes place through a proliferation of textual units without following a firmly established plan; the rich, varied handwritten documents; and even the problems surrounding its publishing, partially imposed by Proust (up to his death on 17 November 1922) and partially compromised posthumously by the arbitrary 'restoration' done by his heirs and publishers.

In 1912, Proust submitted the typewritten documents of the first part of a novel titled *Les intermittences du coeur* (according to the original plan) to various publishers, dividing it into two parts: *Le temps perdu* and *Le temps retrouvé*. After being rejected by Fasquelle, by André Gide on behalf of Gallimard's *Nouvelle Revue Française* (NRF), and by Ollendorf, the first volume appeared with the title *Du côté de chez Swann*, published by Bernard Grasset at the expense of the author in 1913. Although it was to include another two volumes, *Le côté de Guermantes* and *Le temps retrouvé*, their publication was interrupted by the outbreak of WWI. Publication was resumed only in 1919 by NRF, which released a new edition of *Du côté de chez Swann* while the author was still alive (which varied from Grasset's version), and the books *À l'ombre des jeunes filles en fleurs* (1919), *Le côté de Guermantes I* and *II* (1920–1921), and *Sodome et Gomorrhe I* and *II* (1921–1922). *La prisonnière*, the correct typewritten version of which Proust managed to send to Gallimard in time, was issued posthumously, with the subtitle *Sodome et Gomorrhe III* (1923). Other posthumous publications included *Albertine disparue* (1925) and *Le temps retrouvé* (1927), edited by Proust's brother Robert and by scholars Jacques Rivière and Jean Paulhan who, worried about ensuring the text was comprehensible, presented a contradiction-free follow-up novel as if it had been completed by Proust himself, all while quietly implementing their heavy-handed interventions behind the scenes.

This textual arrangement was canonized by the subsequent editions published by Gallimard in the Bibliothèque de la Pléiade. The first was issued in three volumes edited by Pierre Clarac and André Ferré (1954), with the second-to-last part of the novel maintaining the original title of *La fugitive*, which had been previously changed by Proust to *Albertine disparue* to avoid confusion with the equally-titled translation of a work by Rabindranath Tagore performed by Madame Brimont. The second was issued in four volumes edited by Jean-Yves Tadié (1987–1989) that were enriched by a series of *esquisses*, that is, a selection of old drafts extracted from the *Cahiers* manuscripts offered as a simplified transcription. However, the massive editorial reworking of the posthumous volumes of *La recherche* became clear in 1986, upon access to the typescript of *Albertine disparue*, corrected by Proust just before his death and intentionally ignored by the early editors. It was then published in 1987 by Nathalie Mauriac Dyer and Étienne Wolff. The numerous substantial variants that Proust added to the text of *Albertine disparue*, in particular the removal of 250 pages, surpass the last version attested to by the *Cahiers* manuscripts (*Cahiers de mis au net XII–XV*), which the Gallimard editions were based on. They also create undeniable narrative disjunction with the subsequent *Temps retrouvé*, highlighting the unfinished nature of the novel (Mauriac Dyer 2005). By demonstrating the arbitrary nature of the text in the posthumous volumes, this discovery has caused an identity crisis for the entire published *corpus* of *La recherche*, previously untouchable on its lofty pedestal, and has fed into the debate between genetic and textual criticism on the handling of an incomplete, partially posthumous work. The different editions are representative of different positions in the debate: in editing the 1992 Champion edition, Jean Milly published the long version of *Albertine disparue*, typographically differentiating Proust's subsequent changes; on the other hand, in order to adhere as much as possible to the state in which Proust left the novel when he died, Mauriac Dyer suggested publishing — after the last volume that appeared in the author's life, *Sodome et Gomorrhe II* — the typewritten documents of *La prisonnière* and *Albertine disparue* corrected in 1922, which were to be parts of a *Sodome et Gomorrhe III*, followed by their complete preliminary texts, i.e., the *Cahiers di mis au net VIII–XV*, and by the last notebooks in the series, XVI–XX (Mauriac Dyer 2007). In 2017, for the Classiques Garnier edition, Luc Fraisse published the long version taken from the *Cahiers* manuscripts, providing the variants in a critical apparatus. In addition, by making note of the changes imposed by the first publishers, Fraisse provided a more complete analysis of Jean Paulhan's correcting approach, often aimed at flattening the lexicon and Proustian syntax in favour of greater clarity.

In the 1970s, the formation of the Proust team at the Institut des Textes et Manuscrits Modernes (ITEM) led to the steady increase in genetic studies on the Proustian corpus, facilitated by the acquisition of the author's papers by the BnF. After the 1962 purchase of eighty-two notebooks owned by the author's niece, Suzy Mante-Proust (who also gave the library other papers in 1977), in 1983 the BnF acquired thirteen notebooks from the collection of Jacques Guérin (Fau 2013: 135–36). Among those notebooks, a few stand out: first, a series of seventy-five pieces containing the drafts of *Contre Sainte-Beuve* and of *La recherche* written between 1908 and 1922 (*Cahiers de brouillon*), and second, a series of twenty notebooks of clean copies that had often been reworked (*Cahiers de mise au net*), marked with Roman numerals I–XX by Proust himself and enriched by the famous *paperoles*, sheets of paper glued to the original pages (Contini 1947). This second series is datable between 1915 and 1922 and contains the text of the second part of *La recherche*, from *Sodome et Gomorrhe* onward. The collection, digitized on Gallica and freely consultable (www.item.ens.fr/index.php?id=578147), also includes jotter-notebooks, typescripts often made with the involvement of assistants and servants (Brydges 1984 and Pugh 2000), printing proofs with the corrections of the author and others, and loose pieces of paper.

The dynamism of Proust's writing is reflected in the magmatic appearance of the autographs. First Proust used the recto of the paper, then proceeded to eliminate and add text, which he initially inserts between the lines, then in the margins and on the verso, resorting to the *paperoles* for particularly long additions exceeding the material limits of the paper. Sometimes additions were connected to the text with reference symbols ranging from simple to complex (crosses, circles, flowers, a face in profile, etc.). These variations should be distinguished from the author's notes written by Proust on the lines of the paper (interrupting the narrative thread), in the margins, or more frequently on the verso of the paper. They contain critical and aesthetic musings, programmatic instructions, and references, which can be written at the same time as the words on the page (as is the case with the notes on the lines of the paper), or derive from a subsequent re-reading (Herschberg Pierrot 2007). It is thus essential to define the systematic relationships that are established between the text, corrections, and author's notes so that we may identify different layers of variants (of which, however, a diplomatic approach does not offer diachronic representation, contrary to authorial philology). The cross-references between one notebook and another, demonstrating the tightly-woven interdependence of different documents in Proustian working methods, are quite significant, characterized by constant re-writing and re-reading that spans multiple notebooks, where similar or even diametrically opposed narrative nuclei are reworked more than once, without being dated or numbered, until the novel is fine-tuned, which happens more on the level of the typewritten documents and the printing proofs (Brun 2011). Many notebooks, then, are piecemeal, with numerous pages cut entirely or in part and reused by Proust to save time when transcribing passages that had slowly taken shape over time.

A systematic plan to restore Proust's notebooks was launched in 2008 with the critical-genetic edition of *Cahiers 1 à 75 de la Bibliothèque Nationale de France* overseen by Nathalie Mauriac Dyer and co-published by BnF and Brepols. Two volumes are dedicated to each notebook: the first contains a facsimile of the manuscript and useful 'diagrams of textual units' that indicate in numbered boxes the blocks of primary text (1, 2, 3, etc.), additions (1A, 1B, 1C, etc.) and Proust's notes (nr., in French notes de régie), with the scope of helping readers trace the process of writing the manuscript and broadly reconstruct the succession of narrative sequences, without however pinpointing the exact chronology of the variants (Mauriac Dyer 2008a: 159–60). The second volume, on the other hand, contains the transcription of the manuscript. By highlighting the limits of a linear transcription, considered unable to convey the multiple layers of Proust's writing, often difficult to arrange in a hierarchy or set to a precise timeline, the recent publishers have adopted a diplomatic transcription that respects the layout of the words on the page. The rendering of the autograph manuscript is conservative, respecting Proustian spelling and punctuation. Corrections and annotations have been signalled with special diacritical marks: minimal interlinear additions are placed between angle brackets (< >); first and second degree crossed-out text has been indicated by single or double strikethroughs, or by x's, depending on the author's markings; when a word has been written over another or if a variant takes up part of the previous reading, the two readings are separated by a forward slash (/); an asterisk (*) indicates a hypothetical interpretation; square brackets ([ ]) mark the input of the publisher. The transcription is correlated by historical/critical, codicological and genetic notes, which mark the sections derived from previous *Cahiers* or continued within the same notebook (Mauriac Dyer 2001–2002).

Special attention was paid to the reconstruction of the original physiognomy of the notebooks, from which Proust ripped out parts of and even entire pages, reusing them elsewhere. The research done on the paper fragments was based on a careful analysis of their physical qualities, such as the sizes of the fragment and the shape of the tear, the type of paper, the ink, the *ductus*, and even the textual continuity that can be detected between the various fragments (Mauriac Dyer 2008b: 100–02). A project of this scope is incredibly demanding, considering the extensive dispersion that the ripped-out pieces have been subjected to, as shown by the extreme case of the manuscript of *À l'ombre des jeunes filles en fleurs*, spread among fifty copies of a luxury edition (Wise 2003).

The following example of a genetic edition is that of *Cahier 46*, datable to 1914–1915 (André 2009). In the first part of the notebook, Proust introduces the Albertine character to the narrator's worldly Parisian setting, while, starting on folio 57r, he outlines the events of the *Deuxième séjour à Balbec*. The following excerpt offers a brief portrait of Albertine, transcribed from *Cahier 46*, NAF 16686, 52v (https://gallica.bnf.fr/ark:/12148/btv1b6000131k/f59.item.r=NAF%2016686):

```
                                    Il                il
                          Elle n'était pas pâle comme elle
                                        mais rosi de ce rose de verni
                      semblait quelque fois dehors ; un sang vif col[oré] et clair
                                    et t des/d' une matinée d'hiver partiellement ensoleillée que/qui j²
                      colora[it] transparaissait dans ses joues lisses ; sa figure
                                  a m'avait tellement tenté à Balbec
                      tout entie[re] mais semblait un beau globe rose comme
                      il m'avait paru le jour où j'avais voulu l'embrasser
                      paraissait* un beau globe rose, tant un sang vif et
                                            sa peau
                          clair transparaissait sous ses joues vernies/vernie, tant les
                                              joues
                      pentes de son/ses visage étaient courbes et douces. Et
                      Et elles venaient expirer Le regard glissait sur elles
                          et sur son front
                              jusqu'aux premiers contreforts de ses beaux cheveux
                                          que     naturellement naterelle[ment]  qui in saillaient
                                  noirs massés dont les/leur ondulations soulevaient/soulevés comme
                                                  creusés  relevés
  en massifs,              des chaî[nes], creusait, relevait en massifs une chaîne
  à se creusaient          de massifs onduleux¹⁰⁵
  en anfractuosités
  t sans qu'en haut
  cessât de se pour-
  suivre la chaîne
  in ondulée et
  ind ininterrompue
  de leurs crêtes.
  ⌊
```

[105] Proust a ici dessiné une petite tête d'homme avec une moustache qui renvoie à la première note en marge où ce même dessin apparaît après 'voulus'.

The diplomatic transcription conveys the placement of the words on the paper while also making the autograph more accessible and legible, to the detriment of the chronological reconstruction of the editing process. It is worth mentioning that the Proustian example is particularly complex, and formalizing Proust's multi-layered process according to the principles of authorial philology could be too burdensome and unmanageable on the whole. Diachronic formalization could however be applied to single passages with the benefit of providing a more accurate reconstruction. For isolated segments, it would also be useful to reference, each time, the final text with the aim of facilitating a comparison that would be both orderly and in order, as the critical editions of the individual *Cahiers* are published.

As an example, the previous passage of *Cahier 46*, revised in the manuscript, is presented below according to the principles of authorial philology. The last reading confirmed by the manuscript appears first and, in the apparatus, the variants formalized by the different compositional phases:

> Il n'était pas pâle comme il semblait quelque fois dehors mais comme le jour où j'avais voulu l'embrasser paraissait un beau globe rose, tant un sang vif et clair transparaissait sous sa peau vernie, tant les pentes de ses joues étaient courbes et douces. Le regard glissait sur elles et sur son front jusqu'aux premiers contreforts de ses beaux cheveux noirs naturellement soulevés qui ici saillaient en massifs, là se creusaient en anfractuosités sans qu'en haut cessât de se poursuivre la chaîne ondulée et ininterrompue de leurs crêtes.

> Il n'était ... douces] ¹Elle n'était pas pâle comme elle semblait quelque fois dehors; un sang vif col<orait> et clair colora<it> transparaissait dans ses joues lisses; sa figure tout entiè<re> → ²Il n'était pas pâle comme il semblait quelque fois dehors mais rosi de ce rose do<> verni et t<> ⌈d'une matinée *(from* des matinées) d'hiver partiellement ensoleillée ⌈qui m'avait *(from* que j'a<vait>) tellement tenté à Balbec *(with* mais ... Balbec *not deleted)* → ³Il n'était pas pâle comme il semblait quelque fois dehors mais ᵃsemblait un beau globe rose ᵇcomme il m'avait paru le jour où j'avais voulu l'embrasser comme le jour où j'avais voulu l'embrasser paraissait un beau globe rose, tant un sang vif et clair transparaissait sous ses joues vernies, tant les pentes de son visage étaient courbes et douces → ³T{sa peau vernie] *from* ses joues vernies   ses joues] *from* son visage}

> Le regard] *before* Et Et elles venaient expirer   et ... front] *interlinear insertion*   naturellement ... crêtes] ¹massés dont les ondulations soulevaient comme des chaî<nes> → ²que leur ondulation soulevait, creusait, relevait en massifs une chaîne de massifs onduleux → ³naturelle<ment> naturellement soulevés, creusés, relevés en une chaîne de massifs onduleux → ⁴T{ici] *inserted*   en massifs ... crêtes] *inserted in the left margin*   là] *inserted*   sans] *before* t< >   ondulée] *before* in< >   ininterrompue] *before* ind< >}

For reference, the definitive text in *Le côté de Guermantes II* is below:

> J'aurais bien voulu, avant de l'embrasser, pouvoir la remplir à nouveau du mystère qu'elle avait pour moi sur la plage, avant que je la connusse, retrouver en elle le pays où elle avait vécu auparavant; à sa place du moins, si je ne le connaissais pas, je pouvais insinuer tous les souvenirs de notre vie à Balbec, le bruit du flot déferlant sous ma fenêtre, les cris

des enfants. Mais en laissant mon regard glisser sur le beau globe rose de ses joues, dont les surfaces doucement incurvées venaient mourir aux pieds des premiers plissements de ses beaux cheveux noirs qui couraient en chaînes mouvementées, soulevaient leurs contreforts escarpés et modelaient les ondulations de leurs vallées, je dus me dire [...]

As can be seen in the example, this method aims to create a legible body of text of which the entire process of textual correction is recorded in the apparatus, in this case genetic, according to a diachronic and systematic approach that gives priority to the chronology of the markings rather than their layout. This alternate formalization could, perhaps, constitute a useful addition to the model used for the French genetic edition, providing the reader with a truly complete image of the document that doesn't exclude *a priori* an amplified interpretive intervention by the philologist.

Using folios 46v-49r from the same *Cahier 46*, Julie André and Elena Pierazzo have prepared the Proust Prototype, the first prototype of a genetic digital edition of *La recherche* according to the XML-TEI standard (http://elenapierazzo.org/proust_prototype). Pages are displayed in pairs, with the verso of each folio next to the recto of the next folio, where the textual units are grouped into numbered zones distinct from Proust's instructions and notes, following a layout that echoes the 'diagrams of textual units' of the genetic editions on paper. By clicking on the image, the superimposed diplomatic transcription appears. The user can read the manuscript by following the order in which the different textual sequences were written (writing order) or according to the order of the manuscript's final version (reading order). The greater or lesser degree of certainty of the position of a zone within the sequence is indicated by varying degrees of chromatic intensity of the background of the transcribed zones: the darker the colour of an area, the more hypothetical its place in the sequence (André and Pierazzo 2013; André 2016).

The first complete digital edition of a Proustian document, on the other hand, was created in 2015 by Nathalie Mauriac Dyer, Françoise Leriche, Pyra Wise and Guillaume Fau. It is the edition of the *Agenda 1906* — a deep red leather Kirby, Beard & Co. day planner for the first quarter of 1906, though Proust used it only later on — that became part of the BnF collection in 2013 (https://books.openedition.org/

editionsbnf/1457). Of the 80 pages that make up the *Agenda*, only 29 include notes by Proust, some private (concerning, for example, his spying on Agostinelli around Paris) and some relating to work. The latter were made at different times and for the most part *a posteriori*, and focus on specific, historic, botanical, medical, and other matters that required verification and follow up. According to their chronology and their particular purpose, documentary and scheduling notes can be identified, datable between late spring and/or summer of 1909; verification notes taken on the occasion of the clean copy of *Combray* which are from late summer/early autumn of 1909; and verification notes and reminders jotted down when correcting the drafts of *Du côté de chez Swann* in June/July 1913. The diplomatic transcription is followed by a conservative linear transcription linked to the genetic and critical notes that, where necessary (exploiting the connections that define the digital environment), refer to the reproductions of all the cited Proust collection documents, or of other digitized archives (Wise 2017, Leriche 2016).

In the digital environment, it is worth mentioning the Corr-Proust project, which launched the digital publication of the writer's letters under the direction of ITEM, the Université Grenoble Alpes and the University of Illinois at Urbana-Champaign, where most of Proust's letters are kept (http://proust.elan-numerique.fr). The digital interface contains a two-columns display divided in different tabs that can be viewed side by side, depending on the user's needs. The tabs contain the digital images of the letter, a diplomatic transcription of the text and a standardized transcription; notes; and documentary, archival and bibliographic information. The *corpus* can be filtered on various levels, according to different search criteria, such as date, place, people, etc.

These initial, meaningful digital experiments, along with the development of knowledge about Proust's work promoted by the paper edition of *Cahiers*, are the premise of the ambitious digital 'Hyper-Proust' proposed by Mauriac Dyer: a single digital place, interoperable on multiple levels that holds the publication of the *Cahiers* and of all the materials in the BnF's Proust collection, the text of *La recherche* published by Proust, along with letters and the writer's library (Mauriac Dyer 2008a: 168–69). Such a tool would have infinite potential: it could, for example, make it easier to find and compare the various compositional phases of the same passage among multiple manuscripts and typewritten and printed documents, a feature that would be particularly advantageous over the printed reproduction of the single documents that make up each of Proust's avant-textes.

4.5 Samuel Beckett's *En attendant Godot* / *Waiting for Godot*

Olga Beloborodova, Dirk Van Hulle and Pim Verhulst

Genetic Beckett studies have a long history that stretches far beyond the so-called 'archival turn' of the 1990s, although the accessibility of manuscripts was certainly an issue in the first decades of Beckett scholarship (1960s-70s). Things changed radically when he donated a large number of his manuscripts to the University of Reading's archive (UoR) in 1971. Thanks to the efforts of scholars like James Knowlson, John Pilling and later Mark Nixon, the archive has grown throughout the years and now holds the world's largest collection of Beckett manuscripts. Other large repositories are the Harry Ransom Humanities Research Center in Austin, Texas (HRC) and Trinity College Dublin (TCD), Beckett's alma mater.

Even this short list of the largest collections points to one of the biggest problems in genetic Beckett studies, namely the enormous geographical spread of archives and holding libraries. A number of important collections are kept in the United States: Washington University in St Louis (WU), Syracuse University in New York (SU), Indiana University (IU), Ohio State University (OSU), and The University of California, San Diego (UCSD). L'Institut Mémoires de l'édition contemporaine (IMEC) and the Bibliothèque National (BnF) are the two most important repositories in France, where the bilingual Irish author lived for most of his life. The scattered nature of Beckett's legacy was one of the chief reasons, along with preservation, for the establishment of the Beckett Digital Manuscript Project (BDMP) in 2011 (https://www.beckettarchive.org/). The purpose of the BDMP is to reunite the manuscripts of Beckett's works in a digital way, and to facilitate genetic research: by offering transcriptions of Beckett's manuscripts, tools for bilingual and genetic version comparison, a search engine and an analysis of the textual genesis of his works.

As a digital resource, the BDMP uses the affordances of the digital medium to the fullest by foregrounding and visualizing Beckett's rich and layered intertextuality. In this connection, the Beckett Digital Library (BDL) is a crucial feature. The module consists of the 'extant' library (the books that are still in Beckett's apartment in Paris and in a few other collections) and the 'virtual' library (the books we know

Beckett read, based on information in letters and reading notes, but which no longer survive). Both the extant and the virtual library contain links to relevant pages in the genetic editions, and — conversely — one can find references to source texts in the individual modules and enter the library from there (see example below).

Although the focus of the BDMP lies mostly on the *endogenesis* (the succession of draft versions) and *exogenesis* (the author's use of external source texts), it also catalogues and collates different editions of Beckett's works, for which the Bibliography feature, compiled by Breon Mitchell, provides exhaustive bibliographical information. In some cases, the publication history is marked by a complex *epigenesis* (the continuation of the genesis and revision after the first publication). The example discussed below — the genesis of Beckett's most famous play *En attendant Godot / Waiting for Godot* — is a case in point.

Samuel Beckett began writing *Godot* on 9 October 1948, finishing it some four months later on 29 January 1949.[2] Together with 9 December 1948, these are the only three dates recorded in the squared 'Avia' notebook of the original manuscript, now held at the BnF in Paris. The play was completed in the middle of what Beckett referred to as a 'frenzy of writing' or 'siege in the room' to his biographer James Knowlson (1996), a sustained period of intense composition in French which yielded another play, four stories, a novella and three novels. Beckett began *Godot* 'as a relaxation', to get away from the 'awful prose' he was writing (Colin Duckworth, in Beckett 1966: xlv). The only other handwritten material in French are a few lines of dialogue in the 'Tara MacGowran' notebook (OSU). Two typescripts are mentioned in Beckett's letters, but only an annotated playscript based on the second one survives (Morgan Library, New York), which was also used for a radio recording of the play for Michel Polac's *Entrée des auteurs* on RTF's *Club d'Essai* in 1952. Two 'prompt' copies of Minuit's first edition (TCD; IMEC) were heavily used during rehearsals for the premiere at the Théâtre de Babylone in January 1953 and, lastly, a fair copy Beckett made for manuscripts dealer Jake Schwartz (HRC) in 1959 is largely identical to the published text.

Following the play's success in Paris, serious offers started coming in from the USA. Worried about the fate of his text in the hands of others,

---

2   Unless otherwise stated, all the information in this section is taken from Van Hulle and Verhulst 2017, and the online genetic edition.

4.5 Samuel Beckett's En attendant Godot / Waiting for Godot   151

Beckett made his own English translation. Its original manuscript was likely thrown away, but a first typescript was sent to Harold L. Oram, the financial backer, and American publisher Barney Rosset (Grove Press, New York) in June 1953. Despite Beckett's warning that it was only a rushed first draft, it was retyped, duplicated and disseminated for negotiations, but no copy of this playscript has yet come to light. Beckett also sent his first typescript to Britain, for theatre impresario Donald Albery and director Peter Glenville, who likewise had copies made. This playscript did survive, in four versions, all with different annotations — none in Beckett's hand — and some with unique but probably unauthorized variants. The fourth copy was shown to the Lord Chamberlain's office, who censored it for performance (British Library). To complicate matters even more, Alan Simpson wanted to stage *Godot* at the Pike Theatre in Dublin, asking Beckett for a text in November 1953. This time, he made sure to send a copy of his second, revised typescript, which makes it the only English draft to have survived, be it with missing pages (TCD). We know from Beckett's letters to his American publisher that copies of the first and second typescript were given to the New York Public Library in 1961, but these went missing in 1970. Another fair copy manuscript of the English text was made for Schwartz in 1959 (HRC), but this was again based on a published edition, the American one.

Godot's publication history, in both French and English, is long and complicated. The original French edition (1952) appeared before the play's premiere, so it did not include any of the changes that were made for performance. A few small cuts and additions were implemented in the second impression (1953), which was further updated with substantial excisions for paperback and hardback reissues in 1970 and 1971. Another annotated copy that informed this revised edition was the one Beckett made for the *Godot* revival at the Odéon Théâtre in 1961, directed by Roger Blin and featuring the famous tree designed by Alberto Giacometti (IU). By this time, various English editions had appeared. The American version (1954), was based on Beckett's second typescript of the translation and is thus more advanced than the French text. The British edition, however, published by Faber and Faber in 1956, was based on Beckett's by now obsolete first typescript translation, as well as the various playscripts that were used for the play's UK premiere. In addition to unauthorized variants, introduced by Glenville,

Albery and set designer Peter Snow, it also printed the bowdlerized text. Since Beckett was very unhappy with this situation, a new edition was published in 1965. He had carefully marked up a copy of the American edition for this purpose (Columbia University), but instead of setting the text anew from this document, Faber just incorporated Beckett's corrections into their original type, so that many of the old variants were left intact. It was therefore not the 'definitive edition' it claimed to be.

The editorial model we developed for the BDMP is based on a text-oriented approach to the transcriptions in XML, following the guidelines of the Text Encoding Initiative (TEI). The rationale behind this choice is that, since we also provide scans of the document, this text-oriented approach is complementary. The disadvantage of a topographic transcription (in a digital context) is that the transcription does not translate the facsimile image into a searchable text, but into another (unsearchable) image, produced by means of graphic software like Photoshop. In the French tradition of *critique génétique* (genetic criticism), this form of transcription would accord with the principle of *donner à voir* (made for looking), as opposed to the principle of *donner à lire* (made for reading). The latter approach (applied in the BDMP) considers it the role of the transcriber to provide a text that facilitates the reading and therefore tends to linearize the textual features of the manuscript. The linearized transcription still leaves open many possibilities to mark visual particularities as well. For instance, the difference between typed text and handwritten annotations can be rendered by means of different fonts. The line breaks are respected, and the blank space where Beckett did not immediately find the right word can just be marked as such. If the linearized transcription is presented in parallel with a (digital) facsimile, the combination (à *voir* + à lire) is greater than the sum of its parts, as it shows the translation of toposensitive facsimile into chronosensitive linearized sequence.

For genetic editions, one of the most powerful tools is the possibility for users to diachronically compare segments (<seg>) of the text across versions. To enable this type of genetic research, it is helpful to number the segments and it is up to the editor to decide what the size of these segments will be. The BDMP works with the sentence as a unit of comparison, broadly defined as a syntactic unit that ends with a full stop, an exclamation mark or a question mark. The first edition serves as a 'base-text' (or 'anchor text') that determines the numbering of the sentences. In case a segment never made it into the published text, and therefore does not correspond with any sentence in the base-text, a solution for the numbering is to take the number of the preceding sentence that did make it in and add a vertical bar | followed by a second numbering. For instance, [0014|001] means this is a segment that did not make it into the final text and is situated in this manuscript as the first segment after the segment corresponding to sentence 14, which *did* make it in.

By choosing the page as a division (<div>), it is also possible to link the XML transcription to the digital facsimile. In the BDMP, this coupling of text and image happens at the level of the 'zone', a flexible textual unit of about a half dozen lines (depending on the context). The content of the zone can be efficiently linked to the corresponding sentences in the XML transcription. An advantage of this unit's size is that it facilitates the image/text visualization enabling the immediate comparison of the topography of the facsimile (document-oriented) with the linearized transcription (text-oriented). The image/text view is the most frequently used way of reading the transcriptions. The zone can be drawn on the facsimile with a simple, free software tool like ImageJ, and in the BDMP the four coordinates necessary to encode this rectangular selection in the XML are stored in a <div> element.

The transcription work focuses on the microgenesis of 'intradocument variation' (layers of writing within this one draft), while the macrogenenesis opens up the scope across versions ('interdocument variation'). Because segments are numbered, the digital architecture of the genetic edition can be designed in such a way that it retrieves all versions of one particular sentence and visualizes them in a 'synoptic sentence view'. It allows users to compare versions, i.e. what Donald Reiman dubbed 'versioning' (1987: 167–80), but at the level of the sentence, which facilitates comparison. Since Beckett wrote in two languages and translated most of his own works, the edition offers the possibility of bilingual version comparison. In the synoptic sentence view, the sentences in the manuscript that did not make it into the final text, such as segment [0014|001] above, are highlighted in bold type and linked to the preceding sentence that did (here segment [0014]). To turn this form of versioning into the equivalent of a critical apparatus of textual variants, new developments in (semi-)automatic or computer-assisted collation (Juxta, CollateX, HyperCollate) enable editors to highlight variants. By integrating Collatex into the edition, the BDMP offers not only editors but also users the chance to compare differences between versions by means of a collation engine, even in the manuscripts (including cancellations and additions), in both the French and the English texts.

The following manuscript passage, edited according to the principles of authorial philology, illustrates how Beckett revised, cancelling and substituting fragments between the lines, sometimes using the facing verso for additions (both in superscript below). In the digital genetic edition of the play, passages in the manuscripts that refer to source texts in Beckett's personal library are annotated and linked to the relevant pages in his books.[3]

Lévy.	Je me rappelle les cartes de la Terre Sainte.	0151
	En couleurs.	0152
	Très jolies.	0153
	La mer morte était bleu pâle.	0154
	J'avais soif rien qu'en la regardant.	0155
	Je me disais, c'est là que nous ~~passerons~~ $^{\text{irons passer}}$ notre ~~l'x~~ lune de miel.	0156
	Nous serons heureux.	0158
Vlad.	Tu aurais dû être poète.	0159
Lévy.	Je l'ai été.	0160
	Ça ne se voit pas ?	0162
	(Silence).	0163
Vlad.	Qu'est-ce que je disais....	0164
	Comment va ton pied ?	0165
Lévy.	Il enfle.	0166

---

3   This passage is quoted from the French notebook of *En attendant Godot*, module no. 6 in the Beckett Digital Manuscript Project (BDMP6, FN, 05r).

4.5 Samuel Beckett's En attendant Godot / Waiting for Godot

Vlad.	Ah oui, cette histoire ~~du~~ ^{des} larrons.	0167
	Tu t'en souviens ?	0168
Lévy.	Non.	0169
Vlad.	Tu sais où ça vient.	0169|001
~~Vlad~~.	~~Tu sais où ça vient.~~	0169|002
	~~(un instant)~~	0169|003
~~Lévy~~.	~~Ça sent l'Evangile.~~	0169|004
Lévy.	Quelle histoire ?	0169|005
Vlad.	Mais je viens de te le dire.	0169|006
	~~Des~~ ^{L'histoire des} larrons.	0169|007
Lévy.	Quels larrons ?	0169|008
Vlad.	Les deux voleurs crucifiés en même temps que ~~Jésus~~ l'autre. L'un fut sauvé et l'autre (il cherche le contraire de sauvé) damné.	0179
Lévy.	Sauvé de quoi ?	0180
Vlad	Des enfers ?	0181
Lévy.	Je n'ai jamais pu blairer l'Evangile.	0181|001

PHILOLOGICAL NOTES:

0151   Estragon was still called 'Lévy' in the manuscript, which suggests a Jewish heritage or ancestry. The name's potentially political motivation notwithstanding, the author may have decided to change it in order to avoid accusations of Jewish stereotyping in the aftermath of World War II and the Holocaust. Beckett was in Germany from 1936–1937, witnessing the rise of Nazism, and he later helped the Resistance from Paris and Rousillon after German forces invaded the city (see 0181|001 below).

0155   Lévy's comment that the very look of the Dead Sea's pale blue colour made him thirsty, added on the facing verso page, may be inspired by similar maps of the Holy Land in the author's personal library, for example in his Italian Bible (see Fig. 10).

0156   The author changes 'nous passerons' into the more colloquial 'nous irons passer'. This revision also introduces an extra element of movement by adding the verb 'aller', which contrasts with the characters' immobility. The English (self-)translation likewise makes use of the verb 'to go': 'that's where we'll go for our honeymoon' (Beckett 2010: 8).

0158   The sentence 'nous serons heureux' was added inline as an afterthought, which makes it seem more desperate and suggests they are not happy now.

0167   The correction of singular 'du' to plural 'des larrons' suggests the author was first thinking of using a different word, or perhaps just one thief instead of two, which would have made Vladimir seem even more unreliable (see 0180-0181 below).

0169|001-|008   The author first deleted Vladimir's question about the story of the two thieves' source, as well as Estragon's answer that it stinks of the Gospels, after a pause for thought. He then added the question again between the lines, but now Estragon answers with another question instead, a pattern that continues in the following exchange (see 0180-0181 below). The author's revision of 'Des larrons' to 'L'histoire des larrons' also creates more repetition, another central theme in the play. Estragon's deleted comment may connect to Beckett's annotation of Luke 23:34 in his 'schoolboy' Bible, which mentions the crucifixion of the two thieves (see Fig. 11).

0179   By obscuring Jesus as 'the other', the author seems to suggest that Vladimir does not remember his name, adding to the general breakdown of memory in the play, or is reluctant to name him. In the playscript and the published text, the term was replaced with 'le Sauveur' (FP, 07r; 1952, 17), which emphasizes the biblical function of Christ rather than his name. Vladimir also refers to Godot as a saviour in the manuscript — 'qui dit nous délivrer' (FN, 04v) — but this explicit identification with Jesus was cut, possibly because it promoted a Christian reading, which the author discouraged.

0180-0181   Further emphasizing the characters' failing recollection, as well as their lacking knowledge of the Bible or New Testament, in this facing-page addition the one forgets what the two thieves were saved from and the other guesses it was from hell, which gets them no closer to the truth. In the playscript and the published version, Vladimir sounds more assured and Bible savvy: 'De l'enfer' (FP, 07; 1952, 17).

0181|001   Lévy's Jewish-sounding name would have explained why he cannot stand the New Testament and the Gospels, since the Torah or Pentateuch only includes the first five books of the Old Testament. The fact that it was later changed to the more French-sounding name Estragon may be connected to the omission of this sentence from later drafts and versions, although the comment would still have retained blasphemous connotations.

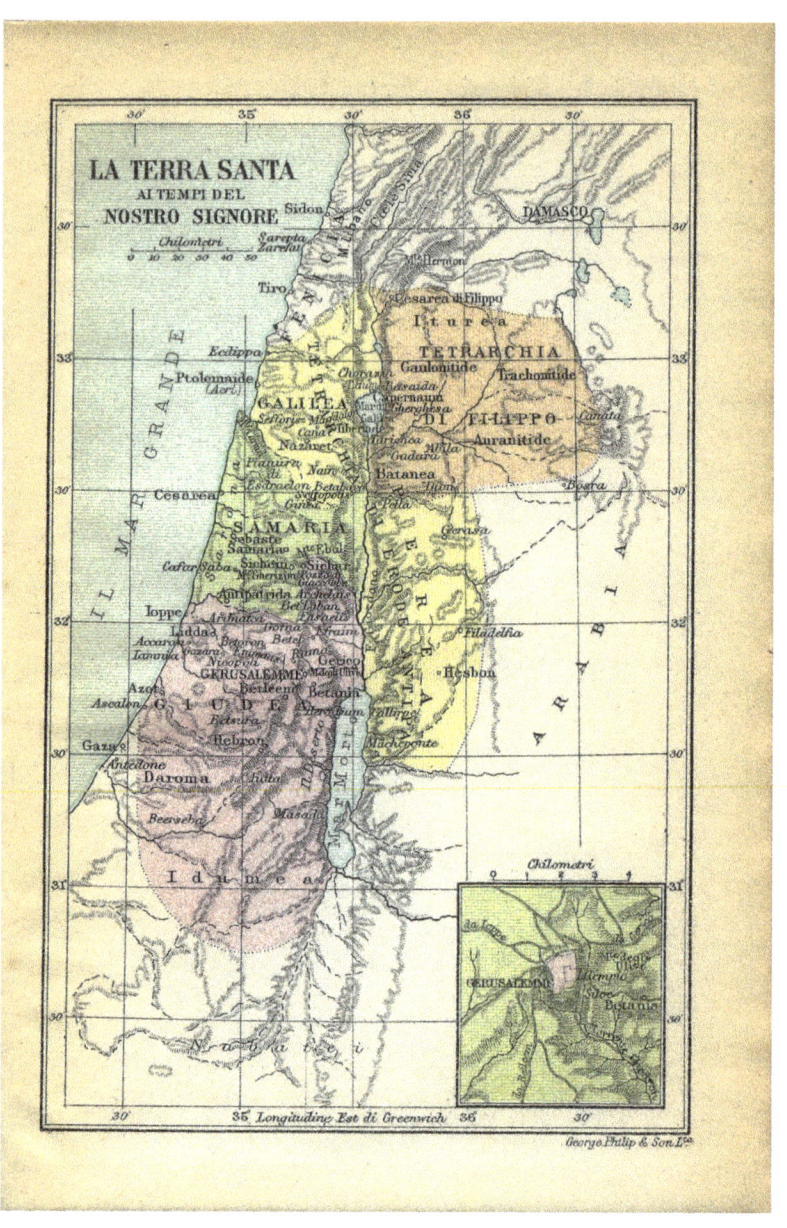

Fig. 11 *La Sacra Bibbia ossia L'Antico et il Nuovo Testamento: versione riveduta sui testi originali*, Società Biblica Britannica e Forestiera, 1924 (n.p.), Beckett Digital Library, https://www.beckettarchive.org/library/SAC-BIB.html?page=map&zone

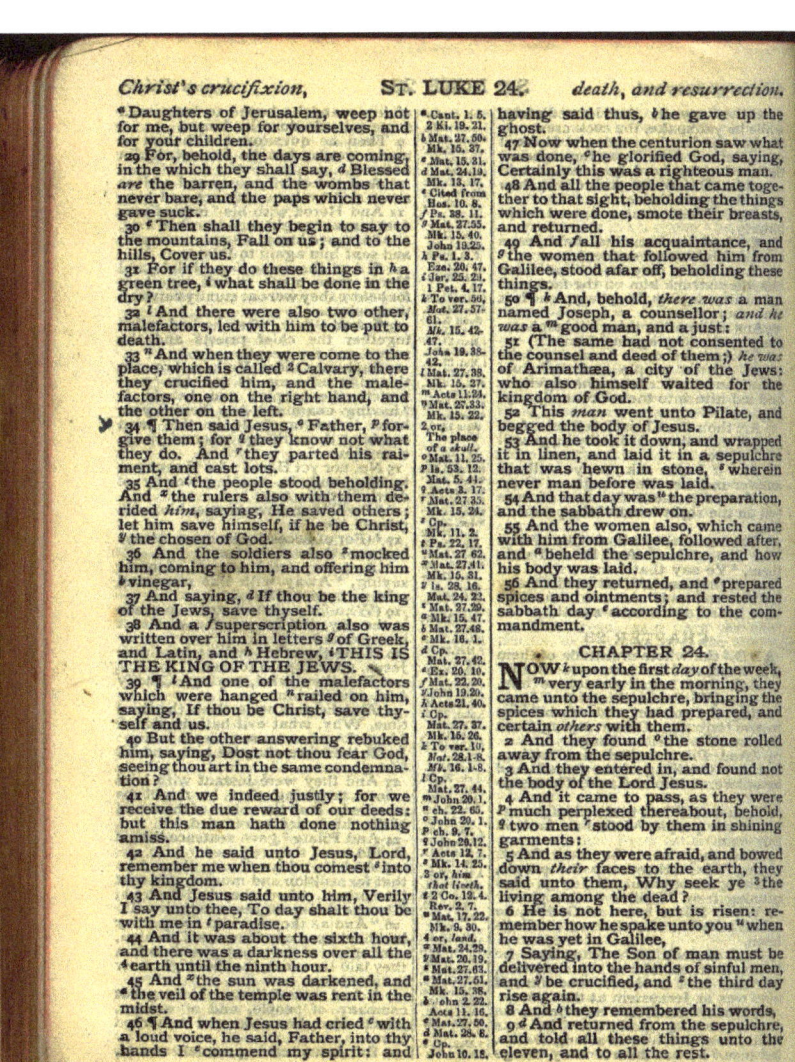

Fig. 12 *The Holy Bible: Containing the Old and New Testaments, Translated out of the Original Tongues and with the former Translations diligently compared and revised, by His Majesty's special command*, Oxford University Press, n.d. (p. 862), Beckett Digital Library, https://www.beckettarchive.org/library/HOL-BIB-1.html?page=862&zone=1

References

Albonico 1999 Simone Albonico, ed., *Due Seminari di filologia. 'Testo e apparato nella filologia d'autore' e 'Critica delle varianti e filologia di Gianfranco Contini 1933–1947'*, Dipartimento di Scienza della Letteratura e dell'Arte medievale e moderna dell'Università di Pavia, Alessandria: Edizioni dell'Orso.

Albonico 2018 Simone Albonico, 'Autografi, documenti, archivi. Solitudine degli originali e configurazioni storiche dei manoscritti letterari', in *La Tradizione dei Testi*, Atti del Convegno (Cortona, 21–23 settembre 2017), ed. by Claudio Ciociola and Claudio Vela, Rome: SFLI-Società dei Filologi della Letteratura Italiana, 31–73.

André 2009 Julie André, *Le Cahier 46 de Marcel Proust: Transcription et Interprétation*, PhD Thesis, Université de la Sorbonne nouvelle, Paris III, https://tel.archives-ouvertes.fr/tel-00713945/document

André 2016 Julie André, 'Proust's Writing. First Drafts as a Digital Representation', in *ECD/DCE, Edizioni Critiche Digitali/Digital Critical Editions*, ed. by Paola Italia and Claudia Bonsi, Rome: Sapienza Università Editrice, 53–62.

André and Pierazzo 2013 Julie André and Elena Pierazzo, 'Le Codage en TEI des brouillons de Proust: vers l'édition numérique', *Genesis*, 36, 155–61, https://journals.openedition.org/genesis/1159

Antonelli 1985 Roberto Antonelli, '*Interpretazione e critica del testo*', in *Letteratura italiana*, dir. by Alberto Asor Rosa, vol. 4 (*L'interpretazione*), Turin: Einaudi, 141–50.

Ariosto 1937 Ludovico Ariosto, *Frammenti autografi dell' 'Orlando Furioso'*, ed. by Santorre Debenedetti, Turin: Loescher.

Ariosto 1987 Ludovico Ariosto, *Satire*, ed. by Cesare Segre, Turin: Einaudi.

Austen 1850 C. Hubback, *The Younger Sister. A Novel*, 3 vols, London: Thomas Cautley Newby Publisher.

Austen 1871 J. E. Austen Leigh, *A Memoir of Jane Austen by Her Nephew J. E. Austen Leigh. Second Edition to Which Is Added Lady Susan and Fragments of Two Other Unfinished Tales by Miss Austen*, London: Richard Bentley.

Austen 1928 Jane Austen, *The Watsons by Jane Austen Completed in Accordance with Her Intentions by Edith (Her Great Grand-Niece) and Francis Brown*, London: Elkin Mathews & Marrot.

Austen 1954 Jane Austen, *The Works of Jane Austen. Volume 6: Minor Works*, ed. by R. W. Chapman, Oxford: Oxford University Press.

Austen 2011 Jane Austen, *Jane Austen's Fiction Manuscripts A Digital Edition*, dir. by K. Sutherland. London: King's College London, https://janeausten.ac.uk/

Austen 2018 Jane Austen, *The Watsons*, in *Jane Austen's Fiction Manuscripts*, ed. by K. Sutherland, vol. 4, Oxford: Oxford University Press, 2–186.

Avalle 1970 D'Arco Silvio Avalle, *L'analisi letteraria in Italia. Formalismo, strutturalismo, semiologia. Con una appendice di Documenti*, Milan-Naples: Ricciardi.

Baldelli and Vignuzzi 1985 Ignazio Baldelli and Ugo Vignuzzi, 'Filologia, linguistica, stilistica', in *Letteratura italiana*, dir. by Alberto Asor Rosa, vol. 4 (*L'interpretazione*), Turin: Einaudi, 451–87.

Balduino 1995 Armando Balduino, 'Varianti d'autore', in *Manuale di filologia italiana*, Florence: Sansoni, 367–410.

Barbi 1938 Michele Barbi, *La nuova filologia e l'edizione dei nostri scrittori da Dante a Manzoni*, Florence: Sansoni.

Barbi 1939 Michele Barbi, 'Piano per un'edizione nazionale delle opere di Alessandro Manzoni', *Annali manzoniani*, 1, 23–153.

Barker-Benfield 1992 Bruce C. Barker-Benfield, *Shelley's Guitar*, Oxford: Bodleian Library.

Basile 1975 Bruno Basile, *Letteratura e filologia*, Bologna: Zanichelli.

Beckett 1952 Samuel Beckett, *En attendant Godot*, Paris: Minuit.

Beckett 1966 Samuel Beckett, *En attendant Godot*, ed. by Colin Duckworth, London: George Harrap.

Beckett 2010 Samuel Beckett, *Waiting for Godot*, London: Faber.

Belanger 1977 Terry Belanger, 'Descriptive Bibliography', in *Book Collecting: A Modern Guide*, ed. by Jean Peters, New York and London: R. R. Bowker, 97–101.

Bellemin-Noël 1972 Jean Bellemin-Noël, *Le texte et l'avant-texte. Les brouillons d'un poème de Milosz*, Paris: Larousse.

Belloni 1992 Gino Belloni, 'Bernardino Daniello e le varianti d'autore petrarchesche'; 'Origine della critica degli scartafacci', in *Laura tra Petrarca e Bembo. Studi sul commento umanistico-rinascimentale al 'Canzoniere'*, Padova: Antenore, 226–83 and 284–320.

Bembo 1991 Pietro Bembo, *Gli Asolani*, ed. by Giorgio Dilemmi, Florence: Per l'Accademia della Crusca.

Bembo 2001 Pietro Bembo, *Prose della volgar lingua*, ed. by Claudio Vela, Bologna: CLUEB.

Bembo 2002 Pietro Bembo, *La prima stesura delle* Prose *della volgar lingua: fonti e correzioni*, ed. by Mirko Tavosanis, Pisa: ETS.

Bembo 2003 Pietro Bembo, *Stanze*, ed. by Alessandro Gnocchi, Florence: SEF.

Bembo 2008 Pietro Bembo, *Le rime*, ed. by Andrea Donnini, Rome: Salerno.

Berisso 2009 Marco Berisso, 'La critica delle varianti nell'epoca della riproducibilità informatica. A proposito di Woobinda di Aldo Nove', *Studi di filologia italiana*, 67, 225–56.

Bentivogli and Vecchi Galli 2002 Bruno Bentivogli and Paola Vecchi Galli, *Filologia italiana*, Milan: Bruno Mondadori.

Bessi and Martelli 1984 Rossella Bessi and Mario Martelli, 'Fenomenologia dell'originale', in *Guida alla filologia italiana*, Florence: Sansoni, 67–90.

Blasucci 2004 Luigi Blasucci, 'Contini leopardista', in *Riuscire postcrociani senza essere anticrociani. Gianfranco Contini e gli studi letterari del secondo Novecento*, ed. by Angelo R. Pupino, Florence: Edizioni del Galluzzo, 33–47.

Boccaccio 1976 Giovanni Boccaccio, *Il Decameron*, ed. by Vittore Branca, Florence: Presso l'Accademia della Crusca.

Bonaccorsco 1983 Giovanni Bonaccorsco, ed., *Corpus flaubertianum*, Paris: Les Belles Lettres.

Bongrani 1982 Paolo Bongrani, 'Appunti sulle Prose della volgar lingua. In margine a una recente edizione', *Giornale Storico della Letteratura Italiana*, 159, 271–90.

Brambilla Ageno 1975 Franca Brambilla Ageno, 'L'elaborazione della forma nei testi letterari'; 'Correzioni d'autore coatte', in *L'edizione critica dei testi volgari*, Padova: Antenore, 195–210 and 211–15.

Brambilla and Fiorilla 2009 Simona Brambilla and Maurizio Fiorilla, eds, *La filologia dei testi d'autore*, Atti del Seminario di Studi (Università degli Studi of Rome Tre, 3–4 ottobre 2007), Florence: Cesati Editore.

Brugnolo 1992 Furio Brugnolo, 'Filologia d'autore ed ecdotica', *Filologia e critica*, 17, 100–06.

Brydges 1984 Robert Brydges, 'Remarques sur le manuscrit et les dactylographies du "Temps Perdu"', *Bulletin d'informations proustiennes*, 15, 11–18.

Brun 2011 Bernard Brun, 'Les Cent Cahiers de Marcel Proust: Comment a-t-il rédigé son roman?', *ITEM* (December 13, 2011), http://www.item.ens.fr/articles-en-ligne/les-cent-cahiers-de-marcel-proust-comment-a-t-il-redige-son/.

Buxton Forman 1876 Harry Buxton Forman, 'Preface', in *The Poetical Works of Percy Bysshe Shelley*, ed. by Harry Buxton Forman, vol. 1, London: Reeves and Turner, xi–xl.

Cadioli 2008 Alberto Cadioli, 'La materialità nello studio dei testi a stampa', *Moderna*, 10.2, 21–38.

Cadioli 2019 Alberto Cadioli, 'Note su alcune riflessioni ecdotiche di Oreste Macrì sugli autori contemporanei', *Prassi Ecdotiche della Modernità Letteraria*, 4.1, 51–68.

Caprettini 1985 Gian Paolo Caprettini, 'Le strutture e i segni. Dal formalismo alla semiotica letteraria', in *Letteratura italiana*, dir. by Alberto Asor Rosa, vol. 4 (*L'interpretazione*), Turin: Einaudi, 495–548.

Caretti 1950 Gianfranco Caretti, *Studi sulle Rime del Tasso*, Rome: Edizioni di Storia e Letteratura.

Caretti 1955 Gianfranco Caretti 'Filologia e critica', in *Filologia e critica. Studi di letteratura italiana*, Milan-Naples: Ricciardi, 1–25 (→ Id., *Antichi e moderni. Studi di Letteratura italiana*, Turin: Einaudi, 1976, 468–88).

Carrai 2010 Stefano Carrai, 'La filologia di Dante Isella', *Filologia italiana*, 6, 9–20.

Carrai and Italia 2018, Stefano Carrai and Paola Italia, eds, 'La filologia e la stilistica di Dante Isella. Per un'antologia', *Ecdotica*, 15, 185–238.

Caruso 2020 Carlo Caruso, ed., *The Life of Texts. Evidence in Textual Production, Transmission and Reception*, London: Bloomsbury, https://doi.org/10.5040/9781350039087

Caruso and Russo 2018 Carlo Caruso and Emilio Russo, eds, *La filologia in Italia nel Rinascimento*, Rome: Edizioni di Storia e letteratura.

Caruso and Casari 2020 Carlo Caruso and Federico Casari, *Come lavorava Carducci*, Rome: Carocci.

Cherchi 2001 Paolo Cherchi, 'Filologie del Duemila', *Rassegna Europea di Letteratura Italiana*, 17, 135–53.

Ciociola 2018 Claudio Ciociola, 'Storia della tradizione e varianti d'autore (Barbi, Pasquali, Contini)', in *La Tradizione dei Testi*, Atti del Convegno (Cortona, 21–23 settembre 2017), ed. by Claudio Ciociola and Claudio Vela, Rome: SFLI-Società dei Filologi della Letteratura Italiana, 3–22.

Ciociola and Vela 2018 Claudio Ciociola and Claudia Vela, eds, *La Tradizione dei Testi*, Atti del Convegno (Cortona, 21–23 settembre 2017), Rome: SFLI-Società dei Filologi della Letteratura Italiana.

Colussi 2011 Davide Colussi, *Figure della diligenza. Costanti e varianti del Tasso lirico. Il manoscritto Chigiano L VIII 302*, Rome-Padova: Antenore.

Contini 1939 Gianfranco Contini, *Esercizi di lettura*, Florence: Parenti (→ Contini 1982 and Contini 1982).

Contini 1947 Gianfranco Contini, 'Introduzione alle "paperoles"', *Letteratura*, 9.6, 122–49 (→ Contini 1970: 69–110).

Contini 1953 Gianfranco Contini, 'Jean Santeuil ovvero l'infanzia della Recherche', *Letteratura*, 1.2 (→ Contini 1970: 111–37).

Contini 1970 Gianfranco Contini, *Varianti e altra linguistica. Una raccolta di saggi (1938–1968)*, Turin: Einaudi.

Contini 1974 Gianfranco Contini, *Esercizi di lettura sopra autori contemporanei, con un'appendice su testi non contemporanei*, Turin: Einaudi (→ Contini 1982).

Contini 1982 Gianfranco Contini, *Esercizi di lettura sopra autori contemporanei, con un'appendice su testi non contemporanei*, Turin: Einaudi.

Contini 1986 Gianfranco Contini, 'Varianti d'autore ("excursus" bibliografico)', in *Breviario di ecdotica*, Turin: Einaudi, 12–14.

Contini 1989 Gianfranco Contini, *Diligenza e voluttà. Ludovica Ripa di Meana interroga Gianfranco Contini*, Milan: Mondadori.

Contini 1992 Gianfranco Contini, *La critica degli scartafacci e altre pagine sparse. Con un ricordo di Aurelio Roncaglia*, Pisa: Scuola Normale Superiore.

Corrente 2017 Eleonora Corrente, '"Un lavoro più da artigiano che da artista". Smisurata preghiera: critica degli scartafacci di un cantautore', *Rivista di Letteratura Italiana*, 35.2, 139–52.

Critica del testo 1985 *La critica del testo. Problemi di metodo ed esperienze di lavoro* (Atti del Convegno di Lecce, 22–26 ottobre 1984), Rome: Salerno.

Croce 1920 Benedetto Croce, *Ariosto, Shakespeare, Corneille*, Bari: Laterza.

Croce 1947 Benedetto Croce, 'Illusione sulla genesi delle opere d'arte documentabile dagli scartafacci degli scrittori', *Quaderni della Critica*, 3.9, 93–94.

Croce 1949 Benedetto Croce, *Nuove pagine sparse. Serie prima. Vita, Pensiero, Letteratura*, Napoli: Ricciardi.

Croce 1951 Benedetto Croce, *Conversazioni critiche*, Serie quarta, Bari: Laterza.

De Blasi 2013 Margherita De Blasi, 'Per l'edizione critica di *Eros*', *Annali della Fondazione Verga*, 6, 147–66.

De Blasi 2018 Margherita De Blasi, 'Leggere *Eros* attraverso le varianti', *Poetiche*, 20.48, 67–85.

D. De Robertis 1990 Domenico De Robertis, 'N.d.D.' ['Nota del Direttore'], *Studi di filologia italiana*, 48, 301–307.

D. De Robertis 2015 Domenico De Robertis, *Gli studi manzoniani*, ed. by Isabella Becherucci, Firenze: Cesati.

D. De Robertis and Parigino 1998 Domenico De Robertis and Giuseppe Parigino, 'Esperimento di visualizzazione informatica dell'elaborazione del testo', *Annali della Scuola normale Superiore di Pisa*, 3.1–2, 242–52.

G. De Robertis 1949 Giuseppe De Robertis, *Primi studi manzoniani e altre cose*, Florence: Le Monnier.

De Maldé 1999 Vania de Maldé, 'Le Rime tassiane tra filologia e critica: per un bilancio dell'ultimo decennio di studi', in *Torquato Tasso e la cultura estense*, ed. by G. Venturi, vol. 1, Florence: Olschki, 317–32.

De Robertis 1967 Giuseppe De Robertis, 'Saper leggere', in *Scritti vociani*, ed. by E. Falqui, Florence: Le Monnier, 155–56.

De Vecchis 2019, Kevin De Vecchis, *Per un'analisi del romanesco delle poesie di Mario dell'Arco attraverso le varianti d'autore*, Florence: Cesati.

Del Vento and Musitelli 2019 Christian Del Vento and Pierre Musitelli, eds, 'Une tradition italienne', *Genesis*, 49.

Dionisotti 1966 Carlo Dionisotti, Introduction to Pietro Bembo, *Prose e rime*, ed. by Carlo Dionisotti, Torini: Utet, 9–56.

D'Iorio 1998 Paola D'Iorio, 'L'edizione elettronica', *Annali della Scuola normale Superiore di Pisa*, 4.3, 253–76.

D'Iorio and Ferrand 1998 Paolo D'Iorio and Nathalie Ferrand, eds, *Genesi, critica, edizione*, Pisa: Scuola Normale Superiore.

Di Iorio et al. 2014 Angelo Di Iorio, Paola Italia and Fabio Vitali, 'Variants and Versioning between Textual Bibliography and Computer Science', in *Humanities and Their Methods in the Digital Ecosystem* (AIUCD '14: Proceedings of the Third AIUCD Annual Conference on Humanities and Their Methods in the Digital Ecosystem), ed. by Francesca Tomasi, Roberto Rosselli Del Turco and Anna Maria Tammaro, New York: Association for Computing Machinery, 1–5, https://doi.org/10.1145/2802612.2802614

Dolfi 2015 Anna Dolfi, *Non finito, opera interrotta e modernità*, Florence: University Press.

Dondero 1998 Marco Dondero, 'Il trionfo degli scartafacci. Le edizioni critiche del secondo Novecento', in *Leopardi a Milano. Per una storia editoriale di Giacomo Leopardi*, ed. by Patrizia Landi, Milan: Electa, 77–97.

Everest 1989 Kelvin Everest, 'Introduction', in Percy Bysshe Shelley, *The Poems*, ed. by G. Matthews and K. Everest, vol. 1, London/New York: Routledge, xii–xxxii.

Falconer 1993 Graham Falconer, 'Genetic Cristicism', *Comparative Literature*, 47, 1–21.

Fau 2013 Guillaume Fau, 'Le Fonds Proust au Département des Manuscrits de la Bibliothèque Nationale de France', *Genesis*, 36, 135–40, https://journals.openedition.org/genesis/1154

Ferrand 2019 Nathalie Ferrand, *La genèse des textes dans l'Europe à l'âge moderne. Questions de méthode et études de cas de Leibniz à Foscolo*, Paris: CNRS Editions.

Ferrand and Del Vento 2018 Nathalie Ferrand and Christian Del Vento, eds, 'I manoscritti italiani del XVIII secolo. Un approccio genetico', *Quaderni de La Rassegna della Letteratura Italiana*.

Filologia testuale 1994 *La filologia testuale e le scienze umane* (Atti del Convegno Internazionale, Roma, 19–22 aprile 1993), Rome: Accademia Nazionale dei Lincei.

Finotti 1994 Fabio Finotti, 'La storia finita. Filologia e critica degli scartafacci', *Lettere italiane*, 46.1, 3–43.

Fiorilla 2010 Maurizio Fiorilla, 'Per il testo del Decameron', *L'Ellisse*, 5, 9–38..

Fiorilla 2013 Maurizio Fiorilla, 'Ancora per il testo del Decameron', *L'Ellisse*, 8.1, 75–90.

Fiorilla 2015 Maurizio Fiorilla, 'Sul testo del *Decameron*: per una nuova edizione critica', in *Boccaccio letterato* (Atti del Convegno Internazionale, Florence-Certaldo 10–12 ottobre 2013), ed. by Michaelangiola Marchiaro and Stefano Zamponi, Florence: Accademia della Crusca, 211–37.

Fiormonte 2003 Domenico Fiormonte, *Scrittura e filologia nell'era digitale*, Turin: Boringhieri.

Fiormonte 2015 Domenico Fiormonte, 'Da "Digital Variants" a "Ecdosis". Filologia digitale vingt ans après', in *ECD/DCE, Edizioni Critiche Digitali/ Digital Critical Editions*, ed. by Claudia Bonsi and Paola Italia, Rome: Sapienza Università Editrice, 85–91.

Firpo 1961 Luigi Firpo, 'Correzioni d'autore coatte', in *Studi e problemi di critica testuale. Convegno di studi di filologia italiana nel centenario della Commissione per i testi di lingua (7–9 aprile 1960)*, Bologna: Commissione per i testi di Lingua, 147–53.

Folena 1953 Gianfranco Folena, 'Statica e dinamica del testo', *Letteratura*, 1.3, 82–84.

Formentin, Inglese and Scaffai 2012 Vittorio Formentin, Giorgio Inglese and Niccolò Scaffai, *Leggere gli apparati: testi e testimoni dei classici italiani*, ed. by Giulia Raboni, Parma: Unicopli.

Fraistat 2000 Neil Fraistat, 'The Workshop of Shelley's Poetry', *Romanticism on the Net*, 19, https://doi.org/10.7202/005929ar

Fubini 1956 Mario Fubini, 'Critica delle varianti', in *Critica e poesia. Saggi e discorsi di teoria letteraria*, Bari: Laterza, 70–84.

Gadda 1983 Carlo Emilio Gadda, *Racconto italiano di ignoto del Novecento*, ed. by Dante Isella, Turin: Einaudi.

Gadda 1988 Carlo Emilio Gadda, *Romanzi e racconti*, in *Opere*, vol. 1, ed. by Raffaella Rodondi, Guido Lucchini, Emilio Manzotti, Milan: Garzanti.

Gadda 1989 Carlo Emilio Gadda, *La meccanica*, in Carlo Emilio Gadda, *Opere*, vol. 2, ed. by Dante Isella, Milano: Garzanti, 461–589.

Gadda 1993 Carlo Emilio Gadda, *Scritti vari e postumi*, in *Opere*, vol. 5, ed. by Andrea Silvestri, Dante Isella, Paola Italia, Giorgio Pinotti, Milan: Garzanti.

Gadda 1995 Carlo Emilio Gadda, *Disegni milanesi*, ed. by Dante Isella, Paola Italia and Giorgio Pinotti, Pistoia: Edizioni del Can Bianco.

Gadda 2002 Carlo Emilio Gadda, *Un fulmine sul '220*, ed. by Dante Isella, Milan: Garzanti.

Gadda 2016 Carlo Emilio Gadda, *Eros e Priapo. Versione originale*, ed. by Paola Italia and Giorgio Pinotti, Milan: Adelphi.

Gadda 2019 Carlo Emilio Gadda, *La Cognizione del dolore*, ed. by Paola Italia and Giorgio Pinotti, Claudio Vela, Milan: Adelphi.

Gavazzeni 2003 Franco Gavazzeni, 'Per l'edizione delle *Rime degli Accademici Eterei*', in *Sul Tasso. Studi di filologia e letteratura italiana offerti a Luigi Poma*, ed. by. Franco Gavazzeni, Rome-Padova: Antenore, 213–28.

Gavazzeni 2006 Franco Gavazzeni, *Studi di critica e filologia sull'Ottocento e il Novecento*, Verona: Valdonega.

Gavazzeni and Martignoni 2009 Franco Gavazzeni and Clelia Martignoni, *Dante Isella e la filologia d'autore*, special issue of *Strumenti critici*, n.s. xxiv, 2.

Gentile 2018 Sebastiano Gentile, 'Tradizioni in presenza dell'autore', in *La Tradizione dei Testi*, Atti del Convegno (Cortona, 21–23 settembre 2017), ed. by Claudio Ciociola and Claudio Vela, Rome: SFLI-Società dei Filologi della Letteratura Italiana, 211–36.

Giaveri 1993 Maria Teresa Giaveri, 'La critique génétique en Italie: Contini, Croce et l' "étude des paperasses"', *Genesis*, 3, 9–29.

Giaveri and Grésillon 1994 M. T. Giaveri and A. Grésillon, eds, *I sentieri della creazione. Tracce, traiettorie, modelli*, Reggio Emilia: Diabasis.

Gibellini 2014 Pietro Gibellini, 'Critica genetica e variantistica continiana: esperienze di lavoro (Parini, Belli, Manzoni, d'Annunzio)', *Ermeneutica letteraria*, 10, 115–25.

Gigante 2001 Claudio Gigante, 'Nel cantiere della Gerusalemme conquistata. Lettura del ms. autografo del poema', *Filologia e Critica*, 26.2, 161–86.

Gigante 2002 Claudio Gigante, '"Un certo volume, dov'era la Gerusalemme ligata". La formazione del testo della Conquistata', *Schifanoia*, 22–23, 183–90.

Gigante 2003 Claudio Gigante, *Esperienze di filologia cinquecentesca. Salviati, Mazzoni, Trissino, Costo, il Bargeo, Tasso*, Rome: Salerno Editrice.

Gigante 2005 Claudio Gigante, 'Le problème critique de l'édition de la Gerusalemme conquistata', *Degrés*, 121–22, 51–60.

Giuffrida et al. 2020 Marilena Giuffrida, Paola Italia, Simone Nieddu and Desmond Schmidt, 'From Print to Digital: A Web Edition of Giacomo Leopardi's Idilli', *Digital Scholarship in the Humanities*, fqaa022, https://doi.org/10.1093/llc/fqaa022

Giunta 1997 Claudio Gunta, 'Prestigio storico dei testimoni e ultima volontà dell'autore', *Anticomoderno*, 3, 169–98, http://www.claudiogiunta.it/wp-content/uploads/2009/04/prestigio-storico-dei-testimoni.pdf

Gramsci 2007 Antonio Gramsci, *Quaderni del carcere 1 — Quaderni di traduzioni (1929–1932)*, ed. by Giuseppe Cospito and Gianni Francioni, Edizione nazionale degli scritti di Antonio Gramsci, Rome: Treccani.

Greg 1950 Walter W. Greg, 'The Rationale of copy-text', *Studies in Bibliography*, iii, 19–36.

Grésillon 1994 Almuth Grésillon, *Elements de critique génétique. Lire les manuscrits modernes*, Paris: Presses Univesitaire de France.

Grignani 2000 Maria Antonietta Grignani, 'Bilancio, con Repertorio bibliografico ragionato', *Moderna*, 2.2, 167–238.

Grignani 2007 Maria Antonietta Grignani, 'Approcci al tema della produzione testuale', in *Lavori in corso. Poesia, poetiche, metodi nel secondo Novecento*, Modena: Mucchi, 257–77.

Harris and Sartorelli 2016 Neil Harris and Emanuela Sartorelli, 'La "Ventisettana" dei "Promessi sposi": la collazione e i "cancellantia"', *Annali Manzoniani*, 7–8, 3–95.

Hatzfeld 1958 Helmut Hatzfeld, 'Recent Italian Stylistic Theory and Stylistic Criticism', in *Studia philologia et litteraria* in *honorem L. Spitzer*, ed. by A. G. Hatcher and K. L. Selig, Bern: Francke, 227–43.

Herschberg Pierrot 2007 Anne Herschberg Pierrot, 'Les Notes de Proust', *ITEM* (March 28, 2007), http://www.item.ens.fr/articles-en-ligne/les-notes-de-proust/.

Hildick 1965 Wallace Hildick, *Word for Word. A Study of Author's Alterations*, London: Faber & Faber.

Inglese 2006 Giorgio Inglese, *Come si legge un'edizione critica*, Rome: Carocci.

Isella 1968 Dante Isella, *L'officina della "Notte" e altri studi pariniani*, Milan-Naples: Ricciardi.

Isella 1987 Dante Isella, *Le carte mescolate*, Padua: Liviana (→ Isella 2009a).

Isella 2009a Dante Isella, *Le carte mescolate vecchie e nuove*, Turin: Einaudi.

Isella 2009b Dante Isella, *Un anno degno di essere vissuto*, Milan: Adelphi.

Italia 2005 Paola Italia, 'L'ultima volontà del curatore. Considerazioni sull'edizione dei testi del Novecento (I) e (II)', *Per Leggere*, V, 8-9, 191-233 and 169-98.

Italia 2007a Paola Italia, Review to Peter Shillingsburg, 'From Gutenberg to Google', *Ecdotica*, 4.4, 299–311.

Italia 2007b Paola Italia,'I tre tempi degli Idilli leopardiani', *Filologia italiana*, 3.3, 173–213.

Italia 2007c Paola Italia, ed., *Editing Gadda*, special issue of *EJGS*, 6, http://www.gadda.ed.ac.uk/Pages/journal/supp6editing/editingcegsupp.php

Italia 2013 Paola Italia, *Editing Novecento*, Rome: Salerno Editrice.

Italia 2016 Paola Italia, *Il metodo di Leopardi. Varianti e stile nella formazione delle Canzoni*, Rome: Carocci.

Italia 2017a Paola Italia, 'Carte geografiche. Prosatori al lavoro', *Autografo*, 57, 23–37.

Italia 2017b Paola Italia, *Come lavorava Gadda*, Rome: Carocci.

Italia 2018 Paola Italia, 'Il testimone anfibio. Il dattiloscritto fra tradizione manoscritta e tradizione a stampa', in *La Tradizione dei Testi*, Atti del Convegno (Cortona, 21–23 settembre 2017), ed. by Claudio Ciociola and Claudio Vela, Rome: SFLI-Società dei Filologi della Letteratura Italiana, 253–74.

Italia 2019a Paola Italia, 'Bassani e Gadda. Quattro varianti per *Botteghe oscure*', in *Cento anni di Giorgio Bassani*, ed. by Giulio Ferroni and Clizia Gurreri, Rome: Edizioni di Storia e Letteratura, 147–64.

Italia 2019b Paola Italia, 'Filologie d'autore', in *La critica del testo, Problemi di metodo ed esperienze di lavoro. Trent'anni dopo, in vista del Settecentenario della morte di Dante*, International Rome Proceedings (23–26 ottobre 2017), ed. by Enrico Malato and Andrea Mazzucchi, Rome: Salerno Editrice, 119–32.

Italia 2019c Paola Italia, 'Un nuovo testimone della lettera sul Romanticismo', *Annali Manzoniani*, 2, 175–202, https://doi.org/10.30451/am.v0i2.34

Italia 2020 Paola Italia, *Editing Duemila. Per una filologia dei testi digitali*, Rome: Salerno Editrice.

Italia and Pinotti 2008 Paola Italia and Giorgio Pinotti, 'Edizioni d'autore coatte: il caso di Eros e Priapo (con l'originario primo capitolo, 1944–1946)', *Ecdotica*, 5, 7–102.

Knowlson 1996 James Knowlson, *Damned to Fame: The Life of Samuel Beckett*, London: Bloomsbury.

Lana 2011 Maurizio Lana, 'Individuare scritti gramsciani anonimi in un *corpus* giornalistico. Il ruolo dei metodi quantitativi', *Studi storici: rivista trimestrale dell'Istituto Gramsci*, 52.4, 859–80.

Latini 2019 Francesca Latini, 'Le carte calviniane di Lina Meiffret', *Per Leggere*, 36, 69–113.

Leopardi 1927 Giacomo Leopardi, *Canti*, ed. by Francesco Moroncini, Bologna: Cappelli [repr. 1978 with an introduction by Gianfranco Folena]

Leopardi 1979 Giacomo Leopardi, *Operette morali*, ed. by Ottavio Besomi, Milan: Fondazione Arnoldo and Alberto Mondadori.

Leopardi 1981 Giacomo Leopardi, *Canti*, ed. by Emilio Peruzzi, Milan: Rizzoli.

Leopardi 1984 Giacomo Leopardi, *Canti*, ed. by Domenico De Robertis, Milan: Il Polifilo.

Leopardi 1991 Giacomo Leopardi, *Zibaldone di pensieri*, ed. by Giuseppe Pacella, Milan: Garzanti.

Leopardi 1994 Giacomo Leopardi, *Zibaldone di pensieri*, ed. by Emilio Peruzzi, Pisa: Scuola Normale Superiore.

Leopardi 1998 Giacomo Leopardi, *Pensieri*, ed. by Matteo Durante, Florence: presso l'Accademia della Crusca.

Leopardi 2002 Giacomo Leopardi, *Appressamento della morte*, critical edition by Sabrina Delcò-Toschini, introduction by Christian Genetelli, Rome-Padova: Antenore 2002.

Leopardi 2009a Giacomo Leopardi, *Canti e poesie disperse*, dir. by Franco Gavazzeni, ed. by Cristiano Animosi, Paola Italia, Maria Maddalena Lombardi, Federica Lucchesini, Sara Rosini, Claudia Catalano, Elisa Chisci, Paola Cocca, Silvia Datteroni, Chiara De Marzi, Rossano Pestarino, Elena Tintori, Florence: presso l'Accademia della Crusca.

Leopardi 2009b Giacomo Leopardi, *Zibaldone di Pensieri*, ed. by Fiorenza Ceragioli and Monica Ballerini, Bologna: Zanichelli.

Leriche 2016 Françoise Leriche, 'Une Première Édition Numérique d'un inédit de Proust: *L'Agenda 1906*', *Genesis*, 42, 183–87, https://journals.openedition.org/genesis/1674?lang=en.

Lope De Vega 1918 Félix Lope de Vega y Carpio, *The Dramatic Art of Lope de Vega, together with 'La Dama Boba'*, ed. by Rudolph Schevill, Berkeley: University of California Press.

Lope De Vega 1935 Félix Lope de Vega y Carpio, *Obras Dramáticas Escogidas de Lope de Vega*, ed. by Eduardo Juliá Martínez, vol. 5, Madrid: Hernando.

Lope De Vega 2007 Félix Lope de Vega y Carpio, *Comedias de Lope de Vega. Parte IX*, ed. by Marco Presotto Lérida: Milenio-Universitat Autònoma de Barcelona.

Manzoni 1916 Alessandro Manzoni, *Gli sposi promessi*, ed. by Giuseppe Lesca, Naples: Perella.

Manzoni 1954 Alessandro Manzoni, *I promessi sposi*, ed. by Alberto Chiari and Fausto Ghisalberti, 3 vols, Milan: Mondadori.

Manzoni 1971 Alessandro Manzoni, *I promessi sposi*, ed. by Lanfranco Caretti, vol. 1 *Fermo e Lucia. Appendice storica su la Colonna infame*; vol. 2 *I promessi sposi nelle due edizioni del 1840 e del 1825–1827 raffrontate tra loro. Storia della colonna infame*, Turin: Einaudi.

Manzoni 1974 Alessandro Manzoni, *Della lingua italiana*, ed. by Luigi Poma and Angelo Stella, Milan: Mondadori.

Manzoni 1985 Alessandro Manzoni, Il *conte di Carmagnola*, ed. by Giovanni Bardazzi, Milan: Fondazione Arnoldo e Alberto Mondadori.

Manzoni 1990 Alessandro Manzoni, *Scritti Linguistici*, ed. by Angelo Stella and Luca Danzi, Milan: Mondadori.

Manzoni 1991 Alessandro Manzoni,*Scritti Letterari*, ed. by Carla Riccardi and Biancamaria Travi, Milan: Mondadori.

Manzoni 1997 Alessandro Manzoni, *Inni sacri*, ed. by Franco Gavazzeni and Simone Albonico, Parma: Guanda.

Manzoni 1998 Alessandro Manzoni, *Adelchi*, ed. by Isabella Becherucci, Florence: presso l'Accademia della Crusca.

Manzoni 2000 Alessandro Manzoni, *Scritti linguistici editi,* ed. by Angelo Stella and Maurizio Vitale, Milan: Edizione nazionale ed europea delle opere di Alessandro Manzoni, Milan: Centro nazionale di studi manzoniani.

Manzoni 2006 Alessandro Manzoni, *Fermo e Lucia*, dir. by Dante Isella, ed. by Barbara Colli, Paola Italia and Giulia Raboni, Milan: Casa del Manzoni.

Manzoni 2012 Alessandro Manzoni, *Gli sposi promessi. Seconda minuta (1823–1827)*, dir. by Dante Isella, ed. by Barbara Colli and Giulia Raboni, Milan: Casa del Manzoni.

Manzotti 2019 Emilio Manzotti, 'I *Viaggi di Gulliver* di C.E. Gadda. Premessa Edizione Commento', *Per Leggere*, 37, 39–120.

Martens and Zeller 1971 G. Martens and H. Zeller, eds, *Texte und Varianten. Probleme ihrer Edition und Interpretation*, München: C. M. Beck Verlag.

Martignoni 2009 Clelia Martignoni, 'Rileggere Sereni (e altre considerazioni novecentesche)', *Strumenti critici*, 24.2, 315–24 (→ Isella 2009c).

Masai 1950 François Masai, 'Principes et conventions de l'édition diplomatique', *Scriptorium*, 4, 177–93.

Mastropaolo 2019 Maria Rita Mastropaolo, 'Riscritture, nuove stesure, nuove edizioni: prassi autoriali e prassi ecdotiche', *Prassi Ecdotiche della modernità letteraria*, 4.1, 157–83.

Mauriac Dyer 2001–2002 Nathalie Mauriac Dyer, 'Comment Éditer les cahiers d' À *la Recherche du Temps Perdu*? L'exemple de "Dux"', *Bulletin d'Informations Proustiennes*, 32, 23–40.

Mauriac Dyer 2005 Nathalie Mauriac Dyer, *Proust Inachevé. Le Dossier "Albertine Disparue"*, Paris: Champion.

Mauriac Dyer 2007 Nathalie Mauriac Dyer, «'Mille Feuilles de l'Écriture: les cahiers manuscrits "au net" de Marcel Proust et la question éditoriale',

ITEM (March 13, 2007), http://www.item.ens.fr/articles-en-ligne/mille-feuilles-de-lecriture-les-cahiers-manuscrits-au-net-de/.

Mauriac Dyer 2008a Nathalie Mauriac Dyer, 'D'Hypo-Proust en Hyper-Proust? Les "brouillons" imprimés de l'édition électronique', in *De l'hypertexte au manuscrit*, ed. by Françoise Leriche and Cécile Meynard, Grenoble: ELLUG, 157–70, https://journals.openedition.org/recherchestravaux/103.

Mauriac Dyer 2008b Nathalie Mauriac Dyer, 'La Reconstitution des cahiers de brouillon du fonds Proust: Points de méthode et principes de foliotation complémentaire', *Bulletin d'Informations Proustiennes*, 38, 99–105.

Montagnani and De Lorenzo 2018 Cristina Montagnani and Pierandrea De Lorenzo, *Come lavorava D'Annunzio*, Rome: Carocci.

Montale 1981 Eugenio Montale, *Opera in versi*, ed. by Rosanna Bettarini and Gianfranco Contini, Turin: Einaudi.

Moreno 2019 Paola Moreno, *Come lavorava Guicciardini*, Rome: Carocci.

Motolese, Procaccioli and Russo 2009 Matteo Motolese, Paolo Procaccioli and Emilio Russo, eds, *Autografi dei letterati italiani. Il Cinquecento*, vol. 1, Rome: Salerno.

Muñiz Muñiz 1996 La genesi del testo: critica delle varianti e critica genetica', in *La costruzione del testo in italiano*, ed. by Maria de las Nieves Muñiz Muñiz, Florence: Cesati.

Natali 2009 Ilaria Natali, *The Ur-Portrait. "Stephen hero" ed il processo di creazione artistica in A Portrait of the Artist as a Young Man*, Florence: Firenze University Press.

Nava 2019 Beatrice Nava, ed., Varianti politiche d'autore, introduction by Paola Italia, Pàtron: Bologna.

Nencioni 1961 Giovanni Nencioni, 'Filologia e lessicografia a proposito della "variante"', in *Di scritto e di parlato. Discorsi linguistici*, Bologna: Zanichelli, 57–66.

Neppi 2016 Enzo Neppi, 'Amore, rapporti di forza e maternità in Lida Mantovani di Giorgio Bassani', *Cahiers d'études romanes*, 33, 101–40, https://journals.openedition.org/etudesromanes/5263.

Neth 2012 Michael J. Neth, *Draft Variants from the Bodleian Shelley Manuscripts and the New Edition of "Laon and Cythna"*, in P. B. Shelley, *CPPBS*, vol. 3, https://romantic-circles.org/reference/laon_cythna.

Pancheri 2007 Alessandro Pancheri, 'Petrarca 1336–1337', *Studi di filologia italiana*, 65, 49–64.

Parodi 1916 Ernesto Giacomo Parodi, 'Gli "Sposi promessi"', *Marzocco*, 21, 9.

Parini 1969 Giuseppe Parini, Il giorno, ed. by Dante Isella, Milan-Naples: Ricciardi.

Pasquali 1934 Giorgio Pasquali, 'Edizioni originali e varianti d'autore', in *Storia della tradizione e critica del testo*, Florence: Le Monnier (→ Pasquali 1974).

Pasquali 1974 Giorgio Pasquali, *Storia della tradizione e critica del testo*, Milan: Mondadori.

Patota 1997 Giuseppe Patota, 'Il "libretto", il Fascicolo B e le *Prose della volgar lingua* di Pietro Bembo', *Studi linguistici italiani*, 19.12, 216–26.

Pellizzari 2013 Patrizia Pellizzari, 'Soglie: le epigrafi latine nelle opere di Alfieri', *Giornale Storico della Letteratura Italiana*, 190, 211–58.

Pellizzari 2014 Patrizia Pellizzari, '(Ancora) su Alfieri, l'Inghilterra e Pope', in *A warm mind-shake. Scritti in onore di Paolo Bertinetti* (a cura del Dipartimento di Lingue e Letterature Straniere e Culture Moderne dell'Università degli Studi di Torino), Turin: Trauben, 483–91.

Petrarca 1891 Francesco Petrarca, *Zur Entwicklung Italienisher Dichtungen Petrarcas. Abdruck des Cod. Vat. Lat. 3196 und Mitteilungen auf den Handschriften Casanat. A III 31 und Laurenz. Plut. XLI N. 14*, ed. by Karl Appel, Halle: Niemeyer.

Petrarca 1950 Francesco Petrarca, *Il codice degli abbozzi (Vat. Lat. 3196)*, ed. by Angelo Romanò, Rome: Bardi.

Petrarca 1996 Francesco Petrarca, *Trionfi, rime estravaganti, Codice degli abbozzi*, ed. by Vinicio Pacca and Laura Paolino, introduction by Marco Santagata, Milan: Mondadori.

Petrarca 2000 Francesco Petrarca, *Il codice degli abbozzi: edizione e storia del manoscritto Vaticano Latino 3196*, ed. by Laura Paolino, Milan: Ricciardi.

Petrucci 1985 Armando Petrucci, 'La scrittura del testo', in *Letteratura italiana*, dir. by Alberto Asor Rosa, vol. 4 (*L'interpretazione*), Turin: Einaudi, 283–90.

Petrucci 1998 Armando Petrucci, 'Dal manoscritto antico al manoscritto moderno', *Annali della Scuola normale Superiore di Pisa*, 4.3, 3–14.

Pierazzo 2014 Elena Pierazzo, 'Digital Documentary Editions and the Others', *Scholarly Editing*, 35, https://scholarlyediting.org/2014/essays/essay.pierazzo.html.

Pierazzo 2016 Elena Pierazzo, 'Le edizioni digitali e l'analisi linguistica: i casi di Jane Austen e Anton Francesco Doni', in *ECD/DCE, Edizioni Critiche Digitali/Digital Critical Editions*, ed. by Claudia Bonsi and Paola Italia, Rome: Sapienza University Press, 13–22.

Proust 1954 *À la recherche du temps perdu*, ed. by P. Clarac and A. Ferré, 3 vols, Paris: Gallimard.

Proust 1987–1989 Marcel Proust, *À la recherche du temps perdu*, ed. by J.-Y. Tadié, 4 vols, Paris: Gallimard.

Proust 1987 Marcel Proust, *Albertine disparue*, ed. by N. Mauriac Dyer and É. Wolff, Paris: Grasset.

Proust 1992 Marcel Proust, *Albertine disparue*, ed. by J. Milly, Paris: Champion.

Proust 2008 Marcel Proust, *Cahiers 1 à 75 de la Bibliothèque nationale de France*, ed. by N. Mauriac Dyer, B. Brun, A. Compagnon et al., Paris-Turnhout: Bibliothèque nationale de France-Brepols, 2008-

Proust 2008 Marcel Proust, *Cahier 54*, ed. by F. Goujon, N. Mauriac Dyer, C. Nakano, 2 vols, Paris-Turnhout: Bibliothèque nationale de France-Brepols (Cahiers 1 à 75 de la Bibliothèque nationale de France).

Proust 2009 Marcel Proust, *Cahier 71*, ed. by F. Goujon, S. Kurokawa, N. Mauriac Dyer, P.-E. Robert, 2 vols, Paris-Turnhout: Bibliothèque nationale de France-Brepols (Cahiers 1 à 75 de la Bibliothèque nationale de France).

Proust 2010 Marcel Proust, *Cahier 26*, ed. by H. Yuzawa, F. Leriche, A. Wada, N. Mauriac Dyer, 2 vols, Paris-Turnhout: Bibliothèque nationale de France-Brepols (Cahiers 1 à 75 de la Bibliothèque nationale de France).

Proust 2012 Marcel Proust, *Cahier 53*, ed. by N. Mauriac Dyer, P. Wise, K. Yoshikawa, 2 vols, Paris-Turnhout: Bibliothèque nationale de France-Brepols (Cahiers 1 à 75 de la Bibliothèque nationale de France).

Proust 2014 Marcel Proust, *Cahier 44*, ed. by F. Goujon, E. Wada, Y. Murakami and Eri Wada, 2 vols, Paris-Turnhout: Bibliothèque nationale de France-Brepols (Cahiers 1 à 75 de la Bibliothèque nationale de France).

Proust 2015 Marcel Proust, *L'Agenda 1906*, ed. by N. Mauriac Dyer, F. Leriche, P. Wise and G. Fau, Paris: Éditions de la Bibliothèque Nationale de France and OpenEdition Books, https://books.openedition.org/editionsbnf/1457?lang=en

Proust 2016 Marcel Proust, *Cahier 67*, ed. by F. Goujon, S. Delesalle-Rowlson, L. Rauzier, 2 vols, Paris-Turnhout: Bibliothèque nationale de France-Brepols (Cahiers 1 à 75 de la Bibliothèque nationale de France).

Proust 2017 Marcel Proust, *La Fugitive. À la recherche du temps perdu, VI*, ed. by L. Fraisse, Paris: Classiques Garnier.

Pugh 2000 Anthony R. Pugh, 'Sur le copiste de la première dactylographie', *Bulletin d'Informations Proustiennes*, 31, 23–30.

Pupino 2004 Angelo R. Pupino, ed., *Riuscire postcrociani senza essere anticrociani. Gianfranco Contini e gli studi letterari del secondo Novecento*, Florence: Edizioni del Galluzzo.

Raboni 2008 Giulia Raboni, 'La scrittura purgata. Sulla cronologia della Seconda minuta dei *Promessi sposi*', *Filologia italiana*, 5, 191–208.

Raboni 2012 Giulia Raboni, 'Per una filologia d'autore meno bederiana', *Ecdotica*, 9, 171–81.

Raboni 2015 Giulia Raboni, 'Verità della storia e verità dell'arte. Sulla prima Colonna infame e la sua elaborazione', *Filologia italiana*, 12, 121–41.

Raboni 2017 Giulia Raboni, *Come lavorava Manzoni*, Rome: Carocci.

Raboni 2018 Giulia Raboni, 'Storia della tradizione in presenza di autografo. Applicazioni manzoniane', in *La Tradizione dei Testi*, Atti del Convegno (Cortona, 21–23 settembre 2017), ed. by Claudio Ciociola and Claudio Vela, Rome: SFLI-Società dei Filologi della Letteratura Italiana, 237–41.

Rea 2000 Roberto Rea, 'Variantistica leopardiana. Origini, orientamenti, problemi', *Filologia antica e moderna*, 10.19, 119–61.

Reiman 1987 Donald H. Reiman, *Romantic Texts and Contexts*, Columbia: University of Missouri Press.

Reiman 1972 Donald H. Reiman, 'Editing Shelley', in *Editing Texts of the Romantic Period. Papers Given at the Conference on Editorial Problems* (University of Toronto, November 1971), ed. by J. D. Baird, Toronto: Hakkert, 27–45.

Rognoni 2018 Francesco Rognoni, 'Nota all'Edizione', in P. B. Shelley, *Opere poetiche*, ed. by F. Rognoni, translated by F. Rognoni and M. M. Mandolini Pesaresi, with the collaboration of V. Varinelli, Milan: Mondadori, 135–39.

Rossi 2007 Luca Carlo Rossi, 'La filologia della letteratura italiana sul confine tra cartaceo ed elettronico', *Studi di filologia italiana*, 65, 401–05.

Rossington and Schmid 2008 Michael Rossington and Susanne Schmid, *The Reception of P. B. Shelley in Europe*, London: Continuum.

Rossington 2013 Michael Rossington, 'Editing Shelley', in *The Oxford Handbook of Percy Bysshe Shelley*, ed. by M. O'Neill and A. Howe, with the collaboration of M. Callaghan, Oxford: Oxford University Press, 645–56.

Santagata 1989 Marco Santagata, *Dal sonetto al canzoniere. Ricerche sulla preistoria e la costituzione di un genere*, Padova: Liviana.

Santagata 2004 Marco Santagata, *I frammenti dell'anima. Storia e racconto nel Canzoniere di Petrarca*, Bologna: Il Mulino.

Schmidt 2015 Desmond Schmidt, 'Ecdosis: Scholarly Editions for the Web', in *ECD/DCE, Edizioni Critiche Digitali/Digital Critical Editions*, ed. by Claudia Bonsi and Paola Italia, Rome: Sapienza University Press, 93–103.

Segre 1967 Cesare Segre, 'La sintesi stilistica (1967)', in *I segni e la critica*, Turin: Einaudi, 29–36.

Segre 1985 Cesare Segre, 'L'avantesto', in *Avviamento all'analisi del testo letterario*, Turin: Einaudi, 79–85.

Segre 1993 Cesare Segre, 'Critica delle varianti e isotopie', in *Notizie dalla crisi. Dove va la critica letteraria?*, Turin: Einaudi, 41–80.

Segre 1995 Cesare Segre, 'Critique des variantes et critique génétique', *Genesis*, 7, 29–45 (→ Muñiz Muñiz 1996: 11–21; Segre 1998b).

Segre 1998a Cesare Segre, 'Critica genetica e studi sulle fonti', *Annali della Scuola normale Superiore di Pisa*, 4.3, 39–48.

Segre 1998b Cesare Segre, *Ecdotica e comparatistica romanze*, Milan-Napples: Ricciardi.

Segre 1999 Cesare Segre, *Le varianti e la storia. Il canzoniere di Francesco Petrarca*, con due interventi di G. Giudici e A. Pancheri, Turin: Bollati Boringhieri.

Segre 2008 Cesare Segre, *Dai metodi ai testi. Varianti, Personaggi, Narrazioni*, Naples: Aragno.

Sereni and Ossola 1990 Umberto Sereni and Carlo Ossola, 'L'atto di Lucifero: Ungaretti apuano', *Lettere italiane*, 52, 388–413.

Shelley 1824 Percy Bysshe Shelley, *Posthumous Poems*, ed. by M. W. Shelley, London: Printed for John and Henry L. Hunt.

Shelley 1839 Percy Bysshe Shelley, *The Poetical Works*, ed. by Mrs. Shelley, 4 vols, London: Moxon.

Shelley 1870 Percy Bysshe Shelley, *The Poetical Works*, ed. by W. M. Rossetti, 2 vols, London: Moxon.

Shelley 1867–1877 Percy Bysshe Shelley, *The Poetical Works*, ed. by H. Buxton Forman, 4 vols, London: Reeves and Turner.

Shelley 1878 Percy Bysshe Shelley, *The Poetical Works*, ed. by W. M. Rossetti, 3 vols, London: Moxon.

Shelley 1904 Percy Bysshe Shelley, *The Complete Poetical Works*, ed. by T. Hutchinson, Oxford: Clarendon Press (reset as Oxford Standard Authors edition 1905).

Shelley 1911 Percy Bysshe Shelley, *The Poems*, ed. by C. D. Locock, 2 vols, London: Methuen.

Shelley 1926–1930 Percy Bysshe Shelley, *The Complete Works*, ed. by R. Ingpen and W. E. Peck [Julian Edition], London-New York: Benn-Scribner's.

Shelley 1961– *SC: Shelley and his Circle, 1773–1822*, ed. by K. N. Cameron et al., 10 vols, Cambridge, MA: Harvard University Press.

Shelley 1985–1997 *MYR: The Manuscripts of the Younger Romantics. Percy Bysshe Shelley*, ed. by D. H. Reiman et al., 9 vols, New York: Garland.

Shelley 1986–2002 *BSM: The Bodleian Shelley Manuscripts*, ed. by D. H. Reiman et al., 23 vols, New York: Garland.

Shelley 1989–2014 Percy Bysshe Shelley, *Longman: Percy Bysshe Shelley, The Poems*, ed. by G. Matthews, K. Everest, J. Donovan and M. Rossington et al., 4 vols, London-New York: Routledge.

Shelley 2002–2012 *CCPBS: Percy Bysshe Shelley, The Complete Poetry*, ed. by D. H. Reiman, N. Fraistat and N. Crook, 3 vols, Baltimore-London: The Johns Hopkins University Press.

Shelley 2002 Percy Bysshe Shelley, *Poetry and Prose*, ed. by D. H. Reiman and N. Fraistat, New York: Norton.

Shelley 2003 Percy Bysshe Shelley, *The Major Works Including Poetry, Prose and Drama*, ed. by Z. Leader and M. O'Neill, Oxford: Oxford University Press, 2003.

Shelley 2017 Percy Bysshe Shelley, *Selected Poems and Prose*, ed. by J. Donovan and C. Duffy, London: Penguin.

Shelley 2018 Percy Bysshe Shelley, *Opere poetiche*, ed. by F. Rognoni, trans. by F. Rognoni and M. M. Mandolini Pesaresi, with the collaboration of V. Varinelli, Milan: Mondadori.

Shillingsburg and Eggert 2010 Peter Shillingsburg and Paul Eggert, eds, 'Textual Studies, Selected Works on Anglo-American Scholarly Editing 1980–2005', *Ecdotica*, 7.

Siciliano 2018 Angela Sicilano, ed., *Laboratorio Bassani. L'officina delle opere*, introduction by Cristina Montagnani and Paola Italia, Ravenna: Pozzi.

Siciliano 2018b Angela Siciliano, 'Una notte del '43 di Giorgio Bassani: edizione e studio critico della versione "originale" (parte prima)', *Studi di Filologia Italiana*, 76, 351–98.

Siciliano 2019 Angela Siciliano, 'Una notte del '43 di Giorgio Bassani: edizione e studio critico della versione "originale" (parte seconda)', *Studi di Filologia Italiana*, 77, 349–92.

Sorella 2008 Antonio Sorella, 'Analisi compositoriale delle Prose di Bembo (1549)', *Tipofilologia*, 1, 31–60.

Stoppelli 1987 Pasquale Stoppelli, ed., *Filologia dei testi a stampa*, Bologna: Il Mulino.

Stoppelli 2008 Pasquale Stoppelli, *Filologia della letteratura italiana*, Rome: Carocci.

Studi e problemi 1961 *Studi e problemi di critica testuale. Convegno di studi di filologia italiana nel centenario della Commissione per i testi di lingua (7–9 aprile 1960)*, Bologna: Commissione per i testi di Lingua.

Stussi 1994 Alfredo Stussi, *Introduzione agli studi di Filologia Italiana*, Bologna: Il Mulino (cf. Stussi 2006).

Stussi 2006 Alfredo Stussi, *Introduzione agli studi di Filologia Italiana*, Bologna: Il Mulino.

Sutherland 2005 Kathryn Sutherland, *Jane Austen's Textual Lives: from Aeschylus to Bollywood*, Oxford: Oxford University Press.

Tanselle 1998 G. Thomas Tanselle, *Literature and Artifacts*, Charlottesville: The Bibliographical Society of the University of Virginia.

Tarantino 2005 Maurizio Tarantino, 'Dagli autografi crociani nella Biblioteca dell'Istituto italiano per gli studi storici. Note sulla composizione di *Un calvinista italiano*', *La Cultura*, 43.2, 311–16.

Tasso 1902 Torquato Tasso, *Le rime di Torquato Tasso. Edizione critica sui manoscritti e le antiche stampe*, ed. by Angelo Solerti, 4 vols, Bologna: Romagnoli Dell'Acqua.

Tasso 1993 Torquato Tasso, *Rime d'amore (secondo il cod. Chigiano LVIII 302)*, ed. by Franco Gavazzeni, Marco Leva and Vercingetorige Martignone, Modena: Panini.

Tasso 2006 Torquato Tasso, *Rime. Terza parte*, ed. by Franco Gavazzeni and Vercingetorige Martignone, Modena: Panini.

Tasso 2010 Torquato Tasso, *Gerusalemme Conquistata*, Ms. Vind. Lat. 72 National Library in Naples, ed. by Claudio Gigante, Alessandria: Edizioni dell'Orso.

Tasso 2016 Torquato Tasso, *Rime d'amore con l'esposizione dello stesso autore (secondo la stampa di Mantova, Osanna 1591)*, ed. by Vania De Maldé, Modena: Panini.

Terzoli 1993 Maria Antonietta Terzoli, 'Problemi di metodo nella filologia d'autore', in *Alle sponde del tempo consunto. Carlo Emilio Gadda dalle poesie di guerra al "Pasticciaccio"*, Milan: Effigie, 131–44.

Trovato 2014 Paolo Trovato, *Everything You Want to Know about Lachmann's Method*, Padova: libreriauniversitaria.it Edizioni.

Ungaretti 1969 Giuseppe Ungaretti, *Vita d'un uomo. Tutte le poesie*, ed. by Leone Piccioni, Milan: Mondadori.

Ungaretti 1978 Giuseppe Ungaretti, *La terra promessa: frammenti*, ed. by Leone Piccioni, Milan: Mondadori.

Ungaretti 1982 Giuseppe Ungaretti, *L'allegria*, ed. by Cristina Maggi Romano, Milan: Fondazione Arnoldo e Alberto Mondadori.

Ungaretti 1988 Giuseppe Ungaretti, *Sentimento del tempo*, ed. by Rosanna Angelica and Cristina Maggi Romano, Milan: Fondazione Arnoldo e Alberto Mondadori.

Ungaretti 1990 Giuseppe Ungaretti, *Il porto sepolto*, ed. by Carlo Ossola, Venice: Marsilio.

Valéry 1957–1961 Paul Valéry, *Cahiers*, Paris: CNRS.

Van Hulle 2020 Dirk Van Hulle, 'Creative Concurrence. Gearing Genetic Criticism for the Sociology of Writing', *Variants*, 15, forthcoming.

Van Hulle and Verhulst 2017 Dirk Van Hulle and Pim Verhulst, *The Making of Samuel Beckett's 'En attendant Godot' / 'Waiting for Godot'*, Brussels & London: University Press Antwerp & Bloomsbury.

Veny-Mesquida and Malé 2013 Joan R. Veny-Mesquida and Jordi Malé, eds, *La filologia d'autor en els estudis literaris. Textos catalans dels segles XIX i XX*, **Aula Marius Torres-Pagès Editor: Lleida.**

Verga 1995 Giovanni Verga, *I Malavoglia*, ed. by Ferruccio Cecco, Milan: Il Polifilo.

Wilkins 1951 Ernst Hatch Wilkins, *The Making of the "Canzoniere" and Other Petrarchan Studies*, Rome.

Wise 2003 Pyra Wise, 'L'édition de luxe et le manuscrit dispersé d'"À l'Ombre des Jeunes Filles en Fleurs"', *Bulletin d'Informations Proustiennes*, 33, 75–98.

Wise 2017 Pyra Wise, 'Due Esempi d'Edizione Genetica di Manoscritti di Proust. Il Chaier 53 e L'Agenda 1906', *Autografo*, 57.1, 71–81.

Zagra, Davini and Kubas 2018 Giuliana Zagra, Monica Davini and Magdalena Maria Kubas, eds, *Archivi letterari del '900*, Parte I, 'Ricerche e interpretazioni', introduction by Paola Italia (I pellegrini degli Archivi), *Quaderni del '900*, 18, 7–11.

Zanon 2007 Tobia Zanon, 'Filologia d'autore e variantistica entro il paradigma digitale. Verso nuove frontiere del testo', *Textual Cultures. Texts, Contexts, Interpretations*, 2.2, 143–49.

Glossary

Apparatus: section of a critical edition containing variant readings.

Derivative apparatus: (see also 'progressive apparatus') an apparatus that represents the chronological chain of variants in which corrections follow a derivative chronological order, i.e., an order in which more recent readings precede the older ones, e.g., 'reading 3 *from* reading 2 *from* reading 1'.

Diachronic apparatus: an apparatus that represents the dynamics of a text through time. In this kind of apparatus, parts of the text are arranged in chronological order, separated and hierarchized by numbers from the earliest to the latest phase (the base-text). Minor variants are usually represented in parentheses. This kind of apparatus preferably shows the chronological order of corrections rather than their place on the page (see also 'photographic apparatus').

Evolutionary apparatus: a graphical way to represent the corrections that have formed over time on a manuscript. This kind of apparatus represents the corrections that were made on the text after the phase that the publisher has chosen as base-text: e.g., reading 1 *corr. in* reading 2 *corr. in* reading 3 (see also 'derivative apparatus').

Explicit apparatus: an apparatus is called 'explicit' when it makes use of abbreviations (cf. section 2.5), rather than symbols (see 'symbolic apparatus') in order to represent variation. Relevant to horizontal but not vertical apparatuses.

Genetic apparatus: (see also 'evolutionary apparatus') a graphical way to represent the corrections that have formed over time on a manuscript. This kind of apparatus represents the corrections that were made on the text, before the version of the text chosen by the publisher as base-text, from the most recent to the earliest.

Horizontal apparatus: (also called 'linear representation') horizontal apparatuses are based on a clear distinction between text and apparatus. The text is located in the upper part of the page, while the apparatus is usually located immediately below it, but can be placed at the end of the book instead. Variants are collected in the apparatus one after the other. The disadvantage of the horizontal apparatus is its separation from the text, which forces readers to shift constantly between text and apparatus (which is especially an issue if the apparatus is located at the end of the book; see also 'vertical apparatus').

Photographic apparatus: in contrast to the diachronic apparatus, the photographic apparatus provides a typographic transcription of the status of a manuscript in question, paying attention to the topographical location of variants rather than the chronological stages in the text's evolution. It gives a synchronic, rather than diachronic, representation of a text.

Progressive apparatus: see 'evolutionary apparatus'.

Symbolic apparatus: (see also 'explicit apparatus') the apparatus is called symbolic when it makes use of symbols, instead of words, to represent variation. Relevant to horizontal but not vertical apparatuses.

Vertical apparatus: (also called 'column representation') the arrangement of variants vertically, in columns. Deletions and insertions are identified through typographic markers such as italics or bold. A vertical apparatus does not need abbreviations or symbols in order to represent variation, since corrections over time are represented by the position of variants vertically in a column. The major advantage of vertical apparatuses is that they allow the reader to visually reconstruct the writing process, since text and apparatus are not divided; the disadvantage is that generally readers cannot read the text in its entirety, free from corrections (see also 'horizontal apparatus').

Apograph copy: version of a text produced by a copyist following an exemplar (known as 'antigraph').

'Approximation to a value': an expression used by Gianfranco Contini to define the literary value of a text as an ever-moving, endless process of refinement, rather than as a product or achievement.

Author's last will: the last known intentions of the author. It is often the favoured base-text used for the production of an edition, providing readers with a work perceived as 'more authentic' than editions which represent a different phase of the text's existence (e.g., editions which incorporate changes made without the author's permission, or which represent an earlier phase of the text's evolution).

Authorial philology: the branch of philology which studies variants introduced into a text by its author, rather than introduced by copyists during the transmission of the text. These variants can be introduced both into manuscripts and print editions. Authorial philology studies the elaboration of a text through time by the authors themselves.

Autograph manuscript: a manuscript considered to have been written by the author, in their own hand.

Avantesto: in Italian authorial philology, this term refers to materials which have a direct relationship with the genesis of the text, such as the early drafts of a literary work. Note the difference with '*avant-texte*'.

Avant-texte: in genetic criticism, this term refers to the entire set of materials that precede the completed manuscript, including materials that do not have a direct relationship with the text, such as lists of words, of characters, maps, etc.

Base-text: (also called 'copy-text') the version of the text used as the basis for a critical edition.

Bédierian philology: a philological practice, born in opposition to 'Lachmannian philology', founded by Joseph Bédier (1864–1938) in which the editor trusts a single 'best' or 'basic' manuscript (*codex* *optimus*), privileging the individual document over the reconstruction of the text.

Column representation: see 'vertical apparatus'.

Copy-text: see 'base-text'.

Critical edition: (*edizione critica*) a critical edition represents the process of correction of the version selected as base-text. For this reason, such editions consider only the part of the *avant-texte* which has a direct relationship with the 'product' (that is, earlier versions of the same text rather than preparatory materials).

Criticism of variants: (*critica delle varianti*) the critical application of the data provided by authorial philology. Originated by Gianfranco Contini (1912–1990), criticism of variants is a critical methodology based on the comparison of two different phases in the genesis of a text. It asks how we interpret corrected texts and considers ways of seeing them as dynamic works.

Critique génétique: a method of analysing literary and/or artistic work, theorised in the 1970s, in France, that aims to study the genesis and the process of creation of the text before the definitive state.

Diacritical marks: symbols such as angled brackets or asterisks used to signal corrections and annotations added by the editor.

Digital edition: enabled by information technology, these editions use the possibilities of digital media to allow for multiple different representations of variants.

Ductus: the way and the speed with which text has been written on the paper.

Ecdotics: (*ecdotica*) the science that deals with the problems related to the editing of texts.

Genetic edition: (*edition génétique*) scholarly edition of a text according to *critique génétique* methods, representing all the *avant-textes*, from initial notes to late corrections on printed proofs. It makes no distinction between these two different types of *avant-texte* and it does not subordinate one type to the other.

Hyper-textual editions: in hyper-textual editions, the 'movements' of the text can be visually represented through specific uses of space and colour, thus offering a representation of a text *in fieri*.

Idiograph: a manuscript or an edition considered to have been written or arranged under the supervision of the author.

Invariant: invariant readings are readings that do not change across different versions of a text.

Lachmannian philology: (also called 'stemmatic philology' or 'genealogical method') the branch of philology founded by Karl Lachmann (1793–1851), which consists of a method aimed at reconstructing the original text by representing the relationships between the extant witnesses to a text (*stemma codicum*) on the basis of shared readings. This *stemma* is ultimately used to establish an archetypal / 'original' version of the text, as close as possible to what the author intended (see also 'Bédierian philology').

Linear representation: see 'horizontal apparatus'

Marginalia: metatextual notes made by the author. In authorial philology editions, the marginalia are not collected in the apparatus, since they do not share the same status and value of the variants.

Philology of the copy: the branch of philology which studies the variants introduced into a text during textual transmission by copyists (see also 'Lachmannian philology' and 'Bédierian philology').

Scartafacci: (*brouillons*) literally, a 'scratchpad' or notebook. The term originates from Benedetto Croce's reductive definition of Gianfranco Contini's 'criticism of variants'. As a general noun it refers to the rough drafts of a text.

Textual Bibliography: a discipline which analyses the technical processes involved in the production of a printed book, evaluating their impact on the evolution of the text itself.

Usus scribendi: refers to the scribal practice — the graphical and phonetical usage of a specific author or copyist.

Varia lectio: in authorial philology applied to the works of Giacomo Leopardi, it refers to textual variants and marginalia added by the author in his original copies.

Variant: the adjustments and corrections made to the text through time, even across different witnesses; they may have been introduced by the authors or others during the transmission of the text (see also 'genetic criticism', 'philology of copy' and 'invariant').

> **Alternative variant:** variants that the author has written in the text without deleting the previous text, showing that he has not decided whether to consider the variant as definitive or not.
>
> **Authorial variant:** variants produced by the author (rather than by copyists or editors). These include changes made by the author both in unpublished versions of the text, and in printed copies.
>
> **Immediate variant:** corrections made at the time of the writing of the text, typically on the same line as the rest of the writing, or interlinear if implicated (see also 'implicated variant' and 'late/later variant').
>
> **Implicated variant:** corrections resulting as a consequence of contextual changes in a text (e.g., the substitution of a singular noun with a plural as the grammatical subject of a sentence will necessarily cause any verb connected to it to change accordingly).
>
> **Late/Later variant:** variants added after writing (part of) the text, during its revision (see also 'immediate variant').

Versioning: a system named by Donald Reiman (1987) that allows readers to compare multiple versions of the same text.

Witness: every handwritten manuscript, whether autograph or not, containing the text to be edited.

List of Illustrations

Chapter 2

Fig. 1   Giacomo Leopardi, *L'Infinito*, 1819 (C.L.xiii.22, p. 2), https://www.wdl.org/en/item/10691/view/1/2/   40

Fig. 2   Giacomo Leopardi, *La vita solitaria*, 1918 (C.L.xiii.22, p. 15), https://www.wdl.org/en/item/10691/view/1/15/   44

Fig. 3   Alessandro Manzoni, *Fermo e Lucia*, 1821–1823 (Manz.B.II, t. I, cap. I, f. 4b), http://www.alessandromanzoni.org/manoscritti/624/reader#page/24/mode/1up   49

Fig. 4   Alessandro Manzoni, *Fermo e Lucia*, 1821–1823 (Manz,B.II., t. I, cap. III, f. 29d), http://www.alessandromanzoni.org/manoscritti/624/reader#page/125/mode/1up   50

Fig. 5   Giacomo Leopardi, *Idillio | La Ricordanza*, 1819 (C.L.xiii.22, p. 1), https://www.wdl.org/en/item/10691/view/1/1/   66

Chapter 3

Fig. 6   Alessandro Manzoni, *Fermo e Lucia*, 1821–1824 (Biblioteca Nazionale Braidense, Manz.B.II, t. I, cap. I, f. 5a), http://www.alessandromanzoni.org/manoscritti/624/reader#page/28/mode/1up   93

Fig. 7   Alessandro Manzoni, *Fermo e Lucia*, 1821–1824 (Biblioteca Nazionale Braidense Manz.B.II, t. I, cap. III, f. 26c), http://www.alessandromanzoni.org/manoscritti/624/reader#page/112/mode/1up   94

Chapter 4

Fig. 8   *La Dama Boba*, 1613 (Vitr/7/5, f. 29r, num. 7, vv. 1422–1452), 117
http://bdh-rd.bne.es/viewer.vm?id=0000051826

Fig. 9   *Laon and Cythna*, Bodleian MS. Shelley adds. e.19, f. 14 (see Bod2; 132
published in *BSM*, XIII, p. 32)

Fig. 10 Jane Austen, *The Watsons*, 1804–1805 (Oxford, Bodleian Library, 138
MS. Eng. e. 3764, b.2-3), https://janeausten.ac.uk/manuscripts/
qmwats/b2-3.html

Fig. 11 *La Sacra Bibbia ossia L'Antico et il Nuovo Testamento: versione* 158
riveduta sui testi originali, Società Biblica Britannica e Forestiera,
1924 (n.p.), Beckett Digital Library, https://www.beckett
archive.org/library/SAC-BIB.html?page=map&zone

Fig. 12 *The Holy Bible: Containing the Old and New Testaments, Translated* 159
out of the Original Tongues and with the former Translations
diligently compared and revised, by His Majesty's special command,
Oxford University Press, n.d. (p. 862), Beckett Digital Library,
https://www.beckettarchive.org/library/HOL-BIB-1.html?
page=862&zone=1

About the Team

Alessandra Tosi was the managing editor for this book.

Adele Kreager performed the copy-editing and proofreading.

Anna Gatti designed the cover. The cover was produced in InDesign using the Fontin font.

Luca Baffa typeset the book in InDesign and produced the paperback and hardback editions. The text font is Tex Gyre Pagella; the heading font is Californian FB. Luca produced the EPUB, MOBI, PDF, HTML, and XML editions — the conversion is performed with open source software freely available on our GitHub page (https://github.com/OpenBookPublishers).

This book need not end here...

Share

All our books — including the one you have just read — are free to access online so that students, researchers and members of the public who can't afford a printed edition will have access to the same ideas. This title will be accessed online by hundreds of readers each month across the globe: why not share the link so that someone you know is one of them?

This book and additional content is available at:

https://doi.org/10.11647/OBP.0224

Customise

Personalise your copy of this book or design new books using OBP and third-party material. Take chapters or whole books from our published list and make a special edition, a new anthology or an illuminating coursepack. Each customised edition will be produced as a paperback and a downloadable PDF.

Find out more at:

https://www.openbookpublishers.com/section/59/1

Like Open Book Publishers

Follow @OpenBookPublish

Read more at the Open Book Publishers BLOG

You may also be interested in:

Dickens's Working Notes for Dombey and Son
Tony Laing

https://doi.org/10.11647/OBP.0092

Tennyson's Poems
New Textual Parallels
R. H. Winnick

https://doi.org/10.11647/OBP.0161

Digital Scholarly Editing
Theories and Practices
Matthew James Driscoll and Elena Pierazzo (eds)

https://doi.org/10.11647/OBP.0095

Text Genetics in Literary Modernism and Other Essays
Hans Walter Gabler

https://doi.org/10.11647/OBP.0120

www.ingramcontent.com/pod-product-compliance
Lightning Source LLC
Chambersburg PA
CBHW042043240426
43667CB00048B/2969